Custom, Work and Market Capitalism

THE FOREST OF DEAN,
1835

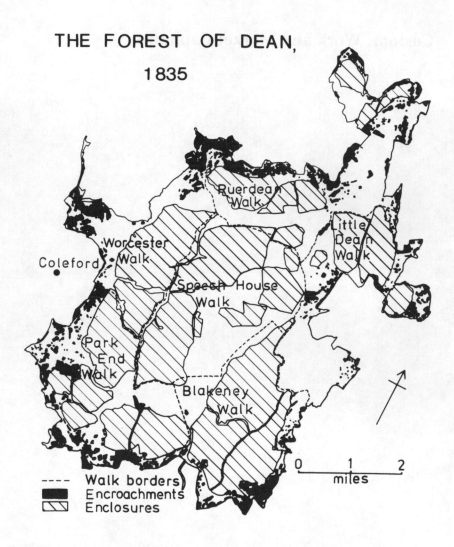

Ruerdean Walk

Little Dean Walk

Worcester Walk

Coleford

Speech House Walk

Park End Walk

Blakeney Walk

- - - - Walk borders
▬▬ Encroachments
▨ Enclosures

0   1   2
miles

CUSTOM, WORK AND MARKET CAPITALISM

The Forest of Dean Colliers, 1788 — 1888

Chris Fisher

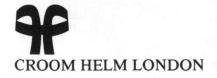

CROOM HELM LONDON

© 1981 Chris Fisher
Croom Helm Ltd, 2—10 St John's Road, London SW11

British Library Cataloguing in Publication Data

Fisher, Chris
    Custom, work and market capitalism.
    1. Mining law — Dean, Forest of, Eng.
    I. Title
    343'.42413'077   KD9312.D42M545

ISBN 0-7099-1001-0

Printed and bound in Great Britain by
Biddles Ltd, Guildford and King's Lynn

Contents

Tables

Introduction

Customary rights are not the invention of Marxist dreamers nor of romantic antiquarians. Customs, and the rights they confer, are recognised and defined in the English law of property. To study customs, the social and economic relationships in which they have been embedded and the ways in which the body of custom has altered over time, is to achieve an insight into the fundamental relations of property, production and law in a society. The ways in which customs are transformed over time and the sorts of adaptations which have to be made in customs which survive are an index of change in the wider society.

That term 'property' refers both to rights of ownership and use and to the corporeal things, land and goods, which are the subject of those rights. Where rights in a thing and possession of a thing reside in the one person, the rights are said to 'corporeal'. Those rights which may be had separately from possession of the thing are called 'incorporeal'. Those incorporeal rights which may be passed to heirs are, in turn, called 'incorporeal hereditaments'. Stephens, in his *Commentaries*, offered this distinction between corporeal and incorporeal hereditaments:

> As the logicians speak, corporeal hereditaments are the substance, which may be always seen, always handled; incorporeal hereditaments are but a sort of accidents, which inhere in and are supported by that substance, and may belong or not belong to it, without any visible alteration therein. Their existence is merely an idea and abstracted contemplation; though their effects and profits may be frequently objects of our bodily senses. And indeed if we would fix a clear notion of an incorporeal hereditament, we must be careful not to confound together the profits produced, and the thing or hereditament which produces them.[1]

In this category of property lie rights of common, rights of way and the rights which the free miners of the Forest of Dean asserted over the lands of the Hundred of St Briavels in the nineteenth century.

Title in incorporeal hereditaments might be claimed, among other ways, by custom. The law recognises three sorts of customs. The first sort are the general customs of the land which, taken together, form the body of the common law. The second sort are those which apply in particular trades. They are not, strictly, customs at all but are referred to as 'usages of the trade'. The third sort, and the one that matters here, is that of particular local custom. Such a custom has the force of law in the locality to which it refers, takes the place of the common law in that locality and, in that, may even be inconsistent with the general common law.[2]

To be valid in law a custom must have four main characteristics. It must firstly have been in existence 'time out of minde'. That is usually taken to mean that the custom existed in 1189, at the start of the reign of Richard I. In effect though it is enough to show that the custom has been exercised as of right so far back as living memory can go. Secondly, the custom must be reasonable. No demonstrated length of use can establish an unreasonable exception to the common law. Thirdly, a custom should have continued without interruption from time immemorial. If a right is surrendered for even a short period it is lost and the custom becomes void. Lastly, a custom should refer specifically to some locality, defined by reference to the limits of a recognised division of land. At the same time, the people who may exercise the custom must be defined with certainty. Customs may belong to a specified group of people in a specified locality and to no others.

These formal criteria, however, go only a small part of the way to providing an adequate account of customary rights. As Stephens wrote, customs exist in idea and abstracted contemplation: they are ideas which men have about their life and work and which are formed in the actual business of living and working. The process in which the idea takes shape precedes the formal recognition or challenge of law and takes little notice of legal boundaries. Whatever the tests of law may be, customs like any other ideas are to be understood in change and in relationship to economy and society. Thus the rights which the free miners asserted in the Forest of Dean centred on the right to dig coal and iron ore. The society of the free miners, however, was not static. The eighteenth century saw a remarkable movement of miners from the parochial areas of the Hundred of St Briavels to its central area of Crown land. In this colonising the miners began to use the Forest in a number of ways which together with the mining right supported a community of small proprietors of land and mines. Those other uses of the Forest, which are examined in Chapter 1, also came to be seen by the miners as part of the body of local custom.

Changeable though they were liable to be in their content, customary rights were inflexible in their form as a category of property. Customs had to be certain in their definition of the people who might enjoy them: equally therefore, customs were certain in excluding all others from enjoyment of the right. For that reason, the rights conferred by custom were not marketable commodities. They could not legally be sold away from the locality and the community whose social and occupational relationships they sustained. Because they encumbered corporeal things like land and because they were not capable of exchange as commodities, customary rights stood as a barrier in the way of 'modernisation' and 'progress'. The resulting conflict, between those who relied on the strength of custom to preserve the old ways and those who would innovate, has been particularly well observed by historians of popular disturbances.

The motivation of those who made disturbances was often conservative in character, informed by what Rudé has called an 'antipathy to capitalist innovation'. As commercialism and the quest of 'improvement' entered the village:

> Common lands were divided and fenced off, turnpikes were erected, and grain was stored in barns and withheld from immediate circulation, while prices were allowed to follow the whims of supply and demand, and find their 'natural' level. Similarly, as industry developed, labour-saving machinery was introduced into mines and mills, and wages like prices, found a 'natural' level by direct bargaining between the masters and their labourers. Thus, gradually, the old protective legislation against enclosure, engrossing, and forestalling, and the export of grain, and the old laws empowering magistrates to fix prices and wages, were rescinded; and the old notions of the 'just' price and the 'just' wage, imposed by authority or sanctioned by custom, gave way to the new prevailing notions of 'natural' wages and prices in a freely competitive market.[3]

The common people protested against the exploitative values and practices of the 'free market' and rational political economy and set against them the force of appeal to ancient rights, custom and statute. Thompson wrote,

> It is possible to detect in almost every eighteenth century crowd action some legitimizing notion. By the notion of legitimation I mean that the men and women in the crowd were informed by the belief that they were defending traditional rights or customs.[4]

In the Welsh disturbances which Jones examined:

> Those who turned to violence were usually a closely knit group of people suffering some kind of economic strain and united by a feeling of injustice because of an attack on, or neglect of, their mythical rights and customs. The 'lower orders' proclaimed that they were determined to defend those rights against the tyranny and oppression of merchants, poor law officers, landlords, employers and the government.[5]

In the Forest of Dean the customary rights of the miners came under siege between 1788 and 1838. The usual explanation of that relies on a sort of geological determinism. After centuries of mining, the outcrop was about worked out and it had become necessary to dig deeper for the coal. Machines were needed for that, capital was needed for the machines and therefore the free miner had to give way to the more conventional figure of the mineowner and employer.[6] Chapter 2 offers an alternative explanation. It is argued there that the State, motivated by the principles of economical and administrative reform, was the prime mover in change. 'Rationality' in administrative procedures is not an absolute value which needs no further justification or explanation. Seen in the context of communities in which the State had a concrete presence as a substantial property owner, reform had more extensive consequences than a change in book-keeping or employment procedures might suggest. In the first three-quarters of the eighteenth century, Crown administration had fallen into decay. In attempting to devise a new administration the State looked to the private sector, to private property, as a model for the management and control of its own property. The reforms of the eighteenth century aspired to import the logic and the values of private economy into the State apparatus and make them the basis of property management. Where the Crown estate was encumbered by ties of custom and right, based on paternalist notions of reciprocity and mutuality in the relationship between the King and his subjects, those ties were to be abolished. The Crown was, for the benefit of the Revenue, to be allowed to enter into contractual relations and to buy and sell and lease its land and minerals on the same sorts of terms as any other owner of real estate: except, of course, so far as explicit statute inhibited those transactions. The consequent struggle between the Crown and the foresters over the rights produced the Dean Forest (Mines) Act of 1838. That Act is a remarkable document in the history of the English law of property. By embodying a version of the rights in a statute, the Crown overrode their basis in custom and at the same time gave those who exercised the rights the authority to buy, sell or lease their coal properties without limit. In doing that the Crown had achieved what Thompson has described as the 'reification' of a customary right. Title in the coal was dislodged from the community of free miners and made a marketable commodity.

There were limits, however, on the extent to which the Crown could have its way. While some of the free miners welcomed change and prospered in it, others offered a resistance which was partly successful and prevented the complete proletarianisation of the miners. That resistance, which is examined in Chapter 3, took both an individual and a collective form. As individuals, foresters refused to behave in ways required by Crown policy; as a collective they sought to overturn that policy, to re-establish their ancient institutions and to regain control of the Forest's resources from the Crown and the new coal masters. At this stage the distinction to be made was not that between employer and employee but that between native and stranger, the old ways and the new. The Crown could not simply ride over the conservatism of the free miners. Crown policy, after all, did not aim at dispossessing particular men of particular properties. On the contrary, there was a scrupulous care to avoid inequitable treatment of particular men in their lifetimes. Change was to come through the careful alteration of general principles and to be effected over a number of generations: change the principle and let the old ways die with the old men. Every step in that process was to be taken in consultation with the lawyers so as to avoid the multitude of traps in law which might invalidate Crown action. Wherever possible, traps in law were to be set for the foresters, with an eye to a future contest in court or before a Royal Commission. Above all, any action which would bring on a legal contest was to be avoided if there was even a slight chance that the Crown might lose. As well as the need for care in matters of law and equity, there was the political problem. To deal with the Forest, if no result in a Court could be hoped for, a government bill was necessary. Since the political balance of West Gloucestershire could be upset by a few hundred voters, government bills had to be constructed carefully and presented in a way that would avoid local political disturbances. Lastly, there was what the masters of the Forest in London believed was the great potential for violence in a desperate and lawless populace. The possibility of fire in the plantations as much as the threat of defeat in court or in the House of Commons, set limits on what the Crown could do.

Up to about 1841, saving the exceptional presence of the Crown, the experience of the free miners was not altogether extraordinary. The pressures on them, in the broadest terms, had been at work in many places where customary rights were part of the fabric of local economy and society. Nor was the backward-looking response of the miners atypical. After 1841, however, the terrain becomes less familiar. The customs and rights which were so important in the history of the common people slip from sight as attention shifts to trade unionism, relations between employers and employees in the workplace and the struggle for working-class representation in the Parliament. That shift, of course, follows a real movement in the modes of collective action used by working people and in the objects of collective action. Yet in some places, and pre-eminently in the Forest of Dean, vestiges of customary practice survived into the second half of the nineteenth century and subsisted among working people alongside their trade unions. The largest part of this book is concerned with the role of the rights in that new environment.

The task of Chapters 4 and 5 is to describe the new environment and to discover the place of the miners in it. When a revived controversy about the foresters' rights arose around 1870, the free miners had become economically insignificant. The largest part of the mining industry had been concentrated in the hands of a few, relatively large companies, whose principal markets were in the highly competitive household-coal trade. Most miners worked for wages in large units of employment. The old control of the market which had allowed the free miners to set the sale price of coal through their 'bargainers' had given way to the competitive mêlée. The unity of ownership of the means of production and the work of production had been broken and labour had become a commodity. A new sense of social division, matching the new reality of the relations of production, informed the development of a trade-union movement and a demand for working-class intervention in politics. In the Forest the distinction between employer and employee came to mean more than the distinction between native and stranger.

Broadly useful though it is, however, this model of dispossession and alienation needs modification. The process of development of capitalist industry may divorce most men from ownership of the means of production but it also offers some men consolations and new standards by which to measure themselves and other men and from which to derive a sense of dignity and self-respect. Such rewards are not, of course, randomly given. Some are given to those whose acquiescence in the work process cannot simply or always be commanded under the threat of replacement. The traditional 'labour aristocrats', the skilled men able to exercise craft control, fall into that category.[7] Differential rewards may be offered too for the purpose of control of the production process. At the simplest level, reward and the speed of work are linked by piecework payments. In other circumstances, where some division of labour within small work gangs may be achieved, speed of work and supervision of work may be controlled by the variable combination of piece- and day-wage payments with the right to employ and direct, and even to determine the level of earnings of, other members of the gang. Among these are the small working masters: Hobsbawm's 'co-exploiters'.[8]

Conventionally it is skill and the highly visible presence of the labour aristocrat which has commanded attention. Skill, after all, allows a measure of independence, organisation and self-defence, which lies beyond the control of the employer, just as much as it provides the means by which a man might distinguish himself from others and perhaps judge them to be less than himself. The differentiation of function in production, however, should not be neglected. It is in the production process that skills are mobilised and people are set into their concrete and routine relationships with one another. If one skilled man, as contractor or sub-contractor, employs another skilled man, it is the fact of employment, not of skill, that matters between them.

In the Forest of Dean, when the relatively large pits began to work in the 1820s, the masters introduced the 'Little butty' method of work organisation. In this scheme the miners worked in gangs led by skilled adult hewers. The hewer and his partner, the butties, worked on contract rates and employed the other members of the gang on day rates. The hewers made their profit from the labour of the daymen. The little butty was an entrepreneur and an employer in his own right, as interested in the condition of the product market and its fluctuations as the master with whom he bargained for the contract. The capitalist-labour process, for a stratum of workers, reproduced in the workplace the conditions of competition and entrepreneurial risk and uncertainty which the firm encountered in the marketplace. The behaviour of miners' organisations in Dean reflected the dominance and needs of the butties. The strategy of the union, its political economy and its relationship with the masters, were conditioned by the fact that the union was primarily a butty union. Thus, the dispossession of the free miners and the new organisation of the mining industry did not create an homogeneous, solidary mass of wage labourers who brooded on their loss. The new generation of miners grew into the altered order, accepted its essential characteristics and struggled to define a place for themselves in it. That, as unionists, they used the language of liberty and of freedom from a tyranny of Biblical proportions, needs to be set firmly within those limits. 'Liberty' had a negotiated value and was to be selective in its incidence.

Organised activity among the Dean miners in the second half of the nineteenth century had not only to do with their role in the workplace and their relations with the colliery masters. It had also to do with the vestiges of the old life in the Forest: with the land, the free miners' rights and the rights of common. These aspects of the miners' experience are examined in turn in Chapters 6, 7 and 8. In this part of their collective life, as in their unions, the miners came to use the rhetoric of freedom and to denounce their rulers as oppressors of the people. Further initiatives by the Crown to eliminate what was left of the rights provoked a new resistance and reinforced that part of trade-union understanding which insisted that working men had a separate social and political identity requiring organised protection and representation in the Parliament. By the time of the general election of 1885 the free miners, as distinct from the coal miners, had begun to couch their discussion of the threat to the rights in republican and anti-aristocratic terms. They had begun to see their difficulties as symptomatic of a general malaise in the social order and to imagine that the remedy was to be found in some alteration of the social order. In that, their experience as free miners transcended the limits of their vision as coal miners.

That said, substantial qualification is again necessary. The character of the rights had changed irrevocably in the 1830s. The rights had lost their basis in custom, through the process of statutory confirmation and had become marketable properties on the terms set down by statute. So far as the rights belonged to the working classes, the controversy about the rights entailed a defence of working-class property. The rights no longer guaranteed the collective livelihood of a native community but were the separate, saleable property of individuals. As Thompson has put it:

> For to the impartible bundle of communal practice capitalism introduces its own kind of partible inheritance. Uses are divorced from the user, properties from the exercise of functions. But once you break the bundle up into parts what becomes inherited is not a communal equilibrium but the particular properties of particular men and of particular social groups.[9]

The defence of the rights in the Forest no longer insisted on the re-establishment of lost institutions and of a lost way of life: there was no demand that a Mine Law Court should be held or that foreigners should be driven from the district. The land was just land. It was the miners who in 1870 wished the Crown land of the Forest to be broken up and sold into private ownership. They justified that with talk of the landless poor but their scheme was meant to give more land to those working men who already had it. This was not a campaign to obtain or defend collective rights in common land but one to do away with such rights by men who understood the value of a building society.

The free miners' rights had a residual symbolic and sentimental value but, as with the land, what mattered was their potential commercial value. Efforts by the Crown, from the late 1860s, to bring about the working of the rich seams of the coal in the 'deep gales' gave the miners' rights a value which they seemed to have lost in the early 1840s. The free miners' rights obstructed the working of the deep gales but the harder the Crown tried to remove the obstacle, the more valuable the rights appeared to be and the more stubbornly the free miners resisted. What was at stake here was the cash value of a mineral lease which might be sold to someone prepared to invest his capital in a new colliery.

The defence of the free miners' rights and the land campaign which preceded it, drew strength from the promise of material benefit for a restricted group of men. The defence of the rights of common had a rather broader base. Even poor working men might object if their few fowls and pigs were to be driven off the Forest. The Crown's persistence in attempting to abolish commoning and the refusal of the Commissioners of Woods to concede that any such right existed, acted throughout the century to maintain ill-will between the Crown officials and the foresters. The Crown's insistence on strict legal definitions of right, for the sake of the 'public interest' threatened anyone who, on however small a scale, supplemented his wages by keeping animals. This part of the Crown's ambition and the feeling that if the free miners lost their fight the commoners would be next, gave the opposition to the Crown a more popular character than it might otherwise have had. The commoners added their weight to that of the free miners, the freeholders and the union men in defining the Crown and the coal-owners as enemies and in promoting the first 'labour' candidate in Dean Forest.

For a small minority of the foresters, however, the flocks of sheep offered substantial rewards and perhaps even some independence of the pit. Like any other sheep-owner anywhere, the flock-master in Dean gambled on the seasons and the fodder of the Forest for the chance of a return on market day. If there were at one end of an imaginary spectrum daymen who lived in rented houses and kept only fowls or a pig, there were also at the other end of the spectrum, butties who owned five or ten acres of land and speculated with a couple of hundred sheep. It was the owner of one of the largest of the flocks, Walter Virgo, who figured in the 'Blakeney Outrages', which brought the dispute over commoning to a climax in the 1890s. Here again, the rationality and legalism of the Crown threatened the commercial opportunity of a few. Virgo the dynamiter is more convincingly a hero of the self-employed than of the proletariat.

The organised miners in Dean are thus seen as men caught between the promise and the lie of capitalist society. On the one hand there was the promise, dear to generations of conservative ideologists, of equality of opportunity and reward for effort in work and before the law. A young man might become a skilled adult and a buttyman. By his work, his acumen and his management of other men, he might face risk and uncertainty and achieve both dignity and profit. He might have access to, and freely exchange, property in land, houses, coal and animals and he might profit from the exchange. Dispossession after all, on the face of it, is a consequence not a defining characteristic of capitalism. The ground rules in law state the terms on which property may be held and exchanged; unlike customary rights, they do not explicitly declare who shall have or not have a particular property. Working men are not excluded by definition and may persuade themselves that calculating and speculating and making the best of the rules is good for themselves and for everyone else. Given the peculiar circumstances of the Forest, which had provided working men with an unusual degree of access to property and had removed the barriers to exchange, the promise seemed to be worth something.

Yet at the same time capitalist society denies equality of opportunity, allows relationships of exploitation and has as its consequence structured and systematic inequalities which persist across generations. The accumulation of wealth by some, the opulence of a few provided by the labour of the many and the multitudes of injustices and denials of dignity which inequalities of wealth and power permit, all give the lie to the notion that the world of commodities and competition truly assures the greatest happiness of the greatest number. The buttyman was exploited as well as exploiting. The free miner stood to lose his chance at the coal, the freeholder his chance at more land and the flock-master his sheep: not through risk-taking but through the unjust power of a parliament and a state administration in which the people were not represented, and through the operation of markets dominated by the large capitals of the wealthy. That provoked the buttymen, the free miners and the freeholders to organise to defend their special interests and it even led some of them to clothe themselves in a passionate radicalism but it did not lead them very far to any greater imagination and understanding. That some of the foresters were day labourers, were landless, had no free miners' rights and could not keep animals was of little matter. Their voices were still to be heard.

This book is based on work done at the Centre for the Study of Social History at the University of Warwick between 1974 and 1978. I wish to acknowledge the help of a number of people in that work, most especially that of Fred Reid, Tony Mason and Royden Harrison. Allen Campbell, John Field, Pat Spaven and John Smethurst also made unique contributions. I am grateful to my wife Anne for patience and persistence. I am greatly indebted too, for support in this work, to Bob Kelly, General President of the Australian Coal and Shale Employees' Federation and to the Central Council of the Federation.

Some of the material in this book has previously appeared in an article in the *International Review of Social History* (1980) and in R. Harrison (ed.), *The Independent Collier* (Harvester Press, London, 1978). That material is reproduced by kind permission of the editors and publishers.

Finally, I also wish to acknowledge the assistance of the staff at a number of libraries: the University of Warwick Library and its Modern Records Centre; the British Library; the Newspaper Library at Colindale; the Public Records Office; the Scottish Record Office; the Gloucester Public Library; and the Gloucestershire County Record Office.

1. The Old System in the Forest

In days of old 'twas here and there a cot,
Of architecture, they'd little knowledge got;
None but a few freeminers then lived here,
Who thought no harm to catch a good fat deer,
Or steal an oak — it was their chief delight.
Old foresters, I'm told, did think 'twas right,
To steal an oak, and bear it clear away,
. . . noble miners, there have been I ken,
By their old works, stout able-bodied men;
They'd not the knowledge then, that now they've got,
To work by steam — hand labour was their lot.

Catherine Drew,
The Forest of Dean in Times Past Contrasted with the Present,
(Coleford, 1841).

When the free miners of the nineteenth century complained of the loss of their rights and privileges, they often looked backwards to a way of life which they imagined had gone on from time immemorial; a way of life in which they had enjoyed a special status and had exercised a peculiar, unlimited right to use the resources of the Forest as they chose. In part they were right about that. The system of administration of the Forest and the institutions and practices of the free miners, were already ancient at the beginning of the eighteenth century. But much of what formed their collective memory and which they wished to reclaim in the nineteenth century was relatively new and had taken shape only in the particular circumstances of the eighteenth century, when a lax Crown administration had allowed the miners to colonise the Forest, establishing its modern pattern of settlement and to begin to exploit the timber and other resources without hindrance.

The Forest of Dean was — and is — part of the domain of the Crown, administered by its officers and hedged in by its rules and regulations. In the eighteenth century there were two main hierarchies of control, under the general authority of the Lords of the

1

Treasury.[1] Overall responsibility for the trees of the Royal Forests, their planting and management, felling and sale or delivery to the Royal Dockyards, rested with a Surveyor General of Woods and Forests. He worked through local resident officers, the chief of whom in each Forest was the deputy surveyor. Below the deputy surveyor came the keepers, each one of whom was responsible for a section of Forest called a 'walk'. (There were six walks in Dean Forest.) The keeper then had the supervision of a body of woodmen and casual labourers. The keeper also acted as enforcer of the old Forest Law, discovering offences against the 'vert and venison', such as poaching, timber stealing and encroaching on the Crown land, and 'presenting' them for trial and punishment at the court of verderers. The verderers, who shared a considerable local authority with the deputy surveyor, were elected by the freeholders of the county from among the minor gentry who lived in the areas close by the Forest.

In Dean, matters other than those concerning the trees were the responsibility of the magnate, usually the Duke of Beaufort or the Earl of Berkeley, who from time to time held the office of Constable of the Castle of St Briavels. Among other things the Constable conducted a court which adjudicated claims of debt among the foresters and maintained a debtors' prison at the Castle. He also governed the mining industry and saw that the King had his share of profit from it, through officers called the 'gaveller' and the 'deputy gaveller' and through a Mine Law Court.

At the beginning of the eighteenth century the Forest was probably in good order and its administration effective. Under the authority of an Act of Charles II, cottages and cabins had been cleared from the interior and the 11,000 acres which the Act allowed the Crown to keep enclosed for new plantations at any one time had been planted and fenced.[2] Over the course of the century, however, administrative control relaxed and the Forest became subject to 'waste and depredation'.

According to the report of a Commission of Inquiry appointed in 1788, the waste followed from the Civil List Act of 1701 which had restricted the right of the Crown to alienate its lands by sale or gift.[3] Gentlemen of substance and property who might once have paid close attention to the Crown lands and forests as potential sources of revenue and grants for themselves as rewards for their services to the Crown, allowed their attention to lapse. Those who held the ancient offices of verderer, forester and woodward allowed the courts which they were bound to maintain to enforce the Forest Law to fall into disuse. The books of the surveyor general, which dealt extensively with the Forest of Dean in the seventeenth century, contained only a few references to it in the eighteenth. Checks on the surveyor general, his deputies and the other resident officers were inoperative. No books were kept and no system of thoroughly regulating the felling of timber maintained. The result was that 'the encroachments there are more numerous, the perquisites and undue advantages taken by the officers more exhorbitant and destructive, and the waste and depredation more rapid than in any other forest belonging to the Crown'.[4]

This situation resulted in part from the system of remuneration of the resident officers. The deputy surveyor and the keepers took their pay partly through salary and partly through a scale of perquisites which must once have been so designed to encourage the officers, under adequate supervision, to attend properly to their duties: a sort of payment by results (see Table 1.1). Consider, for example, the division of an oak tree felled by timber stealers and recovered by the keepers. The keeper was entitled to a share of the offal wood and all

Table 1.1: Perquisites of the Forest Officers

(A) The Deputy Surveyor in Dean Forest

1. The tops of all Naval timber refused by the Purveyor of the Navy as unfit for Naval use.
2. The tops of all stolen timber.
3. All trees felled by wood stealers.
4. One moiety of the cordwood made from the offal wood of timber delivered to the miners and of stolen timber.
5. In some walks of the Forest 4d and in others 6d for every tree felled for the use of the miners.

(B) The Keepers:

1. *On Deer*

   (a) On every warrant for killing a buck: £1 1s
   (b) On every warrant for killing a doe: 10s 0d

2. *On the Herbage*

   For cattle trespassing on the Forest in the fence month and winter heyning:
   viz: for horses, mares and horned cattle: 4d each
          colts, unshod: 1s each
          sheep: 2d each
          hogs, ringed: 4d each
          hogs, unringed: 1s each

3. *On Timber and Wood*

   (a) On every order for delivery of timber to the miners: 1s
   (b) Moiety of all offal wood of timber cut for the miners.
   (c) Moiety of all cordwood of stolen timber.
   (d) All lengths or pieces of stolen timber (called kibbles).
   (e) The bark of timber delivered to the miners.
   (f) A portion of fines imposed on timber stealers.

Source: *LRC* (1788), Appendix no. 24, Examination of the Keepers.

the bark of the tree. The body went to the deputy surveyor. If the stealers had cut the tree into cordwood the keepers had a share of it. Similarly, the keepers received 1s for every order for timber for the miners' use in the pits and a share of the offal wood and the bark of miners' timber. These perquisites, together with a reward to the keeper for every timber stealer convicted, encouraged the keepers to police the plantations and to regulate the supply of timber to the pits. A fee for each animal taken into the pound when the keepers drove the Forest at certain times of the year encouraged them to protect the young growth from grazing sheep and pigs. But obviously enough, without adequate supervision and book-keeping, these same perquisites encouraged the officers to connive at the very offences they were meant to prevent. The more timber stolen, the more delivered to the miners and the greater the number of animals allowed to run in the Forest, the greater the return to the officers in the way of perquisites and fines.

As well as exploiting the system of payment in those ways, the officers engaged in more vigorous and blatant abuses. Thomas Harvey, for example, the Keeper of Speech House Walk:

> (whose son is a dealer in bark and timber) had six men constantly employed in felling and stripping miners' timber during the last spring and summer, as long as the bark would run . . . that practice had been continued with the knowledge and connivance of the Deputy Surveyor, as long as any profit could be made by the stripping of the bark.[5]

The deputy surveyor was himself a man of considerable enterprise:

> In our Third Report to Parliament, we took notice that the Deputy Surveyor in this Forest had a contract with the Navy Board for supplying a certain quantity of timber to the Dockyards, as among other facts acknowledged by him, his having employed agents to buy for his own use, the greatest part of the timber sold by himself as Deputy Surveyor, under warrant issued in 1786 for raising £2,000 towards building Gloucester gaol. This same officer is also a considerable dealer in Bark and exports large quantities of it to Ireland in vessels of his own, built in his own dockyards at Lydney, within a few miles of the Forest.[6]

Some idea of the extent to which the officers benefited from the exploitation of the Forest is given by the returns of income they provided to the Commission of 1788 (see Table 1.2). The basic annual salary paid to the keepers was only £22; with perquisites they admitted to incomes ranging from £95 to £230, excluding the value of their lodges and land. They had each enclosed for pasture, crops or

Table 1.2: Returns to the Keepers from Office, 1788

Walk	Keeper's salary	Annual value of land & lodge	Value of perquisites	Total return from office	Non-salary income as % of total
	(£)	(£)	(£)	(£)	
Speech House	22	40	208	270	91.85
Blakeney	22	33	78	133	83.45
Worcester	22	30	73	125	82.04
Little Dean	22	30	78	130	83.08
Park End	22	30	98	150	85.33
Ruardean	22	24	113	159	86.16

Source: *LRC* (1788), Appendix no. 24, Examination of Keepers.

orchards between 21 and 40 acres of the Forest, the value of which, together with that of their lodges, brought their total returns from office to between £125 and £270 per annum. They also kept substantial numbers of horses, cattle, sheep and pigs (Table 1.3). The deputy surveyor in Dean admitted to a total annual income from office of between £300 and £500 of which only £50 was salary.

Table 1.3: Keepers' Land and Stock, 1788

Walk	Land enclosed (acres)	Stock
Speech House	49	4 horses, 4 colts, 4 bullocks, 6 pigs, 40 sheep
Blakeney	30	20 horses, 6 oxen, 'a few pigs', 80—100 sheep
Worcester	30	3 horses, 2 bullocks, 2 pigs, 30 sheep
Little Dean	30	3 horses, 5 cows, 5 pigs, 40 sheep
Park End	30	2 horses, 4 cows, 6 cattle, 3 pigs, 60 sheep
Ruardean	28	1 horse, 4 oxen, 6 pigs, 8 geese

Source: *LRC* (1788), Appendix no. 24, Examination of the Keepers.

While the Crown had reserved the farming of the trees to itself, for the sake of the Naval Dockyards, it had allowed the coal and ore to be mined by a privileged class of men called 'free miners'. The 'free miners' rights' are obscure in origin but were probably settled in their main outlines by the end of the thirteenth century.[7] The first formal statements of them which are extant date from the seventeenth century; the first printed copy from 1687. The 'Laws and Customs of the Miners in the Forest of Dean'[8] was the result of an Inquisition by 48 free miners at some time before 1610, at which they wrote down all that was remembered about the rights.[9] This was what the miners of the nineteenth century called, for some unknown reason, their 'Book of Dennis'.[10]

The book expounded 'what the Customs and ffranchises hath been that were granted time out of minde and after in tyme of the Excellent and redoubted Prince King Edward unto ye miners of the fforreste of Deane and the Castle of St Briavels and the bounds of the said fforreste'. It asserted the miners' right to take coal and ore from 'every soyle of the King's of which it may be named and alsoe of all other folke without withsaying of any man'.[11] The miner might also, according to the book, build roads in order to carry coal from his mine to the nearest king's highway and might take timber from the Forest for use in the pits without cost. In return for these privileges the miners were to pay a royalty on production to the King through the deputy gaveller, who was also to be responsible for registering the mines and seeing that the customary modes of working were enforced. If the lord of the soil were someone other than the King, he too had a right to a share in the profit of the mine. In more detail, the book also prescribed the distances to be kept between mines, the size of the containers to be used in carrying the coal to market and the procedure to be followed when workings met underground.

Two provisions of the Laws were to become controversial in the nineteenth century. The first reserved the rights to natives of the Hundred:

> Alsoe no stranger of what degree so ever he be but only that been born and abiding within the Castle of St Briavels and the bounds of the forest as is aforesaid shall come within the mine to see and know ye privities of our sou'aigne Lord the King in his said mine.[12]

The second stipulated that all disputes among the miners were to be tried before a Mine Law Court, presided over by the Constable, the Castle Clerk and the deputy gavellers. Matters were to be tried by juries of 12, 24 or 48 free miners whose decisions were to be final and binding. The miners might not take action in any other court about disputes among themselves. No 'foreigner' — a person born beyond the borders of the Hundred — was to take part in the proceedings of the Court or even to be present at its sittings.

The Court operated in the seventeenth and eighteenth centuries as a sort of guild or corporation, governing the industry on behalf of the 'society of free miners'.[13] The Court operated in the manner set out in the Book of Dennis. Cases were decided by juries of miners whose jurisdiction was final and exclusive. The miners were encouraged to hold to the Court and to enforce its decisions by a rule which awarded to any plaintiff half of the fine imposed on a man he successfully sued for breach of the custom. Occasionally, the Court established the size of the measures to be used in selling and carrying the coal and set out and varied the prices to be charged to different customers in different places. To ensure that the miners set their prices in accordance with its scale, the Court sometimes appointed panels of 'bargainers'[14] whose job was to arrange prices with regional and industrial groups of customers. To defend its rules and jurisdiction the Court from time to time declared and collected quarterly levies on all miners and coal carriers.

The Court's primary function was to limit entry to the industry. Unlike those in other 'free mining' districts, as Dobb has pointed out, the Dean miners set up barriers against newcomers.[15] Only the sons of free miners who had been born in the Hundred and had served an apprenticeship to their fathers or to other free miners, of a year and a day, were allowed the freedom of the mine. The sons of those not born free had to serve a longer apprenticeship of seven years if they wished to become free. The only exception allowed to these rules was that the Court might create honorary free miners who were entitled to the usual franchises and privileges. The Court further guarded against the intrusion of outsiders by stipulating that only free miners should carry the coal to market and that no carrier should have more than four horses for his business. There was no ambiguity about the intention of the Mine Law Court to limit the industry closely to natives and exclude foreigners.

The Court ceased to function, probably in 1775, for reasons which are unclear. No contemporary evidence survives to show why the Court disappeared but 50 years later an 80-year-old free miner named Thomas Davis gave evidence to a commission which was enquiring into the free miners' rights, that the dissolution was the result of a quarrel between two Crown officials and the free miners.[16] The officials were John Robinson, the deputy gaveller, and his son Phillip, also a deputy gaveller. Phillip, as Clerk of the Court, had its records in his possession. Davis's evidence and that of other miners suggested that the Robinsons and some others who had been made honorary free miners, had opened three mines, in association with foreigners, the Oiling Gin, the Brown's Green and the Gentlemen Colliers. This had provoked a reaffirmation by the Court of the prohibition against foreigners. At that point the chest containing the Court's records was broken into and the records stolen. The Robinsons then refused to reconvene the Court on the grounds that its records were missing. Davis alleged that the Robinsons had stolen the records in order to protect their mine interest. Some plausibility is given to this account by the fact that the records re-appeared in 1832 in the possession of Phillip Robinson, son and grandson of John and Phillip and himself an assistant to the deputy gavellers.[17]

Whoever took away the records, the cessation of the Court was not immediately of the greatest importance. The three mines in which foreigners had a share were a small minority of the total number of mines and one of them at least, the Oiling Gin, later passed back into the hands of free miners.[18] These cases involving the Forest officers were the only substantial intrusions by foreigners before about 1800. This was probably so because of a successful defence of the custom in 1752. The Governor and Company of Copper Mines in England had enclosed land for their own mining and had attempted to exclude the free miners from it. According to a deposition made in 1832 by a 70-year-old miner, William Collins, 'the miners tried to stop the company and could only do it by cutting under and letting the company's work fall in'.[19] For that the company sought damages from a party of miners in the Court of the King's Bench. The failure of their action left any large-scale, systematic attempt by foreigners to open mines in the Forest vulnerable to undermining, against which they would have no remedy at law.[20]

The industry which worked within the framework of the custom was small in scale. Its pits and levels were shallow, working in the outcrop of the seams in the Forest coal basin and limited in extent by the difficulty of dealing with water in the coal. Roughly contiguous with the borders of the Forest, the field was a basin of 14 seams which outcropped in three rough concentric circles broken in places by faults.[21] Where they could, the miners took advantage of the slope of the seams to help with drainage, driving their levels upwards into the hillsides to meet the crop.[22] When the water in the pits (which were sunk where levels were not practicable and which rarely went below 25 yards) became uncontrollable, the miners abandoned the work and started another. Steam-engines might have solved the problem but the foreigners and the capital which they might have provided for machines were excluded by the custom. Up until 1788 only one steam-engine had been put to work in the Forest.

The miners conducted their works in 'companies'. Until 1824, when David Mushet published a survey of the strata, knowledge of the outcrop depended on local experience.[23] Though any miner might sink a pit wherever he chose, it was a matter of chance and judgement whether he would actually find the coal. Sinking a pit was thus to some extent a speculative venture. This was reflected in the names given to some of the mines: 'Young Men's Folly', 'Small Profit', 'Pluckpenny', 'Hopewell', 'Prosper-On-Time' and 'Venture'.[24] The miners spread the risk and achieved a necessary concentration of effort by forming companies, each partner or 'vern' in which had an agreed share, or 'dole', of the profit. The strict custom required that there should be four verns, each of whom was to be a free miner and who would work the coal by their own labour, assisted only by their sons or apprentices.[25] The King, who actually owned the coal, was considered to be the fifth man in the fellowship, entitled to his dole, his royalty, of one fifth of the profit.

This system spread the ownership of the mines among a relatively large number of men. There are two sources of information about the mines and miners in Dean in the late eighteenth century. The first is the report of the surveyors William and Abraham Driver to the Commissioners of Woods and Forests in 1787. According to that report, there were 98 mines at work, controlled by 66 companies of miners (see Table 1.4). In the following year the keepers compiled

Table 1.4: Ownership of the Forest of Dean Collieries in 1787

No. of mines controlled by each company	No. of companies	Total no. of mines
1	47	47
2	12	24
3	5	15
4	—	—
5	1	5
6	—	—
7	1	7
Totals	66	98

Source: Abraham and William Driver, *Particulars of a Survey of the Forest of Dean in the County of Gloucester* (1787), PRO, F.16/31.

returns of the number of miners in their walks (Table 1.5). Four of them returned answers which distinguished between men, women and boys; one did not distinguish between men and boys; and one provided only the number of miners. These returns showed that in the first four walks there were 71 mines and 229 free miners, an average of 3.22 per mine. The average ranged from 1.86 men per mine in Speech House Walk to 5.5 in Little Dean Walk. The average number of men, women and boys employed in five of the six walks ranged from 3.28 in Speech House Walk to 8.87 in Little Dean Walk.

Table 1.5: Workers in the Forest of Dean Mines in 1788

Walk	Mines	Free miners	Average miners	Boys	Miners & boys	Women	Total	Average workers
Speech House	7	13	1.86	8	21	2	23	3.28
Worcester	17	81	4.77	17	98	—	98	5.76
Little Dean	8	44	5.5	27	71	—	71	8.87
Park End	39	91	2.33	22	113	—	113	2.89
Sub-totals	71	229	3.22	74	303	2	305	4.29
Ruardean	28	—	—	—	133	4	137	4.89
Sub-totals	99	—	—	—	436	6	442	4.46
Blakeney	7	—	—	—	—	—	—	—
Total	106	—	—	—	—	—	—	—

Source: *LRC* (1788), Appendix no. 24, Examination of the Keepers.

It is clear from these numbers that the strict custom of having four verns to a mine had already broken down in part. Ownership of the mines, moreover, was not evenly distributed. Though about two-thirds of the companies held only one mine the other third had more than one. In one case, seven mines belonged to the one company. There is no means of assessing the significance of this distribution of ownership since no record survives of the amount of coal raised from each mine. There is a strong suggestion of inequality of prosperity among the miners in a report from the gaveller that some of the miners were 'so poor that no money can be collected from them, and that there are great arrears of compositions [royalties] due'.[26] But there is nothing to suggest the degree of inequality which would be evident only 40 years later when one man alone would own 30 pits and employ between 400 and 500 men. On the whole, small-scale, co-operative proprietorship characterised the industry at this time.

The miners did not depend upon the coal alone for their liveli-hoods. Because of the lax administrative control they were able to make use of the other resources of the Forest. Firstly, they began to move onto the Crown land from the surrounding parishes to build cottages and enclose land for gardens, orchards and animal raising. By 1788 some 1,433 encroachments of land had been made, taking in about 1,350 acres of Crown land: an average of 3 roods 35 perches per encroachment (Tables 1.6 and 1.7). It is not possible to tell how much land each encroacher held because the same name appears more than once in the survey lists from which the data are taken. The upper limit to individual holdings may be established, however, by consolidating all patches held in the one name. This procedure produces 899 holdings of an average size of 1 acre 2 roods 7 perches: about half of them were of less than one acre; about 95 per cent were of less than five acres. The 899 shared 593 cottages made mostly of stone but also of wood, turf, mud and rushes. Only 8.12 per cent of the encroachers owned more than one cottage.

The most serious weakness of Table 1.6 is that it does not allow for family group working of land. The surveyor's list, through its use of family group names, suggests that a number of members of a family living in the one cottage held land, as does the fact that 45 per cent of the encroachments had no cottage attached to them. On the generous, though arbitrary, assumption that they were part of the economy of the cottage dwellers, we are left with 494 'family' holdings which average 2 acres 3 roods 12 perches each. Small-scale pro-prietorship thus characterised the foresters' working of the land as well as of the mines.

Cultivation on this scale did not make the foresters self-sufficient. Grain in particular they obtained from the farms in the surrounding countryside in exchange for coal. When the government bought-up

Table 1.6: Cottages and Land held by Encroachers in the Forest of Dean in 1787

No. of cottages held by each encroacher	Area of land held by each encroacher (acres)						
	0 — ½	½ — 1	1 — 5	5 — 10	10 — 15	Totals	%
0	174	79	138	13	1	405	45.05
1	130	85	189	12	5	421	46.83
2	1	8	36	6	—	51	5.67
3	—	1	13	6	1	21	2.34
4	—	—	1	—	—	1	0.11
Totals	305	173	377	37	7	899	
%	33.93	19.24	41.94	4.12	0.77		100.00

Note: All land held in the one name has been consolidated as one single encroachment.
Source: Driver and Driver, *Particulars of a Survey* (1787).

Table 1.7: Encroachments in the Forest of Dean, 1787

Total Forest area	(a.r.p.)	24,714 2 29
Encroached area	(a.r.p.)	1,385 3 21
Patches of land enclosed	(no.)	1,433
Average size of each patch	(a.r.p.)	0 3 35
Patches held in the same name	(no.)	899
Average size of patches held in the same name	(a.r.p.)	1 2 7

Source: Driver and Driver, *Particulars of a Survey* (1787).

large amounts of grain for the army in 1795 the resulting scarcity created a disturbance among the miners. They rioted and seized grain from the waggons and barges which were carrying it from the county. Soldiers suppressed the riot and two men went to the gallows. To alleviate distress, the government distributed £1,000 worth of grain amongst the foresters.[27] This incident suggests clearly that the miners in Dean, despite their smallholdings, were vulnerable to shortages of grain and fluctuations in its price.

As well as building cottages and enclosing land for gardens and orchards, the foresters pre-empted to their own use the areas which had been reserved as nurseries under the Act 20 Chas II. They kept animals and turned them loose in the woods to graze and forage. So that the animals might have better pasture their owners burnt-off the undergrowth and carried off the fences of the enclosures for sale in Bristol.[28] Consequently, where there had been 11,000 acres of enclosed land at the turn of the century there were only 'a few acres' in 1788.[29]

Then of course there was the opportunity, or temptation, to turn all that fine timber to good account. For some of the officers concerned with the supply of timber to the dockyards timber stealing had become an important problem. The Purveyor to the Navy in Dean wrote to the Treasury in 1770 that:

> He had discovered and was informed of the most shameful depredations of the oak timber, which was cut every day by persons living around the Forest; and that for some years it had been the custom to steal the body of the tree in the night, and cut it into coopers' ware, leaving the top part on the spot which the keepers take as their perquisite; and that at that time whole trees were conveyed every spring tide to Bristol; and that when he was at Gatcombe, in one day there were 5 or 6 teams came with timber planks and knees winter felled, and other timber among which were several pieces for ships of 64 and 50 guns.[30]

In 1780 the Navy Office had reported stealing by the miners to the Treasury and commented that 'it is well known, they now live more by timber stealing than by any other business'. The Surveyor General, asked about the report, replied dolefully that 'the complaints are but too well founded'.

The Purveyor to the Navy had proposed that rewards should be offered for the capture of timber stealers but rewards proved to be of little use for two reasons. The first was that even if men were apprehended it was difficult to convict them because of:

> The lenity of the Magistrates before whom some of the offenders have been carried, and the unwillingness of the juries, by whom others have been tried, to give a casting verdict (even on satisfactory proofs being adduced) against persons guilty of stealing *only the King's timber*, a practice many of the persons residing in or near the Forest, appear to have been so long habituated to as to render it in their eyes only a trifling misdemeanour, if an offence at all.[31]

Even if a conviction were recorded and a fine imposed, the value of the timber and bark stolen was likely to be greater than the fine. And what if the man could have both the profit on the timber he had stolen *and* the value of the reward offered for his own conviction (less, of course, the value of any fine imposed)? A system of rewards introduced in 1791 had to be discontinued because the timber stealers had conspired in that way 'to direct to their own emolument what had been meant to secure their punishment thus fully defeating the object in view'.[32]

The Forest officers blamed a tendency to violence among the miners for the prevalence of lawlessness. On one occasion violence had broken out in a dispute over the pounding of animals:

Whereas a notorious and villainous gang of persons have several times of late assembled themselves together in a riotous manner and committed diverse disorders by breaking open the pounds at the Castle of St Briavels and Park End Lodge, and discharged from thence several cattle. And upon Saturday night, the 5th instant, the same gang came to the lodge of Mr. R. Worgan, entered his garden, beat down his beans, cut up his cabbages and apple trees, broke his windows, and part of the pound wall; then adjourned to the Speech House Lodge which is in the possession of George James, commonly called Captain Whithorne. Upon their coming they immediately fell to work on the Pound, but being desired by the Captain to desist who rose to the window to disperse themselves, they returned him for answer a brace of sluggs in at the window. The Captain upon that ply'd them warmly with small shot, who sent him in return a great quantity of sluggs and balls, so that almost a continual fire lasted for nearly half an hour, when their ammunition being spent, they had something else to pick besides stones out of the pound wall. On the morrow one of the gang was taken and on Monday committed by Thomas Pyrke Esq. to Gloucester Castle; but his company being apprised of it, seven of them disguised themselves in a dreadful manner, and armed with four guns and three swords, came several miles over the Forest but finding their comrade gone too long before, returned back to pull off their too ragged petticoats and clean off their too much like Devil's faces. But it is to be hoped the gentlemen of the county will lend an assisting hand to put a stop to these desperate and resolute fellows.[33]

In 1780 the Surveyor General reported to the Treasury that timber stealers had 'become so daring and desperate, as to bid defiance to his deputies and render every attempt of his, in a summary way, totally ineffectual'.[34] The miners could not be summarily curtailed because 'they are too numerous and formidable a body to be wantonly refused'.[35] If the timber were not delivered to the miners, the deputy surveyor thought, 'he had not a doubt, but they would take it by force'.[36] Perhaps these reports should be heavily discounted because of the obvious self-interest of the officers who made them.

Many of the questions which might be asked about the miners of the Forest of Dean in the eighteenth century can not now be answered. There is no way of telling, for example, precisely how many miners and other foresters there were and how the returns from mining and the spoil of the Forest were divided among them. None the less it is possible to see in the richness of the Forest's resources and in the laxity and venality of its administration the outlines of varied economic opportunity for those who lived there. The miners could have, and only they could have, the coal and ore under the soil. The laws and customs of the free miners, the Mine Law Court and the decision in the Copper Company's case, acted on the whole to exclude foreigners and to preserve the industry for natives. The Forest also provided cottages, fuel, gardens, orchards and pasture for animals. Timber and the herbage provided income for the men who worked in gangs to steal it or take it ostensibly for use in the mines, as well as employment for women and children in the bark season. The Forest moreover as Crown land was extra-parochial. There were no rates or taxes to pay, no schools or schoolmasters, no churches or ministers, no soldiers in barracks or constables or large-scale employers. Only the Crown officials represented authority and could restrict the miners' ability to use the Forest as they chose — and the officials had an interest in not restricting them. This is a sketch of a community of small proprietors and land holders who had a considerable degree of freedom from established authority.

2. Reifying the Custom

The King with honour did them so regard,
Made them free miners as a just reward;
The Forest Charter to them granted was,
And firm and sure were made the Forest Laws.
In former times, they gloried in the name,
But now the foreigners have got the game.

Catherine Drew,
The Forest of Dean in Times Past Contrasted with the Present,
(Coleford, 1841).

By the end of the 1830s the Forest had undergone a remarkable change. Though some of the social and economic practice which had long given Dean its unique character remained to be seen, there was much that was new. The mines no longer belonged exclusively to the free miners, most of whom were now wage labourers. There were railways, iron furnaces and even churches. There was a new officiousness about the officers of the Crown and the old ways of using the Forest had gone. In part at least, this upheaval had come about because of the demands of those who wished to invest capital in the Forest. It had also come about because of a change in Crown policy. Crown and capital together defined the rights and customs of the foresters as an anachronism, to be eliminated in the interests of efficient administration and the security of property.

The most striking change had been in the ownership of the mines. It is possible to make an assessment of the state of ownership of the coal in 1841 by reference to an Award published by a mining commission in that year.[1] The Award allows a distinction to be made among owners who were free miners, foreigners and 'other foresters' (those who lived in the Forest or the parishes surrounding it but who did not own coal as free miners). The Award also shows the annual tonnage to be taken as the basis for the calculation of the minimum royalty to be paid to the Crown. Those figures, calculated by the mining engineers John Buddle and Thomas Sopwith, say nothing about actual output but probably give a fair average assessment of the minimum capacity of each gale, which may be used in conjunction with the information which the Award gives about the size of shareholdings to obtain a picture of the pattern of ownership.

By 1841 there were 105 gales in Dean whose assessed capacity was 392,680 tons (see Table 2.1). Free miners acting alone or in partnership with other free miners had 34 gales and foreigners had 39, 32.38 per cent and 37.14 per cent of the total number of gales respectively.

Table 2.1: Ownership of the Dean Forest Collieries in 1841

Owners	No.	%	Royalty Tonnage	%
Free miners	34	32.38	77,280	19.68
Foreigners	39	37.14	215,040	54.76
Other foresters	8	7.62	8,600	2.19
Miners and foreigners	10	9.52	67,560	17.21
Miners and other foresters	7	6.67	12,760	3.25
Other	7	6.67	11,440	2.91
Total	105	100.00	392,680	100.00

Source: *Award of the Forest of Dean Mining Commissioners* (1841), PRO F.17/426.

When allowance is made for inequality in capacity of the gales, the foreigners are seen to have had a dominant position: their gales accounted for 54.76 per cent of royalty tonnage as against 19.68 per cent for the free miners. After distribution of the portions of the mixed partnership mines, the proportion of tonnage owned by free miners increases to 27.78 per cent but that owned by foreigners increases to 65.93 per cent (see Table 2.2).

Inequalities had developed within groups as well as among them. Of the 147 shareholders in Forest mines, the 16 whose individual holdings amounted to more than 5,000 tons of capacity, accounted for 76.75 per cent of total tonnage. Of the capacity held by free miners, 74.46 per cent was in the hands of six men. About one-fifth of the foreigners owned about four-fifths of the capacity owned by foreigners.

Those figures refer to the ownership of the gales, the control of the coalfield's productive potential, but what about actual production? There survives a report of the number of tons of coal raised between midsummer 1841 and midsummer 1842. By relating this data to the Award of 1841, the working mines of 1841 — 2 can be grouped according to the ownership categories to which they belonged. Foreigners clearly dominated: 77.61 per cent of output came from mines wholly owned by foreigners; mines wholly owned by free miners produced only 11.06 per cent of output (Table 2.3.)

Inequality between native and stranger had developed in other ways as well. The new men had more machinery at work for them than the free miners. Of the 17 pumping and winding engines for which the Crown had issued licences before 1831, 15 belonged to foreigners.[2]

Table 2.2: Forest of Dean Collieries, 1841 The number of shareholders and the size of total shareholdings within each ownership group

(A) Free Miners

Size of total shareholding (tons)	No. of shareholders	%	Tons	%
up to 250	32	51.61	4,041	3.70
250 — 500	13	20.96	5,509	4.13
500 — 1,000	6	9.68	4,766	4.37
4,000 — 5,000	5	8.07	14,557	13.34
5,000 or more	6	9.68	81,232	74.46
	62	100.00	109,105	100.00

% of total Forest capacity: 27.78

(B) Foreigners

Size of total shareholding (tons)	No. of shareholders	%	Tons	%
up to 250	14	28.57	2,486	0.98
250 — 500	5	10.20	1,540	0.60
500 — 1,000	7	14.29	5,470	2.15
1,000 — 5,000	14	28.57	32,480	12.74
5,000 or more	9	18.37	212,987	100.00
	49	100.00	254,963	100.00

% of total Forest capacity: 64:93

(C) Other Foresters

Size of total shareholding	No. of shareholders	%	Tons	%
up to 250	22	61.11	2,799	9.78
250 — 500	4	11.11	1,266	4.43
500 — 1,000	4	11.11	4,362	15.25
1,000 — 5,000	5	13.89	13,030	45.54
5,000 or more	1	2.78	7,155	25.00
	36	100.00	28,612	100.00

% of total Forest capacity: 7.29

(D) All Shareholders

Size of total shareholding	No. of shareholders	%	Tons	%
up to 250	68	46.26	9,326	2.37
250 — 500	22	14.96	7,315	1.86
500 — 1,000	17	11.57	14,598	3.72
1,000 — 5,000	24	16.33	60,067	15.30
5,000 or more	16	10.88	301,374	76.75
	147	100.00	392,680	100.00

Source: *Award of the Forest of Dean Mining Commissioners* (1841), PRO F.17/426.

Table 2.3: Coal raised by Collieries in each Ownership Group, 1841 — 42

Collieries owned by	Royalty tonnage	Coal raised (tons)	%
Free miners	14,920	28,158	11.06
Foreigners	110,120	197,550	77.61
Other foresters	3,040	5,136	2.02
Free miners and foreigners	6,000	11,306	4.44
Free miners and other foresters	3,800	12,384	4.87
Total	137,880	254,534	100.00

Source: Sir Henry de la Beche, *Observations on the Mineral Produce of Dean Forest and on its Present and Proposed Means of Distribution* (1842), PRO F.20/11.

Eleven of the machines belonged to the one man, Edward Protheroe. By 1832 he had twelve. They allowed him to push his mines to previously inaccessible depths. His Parkend and Bilson mines varied in depth from 150 to 200 yards and he had in 1832 licences for new engines which were to be installed at pits which would go down 250 to 300 yards.[3] Protheroe also dominated the railroads, the Severn and Wye and the Bullo Pill, which had begun to carry in the Forest in 1810. He had about half the shares in the Severn and Wye and acted as its chairman in most of the years before 1831.[4] When the Bullo Pill collapsed financially in 1826, Protheroe bought out the whole of its interests. He kept for himself the Great Bilson Colliery which the company had opened to provide traffic for the line and sold the line itself to the Forest of Dean Railway Company, which he had formed for the purpose and of which he became chairman.[5] Protheroe thus came to control the carriage of coal to the eastern side of the Forest and to the Severn, the field's main outlet. This was the source of later complaints about a railway 'monopoly'. The small iron-making and iron-mining industries which had grown up in the Forest were also controlled principally by foreigners: of the five blast furnaces in operation in 1831 foreigners owned three outright and held the other two in partnership with one free miner.[6] Foreigners owned shares of the iron mines which accounted for 79.22 per cent of royalty tonnage.[7]

Taken all in all it was clear that, so far as the free miners were concerned, 'the monopoly and the customary workings are practically at an end'.[8] Most of the miners were now wage labourers rather than small proprietors. 'By the greater outlay of capital which has taken place under this new system,' a Mining Commission concluded in 1834, 'the custom of working by partners and apprentices has been nearly abolished, and has been succeeded by the practice of working the mines by hired labourers'.[9]

As well as these substantial changes in the nature of industry in the

Forest, there had also been a significant change in the way in which the inhabitants were able to use the land. The clearest sign of that was the restricted access which the foresters now had to the Crown land. Some 11,000 acres of it, about half the area of the Forest, had been effectively fenced off and restricted to use by the Crown for timber nurseries and plantations. Of a total of 2,010 acres 2 roods 6 perches of Crown land which had been enclosed by encroachers before 1834, only 24 acres had been taken in after 1812.[10] As might have been expected, the restriction on encroachments, together with the increase in the population of the Forest from 3,325 in 1801 to 7,014 in 1831, affected the size of land holdings. In 1834 there were 1,512 patches of encroached land with 1,380 cottages. The average of about one-and-one-quarter acres per encroachment was a quarter of an acre less than the equivalent average for 1787. More striking was the decrease of almost an acre in the average encroached area per cottage: from about two-and-one-quarter acres in 1787 to about one-and-one-quarter in 1834 (see Tables 2.4 and 2.5). Over the 46 years the proportion of encroachers holding less than one acre increased from 53.17

Table 2.4: Encroached Land and Cottages in the Forest of Dean, 1787 and 1834

(A) Encroached Land

Area held by each encroacher (acres)	1787 No. of encroachers	%	1834 No. of encroachers	%	% Increase in no. of encroachers in each category 1787—1834
0 — ½	305	33.93	649	40.77	112.79
½ — 1	173	19.24	339	21.30	95.95
1 — 5	377	41.94	535	33.60	41.90
5 — 10	37	4.12	54	3.39	45.95
10 — 15	7	0.77	15	0.94	114.29
Totals	899	100.00	1,592	100.00	77.09

(B) Cottages

No. of cottages held by each encroacher	1787 Cottages	%	1834 Cottages	%	% Increase in each category 1787—1834
0	405	45.05	480	30.16	18.52
1	421	46.83	925	58.10	119.71
2	51	5.67	136	8.54	166.66
3	21	2.34	32	2.01	52.35
4	1	0.11	11	0.69	—
5	—	—	6	0.38	—
6	—	—	1	0.06	—
7	—	—	1	0.06	—
Totals	899	100.00	1,592	100.00	

Source: *The Second Report of the Dean Forest Commissioners* (1834), App. 3; and Driver and Driver, *Particulars of a Survey* (1787).

Table 2.5: Encroachments in the Forest of Dean, 1787 and 1834

	1787	1834
Number of patches	899	1,592
Land encroached (a.r.p.)	1,385 3 21	2,010 2 6
Average area per patch (a.r.p.)	1 2 07	1 1 2
Number of cottages	593	1,380
Average area per cottage (a.r.p.)	2 1 14	1 1 33

Source: *The Second Report of the Dean Forest Commissioners* (1834), App. 3; and Driver and Driver, *Particulars of a Survey* (1787).

per cent to 62.07 per cent; the proportion holding between one and ten acres decreased from 46.06 per cent to 36.99 per cent. There had thus been, along with a capitalist restructuring of mining and the creation of a class of wage labourers, a closing of access to the land. There was no prospect here, so far as the majority of the foresters were concerned, of an unlimited future for smallholders and peasant proprietors.

The primary source of these changes in the Forest had been the pressure for 'economical' and administrative reform in central government which had grown up in the last half of the eighteenth century. Articulated first by the Commissioners on Public Accounts, the philosophy of reform had been applied to the management of the Crown woods and forests by a subsequent Commission which published its findings in 17 reports between 1787 and 1793.[11] The philosophy of reform asserted, among other things, the primacy of the demands of the State and the 'public' over those of office holders under the Crown and private persons: 'The principle which gives existence to, and governs every public office, is the benefit of the State'.[12] Officers should have no right beyond that as a reward for their labour. The Commissioners measured the adequacy of the administration of Dean Forest against those standards and, as Chapter 1 indicated, found the officers wanting in attention to duty and remiss in not protecting the interests of the State. The miners and other 'individuals' were also identified as a threat to the public interest:

Though the Encroachments, Devastation, and Spoil in the Forests were perhaps more rapid, in Times of Public Disturbance, and during the reigns of weak or improvident Princes, than they even now are, yet such was the Power exercised by the Crown, that what was lost or granted away during a relaxed or profuse administration, was resumed, or amply compensated by the first Monarch who gave Attention to that Part of his Property . . . there was formerly more Danger to private Property from the violent exertions of Power, than to the Property of the Crown by the Encroachments of individuals. The situation now is very different: Private Property, happily for this Country, is in perfect security; but the Property of the Crown in the Forests is open to Daily Encroachments; and unless a stop shall soon be put to the Progress of existing Abuses, and some Interruption given to Intrusive Possession, the greatest Part of the Timber now growing in the Forest will be destroyed, and those Rights which are at present retrievable will be gradually lost.[13]

The forests and Crown lands were property and were to have the same status and security as 'private property'.

The Commissioners identified three areas in which reform was necessary. Firstly, there should be proper supervision of the officers, sound book-keeping and an efficient system of planning and management. Secondly, the officers should be paid a wage and not allowed perquisites and privileges to divert them from their duties. Lastly, and perhaps most importantly, efficient administration required that the rights of the Crown in the Forest should be identified and clearly separated from those of others.[14] It was necessary to end the 'perpetual struggle of jarring Interests, in which no party can improve his own Share without hurting that of another'.[15]

> Our Chief Objects have been to give a distinct view of the Rights appertaining to the Crown in this Forest, and of the claims made upon it by Individuals, as well as to explain the Abuses which prevail; in order that a Settlement and Separation of those Rights may take place on just Principles, and that measures may be speedily taken to put an End to those Abuses.[16]

Little was done about these recommendations until Lord Glenbervie took office as Surveyor General of Woods in 1803. By then the demands of the Navy in war had given the problem of timber supply from the Royal Forests some urgency. Nelson himself had visited Dean in 1803. He deplored the condition to which the officers and the miners had brought the Forest and reported that if 'the Forest of Dean is to be preserved as a useful forest for the country, strong measures must be pursued'.[17] Glenbervie agreed with him. 'The two principal objects in the administration of this as well as the other Royal Forests', he wrote, 'ought to be':

(1) To preserve from Depredation and Waste, and to turn to the utmost practicable account the wood growing there.
(2) To adopt such measures, and act upon them steadily and without discontinuance, as shall render the Forest productive of as

great a successive quantity of Navy Timber particularly, and of any other wood not interfering therewith, as shall be compatible with their extent, the nature of the ground, and the rights belonging to the individuals therein.[18]

Accordingly, over a number of years, he deprived the officers of their land and perquisites and subjected timber felling to book-keeping and inspection.[19] In 1808, by means of a new Act of Parliament, he reasserted the terms of the Act 20 Chas II and directed that 11,000 acres of Dean be enclosed and planted.[20] This task he gave out to private contractors who completed it in 1818.[21] Encroaching and timber stealing were brought under satisfactory control by 1829.[22] The appointment of permanent Commissioners of Woods, Forests and Land Revenues in 1810 overcame the problem of the Forest's vulnerability to the whims, venality or inattention of particular Surveyors General.[23]

Concurrently with this reassertion of administrative control, another influence for change had appeared in the Forest: by the time that Lord Glenbervie took office foreigners had entered the mining industry in partnership with free miners. Although the collapse of the Mine Law Court had produced no short-term consequences of any importance, it had deprived the miners of the means of disciplining those of their number who were tempted to break the custom. James Teague was thus free to take foreigners into partnership with him in 1796.[24] Since he was a free miner and had properly registered his gale in his own name, there was no question of the decision in the Copper Company's case affecting his works. Teague built a 'fire engine', a steam-engine, at his pit and more importantly, laid a small tramway to the River Wye.

Teague's line was a crucial precedent and one which neither the Forest's officers nor the largest part of the free miners liked very much. The officers' vision of the future was clear and it told them that tramways and the intrusion of capital which would follow were a threat.

[They] not only expressed their entire disapprobation of the same, and ordered it to be discontinued, but afterwards, with the approbation of the Lord Warden, caused the work to be broken up; notwithstanding which, said Teague, assisted by such partners, had thought proper to continue such railroad . . . if the Crown does not immediately order the same to be thrown up and destroyed the Forest will be laid open to the speculation of every person possessed of money to enter the same without the consent of the Crown or the officers of the Forest, to do what he pleases therein, and terminate in its destruction.[25]

They were aware too that the tramway would not benefit all miners equally:

> Some free miners desired Mr. Jones and myself would meet them at the Speech House, the 4th of this month to hear their complaints against Mr. Teague's railroad made against the consent of the officers of the Forest, which was universally condemned, and agreed, if suffered to go on singly would ruin great numbers of families; But several substantial colliers from the Ruardean side, and likewise a few from the Parkend side, thinking a general railroad . . . would be an advantage to the Forest, and the countries round it, we desired a few colliers to inquire if it could be done without injury to the lower class. They reported that if general railroads were established by an Act of Parliament, in which the rights of the free miners should be confirmed, and that they should have the exclusive right of halling [sic] on the railroads to the Wye and the Severn and carrying to the different places, as by their laws they have a sole right, they thought few carriers would be hurt by it, and the people objecting to it were not many, but since then we have had different lists of free miners, I believe about 150, who have signed against railroads in general, many of whom say it may be a good thing for some of the richer colliers; but as for the poor ones, it will deprive them (they very much fear) of getting the scanty bread they now do . . . I cannot for one, in conscience, join in any Act that is likely to take the bread out of the mouths of the lower class of colliers, who are by much the most numerous.[26]

In this the question of Teague's line has shaded over into that of a general line and there is evidence of a division between the richer and the poorer free miners.

The Forest officers allied themselves for the moment with the poorer miners and appealed to the Treasury Solicitor to prosecute Teague.[27] The Solicitor, however, did nothing. He might have proceeded against Teague on the grounds that the line was a nuisance to be abated and one which was not sanctioned by custom or right.[28] But Teague had argued that he was entitled to build the line by virtue of the free miner's right to link his pit to the nearest king's highway and that the line was not such a nuisance as the practice of driving animals and carts indiscriminately over the Forest. There was, the Solicitor concluded, 'a possible doubt' and an abatement might turn out on trial not to have been justified. He allowed Teague's line, therefore, to go uncontested.[29]

Teague's adventure encouraged foreigners to attempt a more ambitious scheme. In Hereford in November 1800, a most impressive gathering of gentlemen, including the mayor, the Earl of Oxford and the Members of Parliament for county and city, settled that the most effective way of reducing the price of coal in the city would be to build a railroad 'which at the smallest comparative expense would lead to the greatest number of collieries' in the Forest.[30] They commissioned surveys and estimates for the line and began to petition Parliament and the Treasury for a railroad act. Some of the promoters acquired coal holdings along the route proposed for the line and one group of them 'formed a connection with Teague etc. and are now preparing to erect a Steam Engine in the Forest, at or near Syrridge, with a view, no doubt, of getting the coal trade and the mines in their own hands'.[31]

Once again opposition came from the officers. The acting deputy surveyor made three principal objections.[32] Firstly, the line and collateral lines to pits would cut up the Forest into little strips and patches and make necessary deep ditches and raised banks, all of which would effectively ruin the Forest as a nursery for timber. Secondly, the line would be 'singularly serviceable' to timber stealers who would, he feared, be able to get great quantities of their contraband away in coal trucks. Thirdly, he renewed his emphasis on the likely consequences for the mass of miners of capital and the steam-engine:

> As you will know their inability to . . . cope with monied men, the consequence must be that 1,000 poor honest men (who now get but scarce sufficient to maintain themselves and families) would be ruined and must throw themselves at the mercy of those foreigners for employ, who when they have got all the coal works in the Forest into their own hands will in all probability take care to enrich themselves at the cost of the public.[33]

Swayed by this advice, Glenbervie in 1804 refused to allow the railway scheme to proceed.[34]

Frustrated in their first attempt to obtain an Act the foreigners adopted another course.[35] They obtained the permission necessary to build a line on private land from the Severn to the edge of the Forest, thus obviating the need for a railway act. This raised the spectre of each mine owner following Teague's example and constructing his own line from the mine to the railhead. The threat this posed to the Forest was incomparably greater than that of an officially sanctioned and regulated general line. At the same time the promoters had altered their plans for a general line within the Forest so as to remove most of the earlier objections. There would now be two lines: one in the eastern valley and one in the western. They would not be for the use of a privileged few but would carry all coal on equal terms. As well, provision was to be made for £3,000 of the £35,000 of authorised share capital to be reserved in £10 non-voting shares for free miners. New surveys had been made of routes which would run over uniformly sloping ground so that cuttings and embankments or any other destruction of the soil or timber would be avoided.

More importantly, the lines now came to be seen as a means of implementing the plans to improve the Forest as a timber nursery and of disciplining the miners who were cast not as the probable victims of the foreigners but as the chief threat to the interests of the Crown. If many of the roads in the Forest were closed and a railway built, timber stealing could be limited because 'there will be less pretext for their being found with their horses and carts as they now are over the whole tract of forest land'.[36] Inspectors paid for by the railway companies would prevent the use of the line by timber stealers and a provision in the Act that no miner who used the line for the carriage of coal should be permitted to claim free timber for use in his pit would do away with that problem. At the same time the miners' other right, to dig wherever they chose, might also be limited by regulations framed so as

To prevent the opening of new pits at a distance from these railways, in various parts of the Forest where they might interfere with and prevent the enclosures and plantations which may be undertaken under the efficient authority which has now been vested in His Majesty for that purpose.[37]

A clause in the Acts to prevent new lateral lines being opened, or the carriage of coal from any new mine sunk at a distance of more than 100 yards from the main line without the permission of the Surveyor General, would serve that purpose. Moreover, the railways could pay a substantial licence fee, £400 between them, which would help to finance the enclosures provided for by the Act of 1808. A further provision that the railway companies should fence their lines would also fence the enclosures where they marched together.[38] On balance, the railway was now an attractive proposal which by 1808 had won the support of the Forest officers, despite their earlier misgivings about the fate of the poorer miners. In 1808 therefore Glenbervie approved a Bill containing the necessary clauses.[39]

After that discovery of a community of interest between the Office of Woods and the railway promoters, the old system in Dean broke down rapidly. Free miners followed Teague's example and took foreigners into partnership ventures. As the officers had predicted, however, the free miners proved inadequate to the task of dealing with the monied men and soon began to lose their equity in the industry. Edward Protheroe, owner of the largest group of mines by the 1830s, described the process in this way:

As the shallow coal was becoming exhausted, the attention of the miners was directed to the deeper coal, which is accessible only by means of the steam engine, and its expensive pumping and drawing machinery. The free miners took out gales by way of experimental speculation, and in the first instance bargained with strangers possessed of capital for the opening of these works on the terms of holding shares therein themselves; but it was soon found that disagreements and quarrels ensued and the free miners were obliged to be bought out. It was also found that the expense of opening a deep colliery was so enormous, and the difficulty of establishing a new trade so great, that the first adventurers among the foreigners expended their fortunes and received no return to encourage them or others to go on with the system. This was the case with my uncle, who never received back one shilling for his large expenditure. Under these circumstances, he offered his works for sale, and I bought them in conjunction with Mr. Waters upon the express condition that he should get conveyed to us all the shares of the various free miners who were concerned in the different collieries as partners with him. These shares he purchased for different considerations either in ready money or in annuities, some of which I continue to pay to this day . . . The free miners then finding that there was no profit to induce strangers to embark their money in the objectionable mode of partnership with them, adopted the system of taking out gales in the most eligible places, and disposing of them to strangers for a small sum of money paid down and a nominal rent for a long term of years. It is generally acknowledged that these considerations, however small, together with other advantages attending the system, have been much more beneficial to the free miners than their independent speculations. They are mostly working men, and are employed in sinking the pits, in managing the machinery, and in working the mines.[40]

Though the officers had been aware of the likely consequences of an invasion of capital, the Crown made no attempt to prevent the developments which Protheroe described. To the contrary, there was considerable co-operation between the Crown and the new men, so much so that Protheroe felt able to argue that the Crown had in fact established for the foreigners a valid title to their coal:

In what way has the sanction of the Crown officers been given? In the first place by their making the Crown a party to the different Acts of Parliament for forming railways in the Forest at the expense of the foreigners (as they are called), who held coal and iron mines, with whom they concerned all these clauses in the said

Acts designed to give security to the Royal timber, and which have actually produced incalculable benefit to the Crown property, this security being attainable only through our intervention. Secondly by their entering the various conveyances and leases of gales from free miners to or from foreigners, in the Crown books, and receiving the rents and dues from the foreigners. Thirdly, by their granting after such transfers, licences for engines and railroads, etc., directly to such foreigners describing the mines or works as the property of the said foreigners. Fourthly, by their lending to the foreigners so possessed of works in the Forest the protection and direct interference of the power of the Crown in suits against free miners illegally interrupting the proceedings, or injuring the property of the foreigners, as occurred in my own case in the year 1824, when the Attorney General filed a Bill in the Exchequer for my protection against the Churchway Company of free miners and obtained an injunction on the proceedings, which was acquiesced in and obeyed . . . Fifthly by the written explanation and declaration from Lord Lowther, when Chief Commissioner, to myself in a letter dated 8th June 1830, written in answer to a formal inquiry on my part. His Lordship's words are, 'With respect to works carried on under licence from the Crown, we can have no intention of disputing a right exercised under such a licence, as that would be to quarrel with the title which we ourselves confer'.[41]

However convenient those agreements had been for the foreigners and however productive of revenue the development of the mining industry was for the Crown, there still remained for both parties some serious difficulties. Though the Crown had been able to tighten its administration, the problem of 'settlement and separation' of rights in the Forest had not been solved. In particular, those free miners who wished to do so still were entitled, they asserted, to dig for coal wherever they wished. The Commissioners of 1788 had concluded, however, that the miners probably could not sustain this claim to special privilege in a court.[42] The absence of the records of the Mine Law Court was crucial. Without them the miners could base a case for privilege only on what was remembered by individuals and this had become, over time, confused and contradictory. The Book of Dennis contained a basic outline of the rights but said nothing about the regulations made by the Court. To those concerned with the administration of the Forest the rights were obscure, ill-defined, probably illegal and potentially destructive of the Forest.

The survival of the miners' rights posed problems for the foreigners too. They held their coal through arrangements with the free miners. In law, however, it was not clear that the miners were entitled to dispose of their gales in that way. The free miners' rights were use rights not real estate: they accrued to individuals and were contingent upon birth in a defined area and work in the mines for a defined period. The individual who met those tests had the right to use the coal, to dig it up and sell it, but could not alienate the right from himself or transfer its benefits to others who were not already entitled to them. Though gales had in fact been sold, leased and mortgaged — and the Crown had in fact recognised those transactions — the sales, leases and mortgages were probably illegal and the foreigners were not clearly secure in their property. As Protheroe put it:

> However good our titles may be for possession, we know that they are not legally marketable, unless in our own district where the whole system is known and understood. A variety of causes may render sales of importance to us, and for one, I should be quite content to make some sacrifice of profit, by a small addition to the Crown rent in return for a clear title to a definite extent of coal property.[43]

Equally worrying to the foreigners was the fact that the Laws and Customs gave protection to 'water pits', mines worked by shaft, for a distance of only twelve yards around the pithead.[44] A capitalist sinking a pit had no guarantee that someone else would not sink another so close to his own as to render both worthless. For foreigners and Crown alike it was desirable that the free miners' claim to an exclusive right to the coal be eliminated altogether.

In 1828 accordingly the Treasury ordered the Commissioners of Woods to begin an inquiry into the 'nature and extent of the customary rights exercised by the free miners in the Forest of Dean and to ascertain what evidence can be adduced in support of those rights'.[45] The consequent report, which the Commissioners sent to the Treasury in 1829, set out the rights and privileges in a fairly complete form but it adopted a hostile tone. They wrote,

> 'There has long been occasion to observe the great injury that has arisen to the interests of His Majesty, and daily continues to arise, as well as the loss and inconvenience to individuals having invested their property in mining speculations in the Forest, from the undefined and conflicting claims of the persons calling themselves 'free miners'.

The opinions of the best law authorities 'who have been consulted on the subject are, that the exercise of such claims, in the manner and to the unlimited extent urged, cannot now be legally maintained'.[46]

Having stated the probable answer to any question about the legality of the miners' claims, the report urged that:

> Competent professional persons . . . be appointed under the authority of an Act of Parliament . . . to report what rights the miners shall have appeared to have acquired either by grant, prescription or otherwise; and if it shall be found that their claims cannot be maintained to the extent now sought for, then in what manner it may be expedient that they should be limited and defined by legislative enactment.[47]

In an earlier report in 1818 the Commissioners had declared that 'we are not in possession of any Charters, Grants or Documents [concerning the free miners rights] nor have we been able to ascertain that any such documents exist'.[48] That being so — and the records of the Mine Law Court did not come to light until 1832 — all that remained of substance in the Commissioners' recommendations was to discover an expedient manner of defining and limiting the rights by legislation.

The Bill prepared in consequence of the Commissioners' report was presented to the House in October 1829. It was a far-reaching document which went well beyond the initial concern with the free miners' rights, embodying instead the full concern of the Commissioners of 1788 with settling and separating all competing claims on the resources of the Forest. The Commissioners to be appointed under the Act were to report the 'dates, value and other particulars of all other purprestures, encroachments and trespasses in and upon the soil of His Majesty within the said Forest'.[49] Encroachers, cottagers and commoners as well as the free miners were to come under the scrutiny of the Commissioners.

The Commissioners appointed under the subsequent Act began their hearings in the Forest in 1832. They issued five reports between 1832 and 1835.[50] From the fourth of these, on mining, there followed the Dean Forest (Mines) Act of 1838, the appointment under that Act of Mining Commissioners to examine the ownership of the mines in detail and the publication in 1841 of their Awards of gales of coal and iron ore.[51] In considering the mines, the Forest Commissioners, unlike the Treasury officials who wrote the report of 1829, had access to the records of the Mine Law Court which together with other evidence produced established that the mines had indeed once been worked in the manner prescribed by the laws and customs. But, the report concluded, the system had entirely broken down and the industry now operated on an illegal basis. The Commissioners recommended that the few free miners who had works should be given a sum of money in return for giving up their rights. The whole field might 'then be let by the Crown as between landlord and tenant'.[52]

The Mines Act of 1838 did not abolish the miners' rights at a stroke: opposition from the free miners made that course inexpedient. At first sight indeed the Act seemed to give legislative sanction to the miners' rights for the first time, by stipulating that only registered free miners should be entitled to a gale of coal or iron ore. The Mining Commissioners presented the Act in its best light to a meeting at the opening of the Commission in 1838:

> An ancient privilege has been perpetuated from time to time, and one of the first objects contemplated by the Act, is to establish that privilege on a firmer and broader basis than it has hitherto existed. The basis is firmer in as much as it has the direct recognition of Parliament, not merely to the vague and indefinite right of galing, but to the possession of a definite tract of Forest coal.[53]

What they did not stress was that the definition of 'free miner' had undergone alteration. Any male person born and living in the Hundred of St Briavels, at the age of 21 years and upwards, who had worked in the mines for a year and a day, might register under the Act: the critical qualification of the old definition that a free miner had to be the son of a free miner had disappeared. Moreover, there was no provision in the Act that only free miners might be employed in the mines. As well the Act permitted registered free miners to sell or dispose of their gales in any way and confirmed all mortgages, leases or sales made before 1838. In other words the Act, whose provisions the Crown had closely concerted with Protheroe and the other foreigners, gave the foreigners clear title to a definite tract of coal, left them free to employ whomsoever they chose and gave legislative sanction to the processes of sale and lease by which they had acquired an interest in the mines in the first place.

The operative principle in the Act, as the Mining Commissioners proudly pointed out, was the recognition of property rights. Whatever doubt hung over the foreigners' title,

> as regards its origin, or as regards its being an encroachment on the customs, is fully set at rest by the Act, which recognises them as being now proprietors of mines, and entitled to a full enjoyment of that property . . . While, therefore, the rights of the free miner are not only recognised but confirmed and increased, it is due to common justice and to English fairness and uprightness, that the general rights of property shall be respected; this has been our object and it forms a distinguishing, and I have no doubt, when properly considered and understood, a highly popular feature of the present Act.[54]

That dressed up a fairly straightforward trade-off which the Commissioners of Woods had arranged with the foreigners. In February 1838, Commissioner Milne wrote to Edward Protheroe in the course of a long correspondence designed to secure Protheroe's prior agreement to the Clauses of the Mines Bill. He wrote:

> It is not to an immediate Increase of Revenue to the Crown that the proposed Bill is looked so much as to place what the Crown ought to get upon some practically ascertainable principle and when that came fairly into operation, and Capital is protected by good Marketable Titles, I should hope a moderate increase may be afforded and expected.[55]

Public revenue and private property had won the day.

The Crown's assault on the anachronism of the Forest extended well beyond the substantial alteration in the character of the miners' rights. The Commissioners made detailed surveys of the encroachments in 1834 and advised that they should be sold, leased or granted away freehold of inheritance to the occupiers so that, as with the foreigners' title to their coal, property in the Forest might be held in the same way as any other.[56] A further Act of Parliament gave the Commissioners of Woods and Forests the necessary powers.[57] Yet another Act abolished the debtors' court which the Constable had maintained at the Castle of St Briavels and again substituted the general law of the land for the ancient, peculiar, local procedure.[58]

Change also affected the religious life of the forest. As extra-parochial land the Forest had been for a long time without benefit of clergy. Through the eighteenth century both established and dissenting religions had a strong presence in the parishes and villages surrounding the Forest but that had been left behind as the colliers moved in to settle the Crown land. A barrier grew between those who lived on the Crown land and the members of the existing congregations. Ragged and dirty, the foresters were regarded as inferiors who had no rights of attendance at service with their respectable neighbours.[59] The result was the development of what clergymen of all denominations saw as a wild, heathen race, as much in need of redemption as the Maori or Eskimo. As one of the earliest of the Anglican missionaries put it:

> What are the real evidences of a low, debased state of morals? is an habitual profanation of the Sabbath day? are drunkenness, rioting, immodest dancing, revellings, fightings? are the want and ignorance of the holy scriptures? and is an improper state of females on their marriage? if these are *allowed* to be evidences of immorality, I have only to affirm that they are facts . . . they are

rending and harrowing truths. The general state of the women, in an especial manner, gave a convincing proof of a deep-rooted depravity, abhorent to what the world calls virtue: how disgraceful then to the Christian name and profession?[60]

Though there was no power to celebrate marriages in the Forest another sort of formality was available for those who wanted it:

A sort of temporary concubinage was invented, known as a 'lease', binding the parties to live as man and wife for an agreed number of years. Even now there are couples, with no excuse of distance or ignorance, living in this way; and the lawyer is yet living who was in most repute as a drawer of these *leases* in late years.[61]

That, though no doubt an admirable arrangement, did not attract the approval of Christian gentlemen.

From about 1800 the foresters began to attract the attention of missionaries of a number of denominations. Working from their established congregations, missionaries went to preach in the Forest, gradually building up a sufficient body of followers to found a new Church.[62] The role of new converts was important in this process of religious colonisation. P. M. Procter, minister to the Newlands parish on the western border of the Forest, first established contact with Thomas Morgan, a collier who had heard Procter preach in the chapel at Coleford. A little while after the sermon Morgan had sent for Procter. Morgan wished to know what he must do to be saved. After a long conversation Procter agreed to come back into the Forest to preach regularly. From that beginning, preaching to Morgan and his neighbours in Morgan's house, Procter had gone on to build a church and start a Sunday School. Morgan was a useful convert, not least because he had been an outstanding sinner. In Procter's view the greatest sin of all was Sabbath breaking. Morgan took the lead in that and was its chief instigator and promoter in the Forest. That is to say, he arranged cricket matches, to which hundreds came on the Sabbath. Morgan's sinfulness was the greater because he had custody of the bats, balls and wickets.[63] Another of the worst tendencies in the foresters was tamed with the conversion of another collier, Samuel Morgan. Known as the 'Muddlin', he had been famous locally as an unbeaten fighter and wrestler before learning to read and becoming a preacher for the Primitive Methodists.[64] It was an objective of the revival that men like Thomas or Samuel Morgan should give up their idle, blasphemous lives and turn to the Lord, setting an example that others might follow. Thus when the Methodist Society of Colliers in the Forest petitioned for the appointment of a minister to the

Conference of Methodist Ministers in 1823, they emphasised the change which religion had wrought in their lives:

> The doctrine and discipline of the Methodists were first introduced among us by a local preacher whom God in His providence sent to reside in this neighbourhood. Many were brought out of the gloom of hellish night and led to seek redemption in the blood of Christ. In three months a society of nearly 30 persons were formed. A great moral change has taken place among us, the benefits of which extend to hundreds. Our state was once that of lawless heathen, but now we have learned to fear God, honour the King and obey his laws. We no longer lay claim to his Majesty's timber or deer, nor do we attack and murder his keepers. The rising plantations grow unmolested and our neighbours' flocks graze around us unassailed . . . We are no longer the terror of neighbouring towns, neither breaking their bones nor shedding their blood. Horrid blasphemies are changed into loud hosannas, and instead of the lewd drunkard's song we join in hymns of praise.[65]

Thus was religion a civilising influence.

By 1832 there was visible evidence of the Christian presence. The Anglicans had built three churches, with schools attached, and were promoting the building of a fourth.[66] The dissenters had also established a scattering of communities. The Methodists had been especially successful, opening chapels at Joyford, Ellwood, Lydbrook and Littledean Hill.[67] None the less, church discipline remained weak and there was still no power to celebrate marriages in the Forest. Those who preached there, moreover, had to depend on an uncertain private charity for support. So far as money was concerned, the Anglicans had the better lot, since they had been able to obtain the help of the Commissioners of Woods, who had made available a small fund, the proceeds from the investment of which might be used for repairs and maintenance of the Anglican Church buildings. The Commissioners further reinforced the position of the established church and further reduced the peculiarity of the Forest with two more in their series of Acts of Parliament: one of which divided the Forest into formal ecclesiastical districts, made provision for the building of churches and the payment of ministers; and the other of which incorporated the Forest into the adjoining Poor Law Unions of Monmouth and Westbury-on-Severn.[68]

The implications of the movement for reform in government which had begun in the late eighteenth century extended well beyond a concern with efficiency in the taking and stating of the public accounts or with economic administration. Economical reform had meant an explicit repudiation of ties of custom and right between the Crown and its subjects. Such claims of right were to be clearly defined and 'settled', that is to say, extinguished for the sake of protecting private property invested in the Forest and of giving to the Crown's property the degree of security enjoyed by private property. It was expedient for those purposes that Crown and capital should work together. Though rights and privileges might well have been the foundation of the life and work of the miners, and though it was well understood what the consequences of an erosion of the rights would be, the security of property and the 'public interest' were to be served first. And just as peculiar systems of mineral title were to be brought into line with those operating in other coal districts, so in other matters was peculiarity to be eliminated: the land should be held like any other real estate; debtors should be processed in conventional courts; there should be churches and ministers of religion; and there should be guardians of the poor. Despite the energy expended on the Forest, however, these aspirations had not been fully realised: at the end of the 1840s, after all, the free miners still had first claim on the coal. Why had the Crown accepted something less than a complete extinction of the rights?

3. Resistance

Then we were free, no tyrant did oppress,
And although poor did not know distress;
For all industrious, till'd his little land,
And built his cottage, as I understand.
But now there's tyranny enough I know,
And foreigners over we free miners crow.

Catherine Drew,
The Forest of Dean in Times Past Contrasted with the Present,
(Coleford, 1841).

A stubborn and sometimes violent resistance to change by the miners had baulked Crown policy in the Forest. Some of them, it was true, had welcomed the new order. They had petitioned for a railway and had been glad to bring foreigners to work the mines.[1] But other free miners had petitioned against the building of a railway.[2] They resented the steam-engines, the monied strangers and the Crown officers' application of the revised principles of public service.

At one level, opposition took the form of individual refusal to behave in the ways required by Crown policy. After 1808 the Commissioners of Woods had attempted to persuade the foresters to make a symbolic acknowledgement of the authority of the Crown, and its title to the Forest land, by paying a nominal rent for encroachments. The foresters refused to make this important act of submission.[3] Attempts to prevent new encroachments produced 'a constant scene of warfare between the encroachers and the officers of the Crown'.[4] Though the 25 acres encroached between 1812 and 1834 was in sum a small amount of land, it represented the net gain by foresters in scores of attempts to snatch a little of the Crown land through use of the 'rolling fence'. In the ten years after 1837, by which time the Crown's policy had been in force for nearly 20 years, 408 separate encroachments were presented at the verderers' courts. The typical case was that of the rolling fence: 'Benjamin Thomas, collier, for making an encroachment 25 yards long, from 1 to 2 yards wide, at Coleford Meend fined £1 0s 0d'.[5] The foresters persistently put up cabins, pigsties, goose cots and fern ricks and just as persistently the verderers ordered that they should be pulled down and the offenders fined.

35

In 1846 the officers took notice of a form of encroachment which till then seemed to have escaped them: perverse and ill-disposed persons continued to plant fruit trees on the waste land. A census revealed that over the previous 20 years 254 people had planted 2,602 trees on the waste. The Commissioners declared that the practice should cease. Legal proceedings, they warned in a printed notice, would follow future offences.[6]

Poaching had not much occupied the attention of successive Commissioners of Woods, largely because timber stealing was the more important threat to the revenue and because until the new plantations had been completed there were relatively few deer to worry about. As the plantations grew, however, the cover they provided allowed the deer to increase and with them the problem of poaching. It was of course illegal for the foresters to take the deer but, as with encroaching, it was the new rigour of administration which defined poaching as serious crime, to be punished and suppressed, rather than as ordinary behaviour implicitly sanctioned by custom and the forbearance of Her Majesty. The deer were of no importance to the Crown: indeed, they actually harmed the young growth of trees and therefore in 1788 the Commissioners had recommended that what deer there were in the Forest should be cleared out altogether. None the less, the deer were Crown property and had to be strictly guarded and accounted for. Predictably enough, that led to conflict between foresters and keepers. From 1839 to 1848 the Newnham and Coleford Petty Sessions dealt with 95 people for offences against the deer, 17 of the charges concerning assaults upon the keepers.[7] More seriously, Sir James Campbell, a Deputy Surveyor, reported:

> Since I have been at Dean Forest, keepers and others have been absolutely killed by poachers. One man certainly was killed since I was there; that was a policeman. They took to shooting the keepers when they were not allowed to shoot the deer and it was thought better to give the deer up.[8]

Again the Crown was at one with the coal-owners, who saw the deer as a threat to work discipline: 'I think the effect of the deer is very bad upon the general habits and morals of the population: if once a man begins to poach we can never reckon upon them working afterwards.'[9] The Commissioners solved that problem by having the deer killed in 1850.[10]

Up to 1828 there were no signs of collective action among the miners. Perhaps that was because the new enclosures had been made in stages over ten years and the Crown's pressure on the encroachers had been directed at individuals. So far as a free miner was formally required to give up any part of his rights it was through an apparently voluntary act, made in order to obtain some benefit from the railways.

The extent of the Crown's initiative after 1828 did however provoke a collective response from the miners. Initial signs of discontent came in 1828 and 1829, in petitions sent by the miners to the Commissioners, asking — unsuccessfully — for the enclosures to be thrown open.[11] More importantly, on 11 June 1830, the day before the Bill which had resulted from the Commissioners' *Report* of 1829 was due to be considered in Committee, the House of Commons received a petition from Warren James, 'a native and free miner of the Hundred of St Briavels . . . taking notice of the Bill . . . and praying to be heard by his Counsel against the same'.[12] According to a later report in the *Gloucester Journal*, the miners had 'levied large sums among themselves to support James'.[13] Other evidence hints that he represented a 'Fellowship of Free Miners' or 'Committee of Free Miners'.[14] At this time too there appeared in the Forest a new edition of the Book of Dennis, which the Deputy Surveyor described as 'that little book which they consider their Magna Charta'.[15] James' petition did not alter the course of the Bill which came due for another reading on 23 June 1831.

A month prior to that, persons unknown made a number of night attacks on fences around some of the enclosures.[16] The deputy surveyor, Edward Machen, offered a reward of 50 guineas for the discovery of the offenders. The only response to that came from an old miner who declared that he and his three sons had done the mischief and laid claim to the reward.[17] He was not taken into custody.

The night raids were the prelude to a more serious demonstration. On 3 June James had printed a notice which read:

> *Take Notice*, that the *Free Miners* of the . . . Forest, intend to *Meet* on Wednesday next . . . for the purpose of *Opening* the *Forest*, and their *Right* of *Common* to the same, so long deprived and All those persons who may chance to have stock thereon contrary to the Rights and Privileges of the Miners; are here required to remove the same forthwith otherwise they will have their stock impounded without further notice.[18]

Clearly, in James' mind the rights and privileges extended beyond mining and included other uses of the Forest. He posted copies of this notice up 'in the most conspicuous places; and that they might be more extensively circulated, a number were given to the attendants on a funeral from Whitecroft, which took place about that time'.[19]

Machen attempted to persuade James to give up the plan. In a printed notice he contradicted James' assertion that the miners had some right to open the enclosures. Only the Lords of the Treasury had the authority to do that, he warned. Other persons attempting to do so would be guilty of an illegal act and liable to punishment.[20] The invocation of the authority of the Treasury Lords did not deter James: he insisted that he had the support of greater authority. He asserted that he had a charter or an Act of Parliament which set out the rights and privileges of the miners and gave the Forest over to them — the new edition of the Book of Dennis in all probability.[21] According to one of his followers James had:

> through some nobleman in London . . . discovered an old charter or act of Parliament, giving certain rights to the Foresters of which they can never be deprived . . . that it was a document of undoubted authenticity, having been signed by seven English kings, amongst whom was his Majesty George the Fourth, who affixed his signature to it just before he died.[22]

On the morning set for the miners' meeting, when Machen went to see James to demand to know his authority for opening the enclosures, James indulged in no talk of charters and rights. Instead, 'with a face of the most imperturbable gravity' he produced 'as the voucher of his privilege, an enormous pick axe'.[23] He then led the way to the Park Hill enclosures and, with about 80 other miners, began to break down its fences. Machen and another magistrate read the Riot Act but the crowd laughed and jeered at them.[24] The magistrates complained that their presence had seemed to make the rioters work with greater determination. What were the magistrates when such great authority had been claimed for the miners? The impotence of the magistrates seemed to the foresters to confirm what James had told them about the justice of the miners' cause and the powerful men who supported it:

> They are satisfied that the Crown agrees with them in opinion, because they gave formal notice of their intention to lay the Forest open some days ago; and contend that if the Government had been averse to their proceedings they would have sent down military to stop them.[25]

The crowd grew quickly. Before the end of the first day about 300 people had joined it, including 80 women who 'seemed still more intent on the work of destruction than the men'.[26] Over the next two days, as messengers went out to the pits to bring in those miners still at work in them, the crowd grew to between 2,000 and 3,000 people.[27] As well as Warren James and one or two others who may be identified as the working proprietors of small mines, there were workmen from the larger mines, women and children and men who had land and cottages in the Forest but who did not work as miners.[28] One of them, at least, described himself as a 'respectable farmer'.[29]

James and his followers remained in control of the Forest for four days. Using their time to good effect they levelled about 60 miles of fence, breached most of the enclosures in some way and in a number of places and drove cattle and pigs in to graze on the undergrowth and acorns.[30] As the miners came in from the pits, James divided them into parties of from 50 to 300 which accompanied by carts carrying provisions and cider scattered through the Forest to the various enclosures and set to work on the fences 'in the same way as they would have worked at anything else'.[31] And hard work it was, according to a description of it written by James' anonymous biographer:

> Their mode of proceeding was this; they took a few yards at a time, which a large body rushed on, and by mere muscular strength overthrew. This appears still more worthy of note, from the thickness of the walls, which were mostly composed of clayey earth, in some places seven or eight feet thick. Gorse of many years growth had strengthened these boundaries by shooting down roots into the earth of a prodigious size, and interlacing its branches in such a manner on the top, that it appeared to a spectator to require a work of time to effect its overthrow, and not that of two or three days. They first cut away some of the strongest of the roots and then proceeded in the way mentioned, tearing down all before them, and at the fall of each fresh piece giving loud and repeated cheers.[32]

There were few threats of violence to people or to private property; the rioters were 'civil in their deportment but resolute in their purpose'.[33] According to the magistrates 'the mob offered no personal violence and indeed confined themselves wholly to the destruction of the fences'. The only exception they noted was that on the Saturday night some of the miners went in straggling parties to beg for food and beer, which 'the farmers in general supplied them willingly'.[34] The *Journal*'s correspondent wrote similarly that the 'rioters committed no other outrage, either in language or deed, than that of destroying the enclosures'.[35] Pressing his point, he reported that when the magistrates left the enclosures after reading the Riot Act to no good effect on the first morning of the disturbance, 'James sent for a constable and in his presence superintended the work of destruction, observing that he had sent for him to keep the peace'.

This picture of a peaceful riot should be modified a little. One member of a party of rioters was very rude to John Langham, the assistant surveyor of the Forest. 'I should like,' he said to Langham, 'to cut your b----y head off.'[36] Another party threatened to put a woodward down a coal pit when they saw him taking down the names of the leaders and offered to treat an unpopular bailiff in the same way if he appeared at the enclosures. A little later the crowd levelled the fences around the house of Edward Protheroe's agent, Aaron Goold, and turned cattle in to graze in his garden. A threat to more substantial private property arose when some in the crowd set up the cry to tear up the railways but nothing developed from that. These few incidents aside, there was nothing to contradict the *Journal*'s assessment that 'altogether they [the rioters] have behaved very temperately except in the act of destroying the enclosures'.[37]

The magistrates could offer little resistance to the destruction because 'the feelings of the inhabitants in general are rather in favour of the proceedings of the mob and we have not been able to establish a constabulary force'.[38] To compensate for the want of constables the magistrates sent a messenger to bring soldiers. But since the regular troops in the Monmouth area were concentrated at Merthyr dealing with another disturbance, only a makeshift group of men, composed of pensioners, militia and a marine recruiting party could be spared for the Forest. Though armed, they did not overawe the foresters who

> having had intimation of their approach, hastened down to welcome them, and whilst they waited in the yard of the 'Angel' for orders, greeted them from without by the appellation of the 'ragged regiment', and invited them up to the Forest to see them at work.[39]

The Monmouth party marched out again the following morning after spending the night in a room above the Coleford market house while the carousing crowd cheered and jeered at them from outside.[40] The magistrates wrote later that they had not used the Monmouth soldiers to execute the warrants sworn for the leaders of the riot because they feared that they 'could not without shedding much blood'.[41] To the foresters the magistrates appeared to act from weakness. The departure of the troops

> was no sooner announced in the forest, than the most enthusiastic joy was felt. They considered that they had now completely prevailed, and their rights were by this bold effort restored to them. They looked upon themselves as masters, where they had long been servants.[42]

Their triumph was shortlived: they had the Saturday night to celebrate but regular troops arrived on the Sunday. That event overawed the *Merlin*'s correspondent:

> The arrival in Coleford, on Sunday, of a squadron of the 3d [sic] Dragoons, with their loaded pistols and carabines — their naked

swords glittering in the sun — their limbs of Herculean mould — and their dashing military appearance, struck terror into the hearts of the bravest.[43]

A little after the advance guard, the rest of the Dragoons arrived, in company with the Duke of Beaufort, the Marquis of Worcester, the High Sheriff of Gloucestershire, 'every magistrate and gentleman of influence in the neighbourhood' and a party of special constables and woodwards.[44] This was a rather more daunting force than Monmouth's ragged regiment and the rioters responded accordingly, scattering to hide in the woods and coal pits.

Authority, present now in full strength and with proper show, settled down to a selective and calculated punishment of the rioters. The distribution of punishment reflected a distinction which the magistrates and the press had made from the beginning between James and his followers. They saw James as having a direct and personal responsibility for the riot.[45] The others were essentially good and loyal men who had been deluded by the talk of charters and rights. Most of the rioters consequently were allowed to expiate their disloyalty by rebuilding the fences they had levelled.[46]

Not all could be treated so leniently. It was necessary, the presiding judge said in his introductory remarks at the opening of the Gloucester Assizes, to 'satisfy all persons, that the law will protect those who are in peaceful enjoyment of property, and punish such as assemble riotously together, to the terror of his Majesty's subjects, to attempt to enforce their rights'.[47] To that end, seven men were indicted for causing riot and tumult. They were not charged as capital offenders because 'his Majesty's Attorney-General was of opinion that they had been acting under misguided notions'.[48] Found guilty, they received sentences ranging from one month to two years at hard labour with, for four of them, strong recommendations from the jury for mercy.

Warren James had not disclaimed his leadership of the riot after the arrival of the Dragoons but according to his biographer played his part faithfully and with a full sense of its dramatic import right to the last. The soldiers did not take him until the Wednesday following their arrival when he was, in the correct manner, betrayed. At about midnight a party of foot soldiers concealed themselves aroud the pit in which James was hiding. William Watkins, one of the keepers of the Forest, then gave the signal which James' sister used to 'draw him to bank'. When James appeared in his pit dress, 'almost as black as the coal he worked', the soldiers surrounded him. 'I'm betrayed by treachery', he cried, 'was not this the case, nine hundred men would have surrounded and defended me with the last drop of their blood! But do your duty; I have nothing to fear.' Properly proud and defiant, he refused to change from his pit dress to appear before the magistrates: 'No, I shan't; my dress is good enough for the company I am going in'.[49]

At Gloucester, James faced the capital charge of remaining with rioters for one hour after the reading of the Riot Act. The jury found him guilty but recommended mercy. Accordingly the judge undertook to make as favourable a representation of the case to His Majesty as he could and then recorded judgement of death.[50] James made no statement about the riot but said simply: 'I don't care if they hang *me*, only let it lead to the good of my countrymen'.[51] They did not hang him but instead allowed him the appalling mercy of transportation to New South Wales for life.[52]

The accounts of the riot which have survived seem less concerned with accurate reporting than with creating a sense of drama or displaying a condescending refusal to believe that the rioters really knew what they were about. Still it seems clear that the riot was not simply a spontaneous, casual outburst of violence. Nor was it what Nicholls believed it to be: an outbreak of that excitability to which the Celtic peoples are prone.[53] The miners and the others with them had deliberately and in an orderly and disciplined manner set themselves against the authorities. The event had been planned in advance and warning given to and received from the magistrates. The rioters were a 'mob' in the sense that they had ignored the reading of the Riot Act but not in the sense that they were a disorderly rabble.

Confrontation with the authorities had begun with James's notice about the rights and privileges of the miners. Concern for the rights was the main element in the making of the riot but there were others. Two obvious questions to ask of an event in 1831 are about the economic and political background. Was this riot a 'slump explosion': the product of distress, hunger and unemployment?[54] Or was this riot of a kind with others in that year described by Thompson as 'insurrectionary climaxes to Radical agitation'?[55]

Some evidence suggests strongly that the Dean miners were suffering distress in 1831. In their report to the Home Office on the causes of the riot the magistrates remarked that: 'the men in general have for the last 2 or 3 years suffered considerable privations for want of full work having many of them not more than 2 or 3 days work in a week. This has caused dissatisfaction.'[56] The *Gloucester Journal*'s correspondent wrote similarly that the 'real cause of the evil is a want of labour and of sufficient wages, so as to enable a man to live, and procure for himself and family the necessaries of life'.[57] In March 1832 a meeting of free miners at Yorkeley in the Forest made much the same point. The meeting resolved that 'a large portion of the Working Class of this Forest, together with their numerous Families, are great Sufferers for *Want of Employment*; to which cause they ascribe entirely the recent Disturbances which took place in the Forest'.[58]

There is also evidence of Radical agitation. The *Monmouthshire Merlin* printed, at the beginning of 1831, a report that 'an orator of the Cobbett School has lately been gulling the poor miners in the Forest of Dean by inflammatory speeches'.[59] A number of the miners had collected together at Bream village to hear the orator 'harangue them on some topics which they would not understand, and then obtained a number of signatures to different blank sheets of paper, which he represented as intended petitions for doing away with the truck system'. The clever orator, moreover, persuaded 'many of the poor creatures' to subscribe money to promote his campaign.

The orator was perhaps one William Birt, who published the first edition of his unstamped newspaper, the *Forester*, on 26 May, a fortnight before the miners' riot. The *Forester*'s principal content reflected two main purposes: firstly, to demonstrate that the English social and political system was immoral and secondly to argue that a number of problems peculiar to the Forest were symptoms of the oppressive working of the general system. Birt hoped for a society based, not on the individual selfishness which he identified as the source of poverty and degradation in England, but on a collective regard for the welfare and rights of all men:

> The hostility generated by the fancied reality of individual advantage, has been universally diffused, and men have employed their inventive energies to create means for the disadvantage and destruction of their fellow-creatures. But a bitter climactic — an ultimate demonstration of the *insanity of selfishness* — is now beginning to dispel the doctrine which assumed that private interest and individual aggrandisement are compatible with *general* welfare. In the unnatural inequality of fortune, in the ferocious delights of despotism, in the constant efforts for increasing individual power is the effect of this doctrine discovered.[60]

English society, dominated by the passions of sensual gratification and despicable avarice, worshipped at the shrine of sordid gain and bestial licentiousness. Immorality in society produced, and was supported by, an unnatural, artificial concentration of power and property in the hands of the few men who had dispossessed the majority.[61]

But though profoundly corrupt, England had not lost all hope of redemption. A new political era had dawned and brought with it the chance of regeneration:

The intensity of social evil has hastened the period of its decay. Extremes have arrived, and the balanced medium *must* be restored. There is an incipient but advancing perception, that the present perverted state is not unchangeable, that some analogy, between the advance of intelligence and the improvement of the social compact must be gradually and extensively realised . . . the chains which bound mankind in darkness are rapidly corroding away, and the reign of despotism is verging to its close.[62]

England's hope was, in general, moral reform and, in particular, a Reform Bill from a Whig ministry.

Birt's newspaper was the first ever published in the Forest. Aiming at the foresters in general as his readers, he discussed within the framework of his general analysis problems peculiar to the Forest. He began with a discussion of the truck or 'tommy' system of wage payment in the mines, the use of the waste land to help the poor and the operation of the Forest mining and game laws. Birt aligned himself with 'my poor fellow creatures, labourers in the Forests', against the 'base and contemptible dastards' who operated the tommy shops, 'many of whom I knew to be steeped in poverty to the very lips, a few short years ago . . . [who are now] snorting and looking down upon your plain but honest wives and families with heartless contempt or filthy pride'. The hard working forester, Birt declaimed, should not be 'treated like a Negro, and merely receive victuals for his work'.[63] He described the laws which regulated mining and commoning in the Forest as a 'chaos of mixed plunder, meanness, oppression and litigation, from which he can best extricate himself who has the amplest means of establishing might against right'.[64] It had not always been so:

> The good old straight-forward Foresters appear to have had a code of their own, which worked well and yielded a just apportionment of the Forest resources to the inhabitants at large, but now, from some cause or other, new laws and new results have the predominance.[65]

This contrast between the fairness of the old laws and the oppression of the new he linked again with the contrast between the wealth of the few and the poverty of the many. The present laws produced, on the one hand, 'pale and wan looking colliers' and, on the other, men who 'appeared as frequently, spruce, gay and waxing fat with the same temper as the ass emphatically alluded to of old. The Noblesse and Beggary of Italy in a petty way'.[66]

Birt declared in favour of the 'Foresters, the real Foresters, *Those who work and toil for their bread*':[67] their condition had to be reformed. One way of doing that was to throw open the Forest's waste lands for cultivation by the poor. Another was to remove the restrictions on the taking of game, whose effect was to tempt the 'starving peasant' to crime and then to punish him for it with transportation to the Charmless Antipodes. That should not be tolerated in the reign of the Fourth William, 'the King who has so wisely identified himself with the people'.[68]

However strident this new voice in the Forest, it is difficult to connect Birt directly with the riot. His catchphrase, 'King William and Reform', appeared only once at the enclosures, on a piece of paper handed to a banker from Monmouth by one of the rioters. But this was the only reported reference to Reform in the event. If the riot had been directly promoted by Birt, more than that might have been expected. Birt, moreover, was in a difficult position: although his writing had been inflammatory, it had been tendentious. If he wished to stir up the foresters it was for the cause of Reform and the return of a Whig Ministry. But it was obvious before the riot that those opposed to Reform had fared badly in the general elections of 1831 and that a Reform Ministry would regain office.[69] That being so, Birt could not advocate, without monstrous inconsistency, anything resembling a want of confidence in the enlightened leadership. His advice to the foresters was, therefore, to be calm and rational:

> I have heard that threats have been used to enforce the re-opening of the enclosures, these are very blameable — to give them effect would be decidedly illegal and wrong. The time now is, when just complaints will not only be received but redressed . . . Never mind my good fellows, don't get waspish and angry with the flip-flaps and popinjays of things as they have been, just as they are about to die a natural death . . . Try to get relief by every rational and constitutional means, but by no other . . . Our old ship has been a long time on her beam ends, but we have got a good commander aboard and a capital pilot at the helm now, who . . . will soon put her on sailing trim again.[70]

That was the theme of all Birt's subsequent comment on the affair and none of it contributes to an impression that he was in some way an instigator of it.

On balance, despite rumours current at the time, it does not seem likely that the Dean riot was 'political' in the sense that it was intended to promote the Reform Bill or was the result of direct political agitation. The magistrates certainly did not believe in a plot. Warren James, they reported, had gained great influence among the miners by '*Stating that he was countenanced by persons high in authority* and by the Government *itself* . . . but we have no idea that [the miners] *were assisted by any person of higher rank, or that the riots have any connection with any political cause*.[71] There is nothing in the surviving Home Office or Treasury Solicitor's papers to suggest that the Government took seriously any suggestion that political agitation lay behind the riot. The Solicitor's lenient treatment of the rioters who were taken into custody suggests the contrary.

That is not to say that the general political context was irrelevant. Explicit criticism of government and the condition of the poor may well have encouraged the foresters to attend to their grievances, to articulate them and seek redress. The environment in 1831 of general political unrest, of agitation, Cobbetites, Swingites, incendiarists and attacks on the popinjays of things as they have been, probably made the use of riot to draw attention to the miners' grievances seem a less extraordinary course of action than it might have in more settled times.

But the riot had been, first and foremost, an attempt to reassert against the Crown what the miners believed to be their rights in the Forest:

> The miners say that when Lord Lowther was the Chief Commissioner, the Foresters had applied to him for the throwing open of the Forest, and he was disposed to listen to their application: that the Duke of Wellington had appointed to meet him in the Forest for the purpose of inspecting the state and condition of the trees. The death of the late King, and the consequent dissolution of the Parliament, and breaking up of the Wellington Administration, prevented any further proceedings. It is said that since that time the Foresters have memorialized the present Commissioners of Woods and Forests on the subject, but without success . . . Under the persuasion that they have been unfairly dealt with . . . they have taken the work of their real or supposed grievances into their own hands.[72]

The press, the Government and the magistrates all, so far as it is possible to tell, believed that 'the war word, as usual, is restitution of rights, which the foresters complain have been wrested from them by the Crown'.[73] Thus the deputy surveyor wrote that he 'saw Henry and Richard Dobbs pull the bushes out of a gateway, and turn their cow into Cockshoot's Enclosure, and when I went out and expostulated with them they said that they had been deprived of their rights long enough'.[74]

The riot drew upon and expressed hostility to the foreigners as well as to the Crown. In their account of the riot to the Home Office, Beaufort and the magistrates reported that the miners were aggrieved by 'the influx of foreigners of whom they are very jealous . . . It is difficult to explain why a dissatisfaction on this ground should lead to an attack on the Forest Inclosures but this was certainly the most prominent ground of complaint'.[75] Along with petitions asking for the opening of the Forest, the miners had sent others praying for the restoration of the Mine Law Court. The Commissioners of Woods referred them to their Solicitor's Department, explaining that:

> The works thus carried on [by foreigners] are much complained of by such of the free miners as are not connected with the adventures. These men (more than 1,000 in number) state that they are thrown out of employment by means of the new works in which they are not engaged; and being thereby (as they alledge) [sic] reduced to a state of penury . . . imagine that the speediest means of putting a stop to the Encroachments which have been made by the adventurers is to revive this Court.[76]

The *Forester*'s 'explanation' of the riot also complained that:

> His Grace the Duke of Beaufort, as Constable of the Castle of St Briavels and Lord Chief Ranger of the Forest, has been for nearly three years past trifling with the patience of the free miners by denying their just demands of opening their free miners' Courts according to their rights and privileges, and which they usually enjoyed from time immemorial, the grants made to them by Edward the 3rd.[77]

The rioters had declared that they would drive the foreigners from the Forest.[78] The crowd destroyed the fences around the house of Edward Protheroe's agent and on the Saturday night, celebrating their success in cider, the rioters drank the toast 'Confusion to all foreigners'.[79]

For some of the richer free miners a more direct form of self-interest was at stake. About 1826, at about the time the Crown was preparing its new assault on the free miners' rights, the Purton Pill Railway Scheme had taken shape. This line was designed to run from Purton Pill on the Severn to roughly the centre of the Forest at Foxes Bridge. It was to run about midway between the existing Severn and Wye and Bullo Pill lines, across an area of coal which had been little mined.[80] The scheme offered new opportunity for free miners to register gates along a railway which would make the gales worth having. Little is known about this scheme except that its main promoter was Moses Teague, one of the few free miners who had prospered in partnership with foreigners and who owned a mine at Foxes Bridge.[81] For Teague and for other free miners the Purton Pill scheme gave the miners' rights a new value at the very moment that the Crown had put their existence in question.

The foreigners, notably Protheroe, had opposed the Purton Pill scheme.[82] This gave both rich and poor free miners a common interest in opposition to the foreigners. The working miners believed that the 'monopoly' of the railways held by Protheroe was an important cause of unemployment and distress in the Forest. The problem was that the railways did not operate as a subordinate or complementary service to the pits. As Protheroe wrote, 'the truth is that the only persons who have ever ventured to open deep coal works have done it to serve their interests as rail road proprietors'.[83] Protheroe had to strike a balance between the wish to profit from the mines and the wish to profit from his railways. For those who depended on the mines alone, as owners or workers, a price for the carriage of coal which would provide the railway with a good return could only be a source of grievance.

There was one other important grievance against the foreigners and one which probably affected the largest number of miners: 'those foreigners introduced foreign miners in preference to the natives'.[84] The Dean Forest Commissioners concluded that:

The claims of the free miners to the exclusive holding of gales, and to be exclusively employed as labourers in the mines, occasion constant and never ending jealousy and dissatisfaction on their part. The foreigners who have got into possession of extensive works, although they in general give preference to the free miners, consider themselves quite at liberty to employ and do employ some foreign labourers.[85]

A free miner, Thomas Davis, had given evidence to the Commissioners that:

What is the grief among the miners is, that foreigners should employ foreigners instead of free miners. We should not object to foreigners, if they were obliged to employ free miners to work. I have known many free miners distressed for employment when foreigners have been in work by preference.[86]

Another free miner, John Worgan, had testified similarly that:

I think free miners are imposed upon very much by foreigners. They bring in their own foremen and their own foreign work men; I was myself turned away to make room for a Bristol man and we cannot remedy ourselves, unless our Mine Law Courts be revived. I think the Mine Law Courts would enable us to tell who was free and who was not; it would prevent foreigners managing everything their own way.[87]

A considerable hostility to foreigners had thus grown up among the free miners. Distress and unemployment were the product of the monopoly which the foreigners had created by destroying the Mine Law Court and usurping the miners' rights. Not content with owning the mines, foreigners had brought other foreigners to work in the Forest. Here was a sense of injustice and dispossession which found expression in the riot along with resentment of the State's intrusive assertion of control and its refusal to re-open the Forest. The campaign for the restoration of the Mine Law Court and the riot in which it culminated represented in sum a demand by the free miners to have control of the Forest economy returned to them: a control which miners had exercised in living memory. That the Crown and the foreigners should have been linked in the minds of the foresters was not such a difficult problem: they believed — with good reason — that the Crown had 'favoured' the foreigners and had 'materially assisted' them.[88] Crown and capital were seen as allies in dispossessing the foresters and usurping their rights.

With the closing of Gloucester Assizes and the banishment of Warren James to New South Wales, the miners' attention shifted to the hearings of the Dean Forest Commissioners. The miners' mode of action in this new phase was the public meeting, the petition and the representative committee, rather than the riot. And despite some initial wavering their demand continued to be for the revival of the Mine Law Court and the exclusion of foreigners.

A memorial presented to the Commissioners in April 1832 expressed the opinions of the working miners:

That the free miners most respectfully wish . . . the Commissioners to take into their consideration the distress to which they have been reduced by the demise of the Mine Law Courts, by which their rights and privileges were formerly protected, and which they have repeatedly solicited to have restored; the consequences of which disuse have been, that foreigners, who had originally no right to enter the mines, have gradually possessed themselves of property therein, and again sold the same to other foreigners, to the exclusion of the free miners themselves; that the free miners have not been able to obtain redress, owing to there being no tribunal except the Mine Courts which could legally investigate their claims; that in many instances they have been arbitrarily despoiled of their possessions by foreigners, and altogether, from the numbers of strange workmen and others introduced into the Forest, and employed in the hauling of mine, coal and ore, the free

miners have been deprived of work, and themselves and their
families reduced to the utmost distress.[89]

There followed a statement of the claims of the free miners. They
wished to have restored all their rights and privileges, including the
right to mine wherever they wished in the Forest and to have timber
for the pits. They wanted the Mine Law Court revived to adjudicate
disputes and 'for the purpose of ascertaining what persons have
usurped the privileges of free miners'. They were uncompromising in
their insistence that only free miners had a right to work mines in the
Forest.

The Commissioners conceded nothing to the free miners. It might
well have been true that the working of the mines by the foreigners
under the cover of the free miners' rights was fraudulent but free
miners had assisted in the perpetration of that fraud. The free miners,
therefore, could not now equitably demand that the foreigners should
be dispossessed. The Crown moreover, as a matter of equity, was 'in a
great degree' barred from interference with the foreigners because it
had for so long recognised in fact their ownership of mines. The customary workings were at an end and the only way out of a difficult
situation was to extinguish the free miners' rights altogether, with
suitable compensation, and to make the relationship of the Crown
and mine owners the same in law as that between any landlord and
tenant.

Their demands completely rejected, the free miners sent a
memorial to the Commissioners of Woods in 1836, complaining that
the proposed Mines Act was for 'the purpose of entirely destroying the
rights and privileges of the free miners, and of depriving them and
their children of the customs and franchises which have been exercised by the free miners from time immemorial'.[90] They prayed yet
again that the Crown would restore the Mine Law Court and
threatened that the miners 'cannot voluntarily consent to the arrangements proposed by the Commissioners'.[91]

The Commissioners had other cards to play in the face of this
intransigence. In November 1836 the foresters were 'startled by the
apparition of the agents of the solicitors to the Board of Woods and
Forests, traversing the district in all directions'.[92] These gentlemen
placarded the Forest with notices of intention to bring in Bills in the
next session of Parliament, two of which were to concern the
encroachments and the right of common. Alexander Milne, one of the
Commissioners, came to the Forest himself in June 1837 to consult the
landholders of the surrounding parishes about Commoning. So far as
the Commissioners were concerned the encroachers of Crown land
had no right of common at all. Milne therefore did not invite them to
meetings of parishioners which he called to discuss a proposal to

disafforest the waste and to extinguish Commoning altogether.[93] None the less, about 1,000 of the encroachers came uninvited to his meeting in Newland parish, where they loudly proclaimed that they were as entitled to common as any other of the inhabitants of the Hundred and made it impossible for Milne to carry on the meeting.[94]

Shortly afterwards the free miners met to discuss the Mines Bill. They received this time a Bill which had been modified so as to retain the free miners' privilege in a diluted form and decided unanimously to accept it, even though it meant the end of any hope for a renewal of the Mine Law Court and though it confirmed the foreigners' possession of the coal.[95] Milne almost immediately announced the withdrawal of his plan to abolish Commoning.

Government also made useful concessions on its Bill to deal with the encroachments, in order to meet objections from the foresters. The Commissioners dropped earlier plans to impose restrictions on building on land after it had passed freehold into the hands of its occupiers and agreed to make all conveyances under the Act free of legal expenses and stamp duty.[96] The holders of land encroached after 1812, to whom it was originally intended to grant relatively short leases, were given the option to purchase at a nominal sum:

> The announcement of these liberal concessions, which have the effect of giving the owners of upwards of 2,000 acres of land quiet titles to their possessions, and placing them on a footing with other freeholders of the empire, was received with loud cheering.[97]

That Government did make concessions may partly be explained by the political context of these events as well as by the wish to carry through the Mines Bill. The balance in Gloucestershire politics between the Tory followers of the Duke of Beaufort and the Whigs, led by the Earl of Berkeley, had been upset in 1831 and 1832 by the return of two Whig reformers for West Gloucestershire.[98] The Duke of Beaufort's eldest son, the Marquis of Worcester, took a seat back for the Tories in 1834 but the balance having once been upset it might be again.[99] And might not circumstances so alter that the Tories could take both seats?

Certainly there had been great enthusiasm for Reform in the Forest in 1831. When the Whig candidates came to Coleford in 1831, 500 people came out to meet them and drew their carriage into the village, cheered their speeches and went on to break some Tory windows.[100] The Tory party, led by Lord Granville Somerset, had a different sort of reception. A crowd harassed them, thrust green boughs (the Whig emblem) into their faces, pelted them with stones, prevented them from speaking and broke some more Tory windows.[101] The passing of the Act produced celebration 'which was never before witnessed'.[102]

The houses of Coleford displayed illuminations and transparencies. Banners decorated the market hall, a band paraded in streets which were lined with freshly cut green boughs and the better-off inhabitants distributed 750 loaves to the poor. Within the Forest proper, gatherings of several hundred sat down to whole roast oxen and carried on to 'a country dance on the green'.[103] The confidence of the Whigs in their support among the foresters was clearly demonstrated in 1832. When the barristers who were to revise the electoral roll for West Gloucestershire came to Newnham, a village on the western side of the Forest, 991 foresters attempted to register: of those the Whigs objected to 113 and the Tories to 559.[104]

The Tories won the day in 1832. The foresters had claimed the vote on the grounds that they occupied land and cottages. The Tories objected that these people were encroachers on Crown land, that their occupation of land and cottages was illegal. The barristers upheld that objection. In 1835, however, the barristers reversed their decision after complex legal argument which showed a precedent for allowing the vote to occupiers of Crown land where the encroachment was ancient and possession had not been contested.[105] By 1836, moreover, it was probable that the plan of the Commissioners of Woods to create a freehold title to the encroached lands would add 500 to 1,000 voters to the roll for West Gloucestershire. It was a delightful irony that the anxiety of the Commissioners of Woods to eliminate the problem of irregular occupation of land in the Forest should, in a clearly unstable electorate, give the foresters the means of resistance to the complete separation and settlement of their rights.

The compromise settlement of the problem of the rights helped to re-establish for the authorities in Dean some of the self-confidence which had been lost in the disturbances of 1831 and the quarrelling which followed them. There was still, of course, some doubt about the loyalty of the foresters and their potential for violence. Those doubts were reflected in the response of the authorities to the visit of a Chartist lecturer to the Forest in 1842. In August the Chief Constable of Gloucestershire reported to the Home Office that some five to six hundred people had gathered to hear the lecturer.[106] That meeting was dispersed by the appearance of the superintendent and constables of police who had been appointed to work in the Forest after the riots at the enclosures. The lecturer was Ruffy Ridley, a dyer of Sloane Street, Chelsea, who had come to present himself to the miners as a suitable man to act as their delegate to a Chartist convention which was to be held in Birmingham.[107] At Circencester, on his way to the Forest, he had spoken

in abuse of the Government and authorities stating that the working classes were living in a State of Anarchy and that if the middle classes of society would join the working classes they would soon have it their own way, he adverted to the Riots and the conduct of the red coats and blue bottle Police and called on the People to hold them up to public scorn.[108]

Fearful that the unemployment and distress which had reappeared in the Forest would lead the people to listen too carefully to Ridley, the authorities acted quickly and confidently. After Ridley had held a second meeting of about 700 people, who elected him delegate to Birmingham, the magistrates issued an extraordinary proclamation which, firstly, referred to Ridley's lectures on the principles of Chartism and then proclaimed that assemblies of 'persons in considerable numbers, having a manifest tendency to endanger the public peace, and to excite the fears of her Majesty's subjects' were illegal.[109] They were illegal, moreover, even though they were not 'at the time attended with acts of open violence'. The proclamation further requested that all masters caution their workmen and servants against attending such meetings. The magistrates then arrested Ridley on a charge of using seditious language. They complained that he had said at one of his meetings that: '*It was a great shame as the Queen do not maintain her own Mother, as you poor Foresters are obliged to do*'.[110] Released on bail, Ridley disappeared in the company of some Staffordshire men and no more was heard of the matter.

4.   The New System I: Mining and the Little Buttymen

The forest now is numerous got of late,
Since monied men come here to speculate;
Where once a little turfen hut did stand,
You'll see a noble house and piece of land.
Rail-roads you see, and tunnel through Hay hill;
From Bilson coalworks, down to Bullo Pill.
Protheroe! thy name is to the Forest dear,
For many thousands thee hast ventured here;
Deeper thy pits than any here before,
The lowest vein of coal for to explore.
They were but shallow pits in days of old —
They'd not the knowledge then, as I am told;
But though here was not then great learning's store,
It was much better for the labouring poor;
Men loved their masters — masters loved their men,
But those good times we ne'er shall see again.

Catherine Drew,
The Forest of Dean in Times Past Contrasted with the Present,
(Coleford, 1841).

In the second half of the century, when controversy about the rights and customs revived, the Forest still seemed to outsiders to be in some ways different from the rest of England. The nature of that argument though had changed. Once, the foresters had been feared as a savage and lawless people who might do hurt to their neighbours when work was scarce or the price of corn too high. With that there had gone a sort of contempt. If the foresters were dangerous it was because they were ignorant, pagan, superstitious and generally not fit to go among civilised people. It was in that spirit that the *Monmouthshire Merlin* reported in 1834 the efforts of a forester to free his pig from the influence of witchcraft.[1] That contempt gave way to the detached curiosity of the observers of odd and old customs, like that of the

54

clergyman in the 1860s who recorded the practice of dual naming: some surnames had become so common in the Dean that families adopted other names for everyday purposes.[2] If the Forest was odd, it was no longer dangerous in any special way. It had become a coal and iron district much like any other.

In 1871 the census takers described about half of the 6,782 males employed in the Forest as coal or iron miners (see Table 4.1). Four employed males in ten were coal miners and one was an iron miner.

Table 4.1: Occupations of Employed Males in the Forest of Dean, 1851 and 1871

	1851		1871		Increase 1851—1871	
	No.	%[a]	No.	%[a]	No.	%[b]
Clerical, non-mining professional	38	0.9	67	1.0	29	76.3
Shopkeepers, merchants	337	7.9	509	7.5	172	51.0
Industrial trades[c]	215	5.1	329	4.9	114	53.1
Metal workers	171	4.0	388	5.7	217	126.9
General labourers	573	13.5	957	14.1	384	67.0
Colliers	1,712	40.3	2,864	42.2	1,152	67.3
Iron-ore miners	230	5.4	740	10.9	510	221.7
Other mining[d]	76	1.8	119	1.8	43	56.6
Stone and quarry	295	7.0	340	5.0	45	15.3
Agriculture	350	8.2	237	3.5	−113	−32.3
Wood and timber	124	2.9	128	1.9	4	3.2
Miscellaneous	127	3.0	104	1.5	−23	−18.1
Total	4,248	100	6,782	100	2,534	59.65

Notes: a. Proportion of all employed males in the Forest.
b. Percentage increase, 1851—71.
c. Blacksmiths, carpenters and other tradesmen who might have been employed in mines or iron works but who might equally well have been independent tradesmen.
d. Mining management and professional.

Source: *Census of England and Wales*, 30 March 1851, PRO HO 107/1, 959/1, 976/2, 444; 2 April 1871, PRO RG 10/2, 596—2, 605/2, 686/5, 296—5, 300.

Though employing in absolute numbers far more many men, coal mining had not grown at as fast a rate as metal mining and metal processing. The proportion of colliers in the workforce had not altered much between 1851 and 1871 but the number of iron-ore miners more than tripled and the number of metal workers more than doubled. The timber, stone and agricultural workforces, by contrast, all fell as a proportion of the workforce. Where those groups made up about a fifth of the total male workforce in 1851 they were only about a tenth of it in 1871. Agriculture suffered an absolute decline, losing about one-third of its workforce over the two decades.

Those figures, however, though indicative of the basic trends in employment in the Forest, underestimate the numbers employed in mining. Some miners lived in the parishes surrounding the Forest: in Abbinghall, Little Dean, Flaxley, Lea Bailey, Mitcheldean, Newland, Ruardean and Staunton. Bringing together the miners in the parishes and the Forest, as well as workers in the industry other than 'coal miners' and 'iron miners', allows the construction of a table showing the number of males employed in mining in the Hundred of St Briavels at each of the census dates between 1841 and 1871. The same information may be obtained from the annual reports of the Mines Inspectors for each year from 1874 to 1880 (Table 4.2). The total coal mining workforce had more than doubled from 1841 to 1871. More striking was the fivefold increase in the number employed in iron mining.

Table 4.2: Employment in Coal and Iron Mining in the Hundred of St Briavels, 1841—1885

Year	Coal	Iron ore	Total
1841	1,544	236	1,780
1851	2,066	289	2,355
1861	2,732	533	3,265
1871	3,375	1,114	4,489
1873	—	2,322	—
1874	5,050	2,055	7,105
1875	4,694	1,860	6,554
1876	4,433	1,790	6,223
1877	4,148	1,814	5,962
1878	3,985	1,683	5,668
1879	4,291	1,627	5,918
1880	3,830	1,758	5,588
1881	4,419	—	—
1882	4,115	—	—
1883	4,167	—	—
1884	4,213	—	—
1885	4,240	—	—

Source: *Census of England and Wales*, 1841—71; R. G. Hunt, *Mineral Statistics of the United Kingdom* (Geological Survey, 1873—85).

At the time of the 1831 riot many of the miners had feared that the new capitalists would introduce foreign workmen who would exclude the natives. That in fact had not happened. The miners who worked in the Forest had mostly been born there or in neighbouring areas. In 1871, 70.8 per cent of the colliers resident in the Forest had been born there (Table 4.3). Gloucestershire and Herefordshire contributed another 23.1 per cent. Small groups had come from distant English counties and from Wales but there were only three Irish miners. That meant that there were not in the Forest the sorts of conflicts which divided the Scottish mining workforce after the influx of the Irish.[3]

Table 4.3: Forest of Dean: Place of Birth of Colliers in 1871

Place of birth	Number	%
Forest of Dean	2,029	70.8
Other Gloucestershire	564	19.8
Herefordshire	95	3.3
Other English	97	3.3
Wales	74	2.6
Ireland	3	0.1
Not Known	2	0.1
	2,864	100.0

Source: *Census of England and Wales*, 2 April 1871, PRO RG 10/2, 596—2, 605/2, 686/5, 296—5,300.

Between 1841 and 1871 the Forest's output of coal increased almost sixfold from 145,136 tons to 837,893 tons. Up to 1860 output had grown steadily with few setbacks, from an index number of 22 in 1841 to 89 in 1860. There was a marked slump, however, in the early sixties and, from 1863 to 1869, little increase in production. Though a good deal more volatile the output of iron ore showed the same rough trends: expansion, though uneven in character, to 1860; a trough from 1861 to 1863; and then a plateau in the late sixties (Tables 4.4 and 4.5).

Table 4.4: Coal Raised in the Forest of Dean, 1841—1885

Year	Tons	Index (1874=100)	Year	Tons	Index (1874=100)
1841	145,136	22	1864	676,627	101
1842	255,592	38	1865	778,428	117
1843	220,777	33	1866	773,447	116
1844	264,571	40	1867	774,593	116
1845	309,228	46	1868	779,839	117
1846	284,227	43	1869	761,843	114
1847	316,404	47	1870	837,184	126
1848	316,571	48	1871	837,893	126
1849	337,119	51	1872	730,409	110
1850	337,948	51	1873	790,400	119
1851	335,687	50	1874	667,069	100
1852	363,157	54	1875	700,648	105
1853	402,623	60	1876	670,009	100
1854	412,028	62	1877	638,319	96
1855	460,280	69	1878	655,605	98
1856	460,432	69	1879	779,428	117
1857	487,686	73	1880	755,156	113
1858	491,284	74	1881	813,327	122
1859	527,219	79	1882	777,497	117
1860	590,470	89	1883	709,294	106
1861	573,159	86	1884	778,046	117
1862	474,168	71	1885	826,167	124
1863	747,971	112			

Source: Dean Forest, Coal and Iron Mine Rentals, PRO LRRO 12/113, 114.

Table 4.5: Iron Ore Raised in the Forest of Dean, 1841—1885

Year	Tons	Index	Year	Tons	Index
1841	18,872	17	1864	179,292	163
1842	27,537	25	1865	130,179	118
1843	19,795	18	1866	136,893	124
1844	43,717	40	1867	142,174	129
1845	49,463	45	1868	135,604	123
1846	66,032	60	1869	133,595	121
1847	76,199	69	1870	137,795	125
1848	54,507	50	1871	170,611	155
1849	63,134	57	1872	153,255	139
1850	73,990	67	1873	150,887	137
1851	80,531	73	1874	110,203	100
1852	80,907	73	1875	92,835	84
1853	69,570	63	1876	98,133	89
1854	76,205	69	1877	79,646	72
1855	73,370	67	1878	69,034	63
1856	75,042	68	1879	52,061	47
1857	82,140	75	1880	83,198	76
1858	76,622	70	1881	78,876	72
1859	91,384	83	1882	68,075	62
1860	192,074	174	1883	195,199	177
1861	95,770	87	1884	46,473	42
1862	109,056	99	1885	35,249	32
1863	62,473	57			

Source: Dean Forest, Coal and Iron Mine Rentals, PRO LRRO 12/113, 114.

The tendency, evident before 1831, for production to be concentrated in the hands of a few companies, had continued. Most of the Forest's output came from a small number of relatively large pits. Table 4.6 shows the pits in Dean in groups according to the size of their annual outputs at five-year intervals from 1865 to 1885. There were still many tiny pits whose annual output was less than 5,000 tons: in 1870 almost half of the Dean mines were in that category. Those were the levels and shallow pits which free miners still worked in the outcrop of the main seams, supplying the winter trade in house coal to the farmers in the surrounding countryside. In 1870, however, those pits raised only 3.9 per cent of total output. Most of the coal raised came from those which produced more than 50,000 tons in each year. Half a dozen of them in 1870 accounted for about three-quarters of the field's output. In other words, most of the colliers in the Forest worked in relatively large-scale employment units such as the Trafalgar Colliery which employed 800 men and boys in 1871 and the Parkend Coal Company which employed 600.[4]

The six pits which produced more than 50,000 tons in 1870 were the Resolution (and Safeguard), the Soundwell (Lightmoor), the Foxes Bridge, Crumpmeadow, Trafalgar and New Fancy. The first two of

Table 4.6: Number of Collieries and Coal Raised in Each Size Category in the Forest of Dean, 1865—1885

	Up to 5,000 tons				Size category[a] 5,000 – 50,000				50,000+				Total no. of mines
	No.	%[b]	Output[c] (tons)	%[d]	No.	%	Output (tons)	%	No.	%	Output (tons)	%	
1865	20	43.5	22,068	2.8	22	47.8	390,059	50.1	4	8.7	366,301	47.1	46
1870	19	47.5	32,614	3.9	15	37.5	198,681	23.7	6	15.0	605,889	72.4	40
1875	27	51.0	42,355	6.0	22	41.5	345,770	49.4	4	7.5	312,523	44.6	53
1880	43	68.3	48,558	6.4	14	22.2	214,657	28.4	6	9.5	491,941	65.2	63
1885	34	65.4	43,719	5.3	11	21.2	181,851	22.0	7	13.4	600,597	72.7	52

Notes:

a. Collieries raising that many tons of coal in each year.

b. Proportion of total number of collieries in the Forest of Dean in that year.

c. Tons of coal raised by collieries in that size category in that year.

d. Proportion of the total of coal raised in Dean in that year which were raised by collieries in that size category.

Source: Dean Forest, Coal and Iron Mine Rentals, PRO LRRO 12/113, 114.

these belonged to Henry Crawshay, a son of William Crawshay, the Welsh iron-master. Henry Crawshay, in partnership with Osman Barrett, also owned Foxes Bridge. The Crumpmeadow had belonged to Aaron Goold, Edward Protheroe's agent in 1831, and had come by inheritance to his sons Alfred and Thomas. All these men were foreigners, as was James Sully, whose Parkend Coal Company owned the New Fancy. Only the brothers Thomas and William Brain, masters at Trafalgar, were free miners.[5]

The coal, iron-ore and iron-processing industries of the Forest depended closely on each other. Iron mining and making were of course closely related: furnaces in Dean took almost two-thirds of the ore raised there in 1869. The furnaces in turn supplied iron to the tin and wire works at Lydbrook, Cinderford, Parkend and Soudley.[6] In the years for which there are any data, local mills and furnaces took about one-fifth of all the coal raised in the Forest.[7]

The most important markets for coal, however, were those outside the Forest. Perhaps two-thirds of the coal went to the household coal trade of southern and south-western England. That trade varied with the seasons, demand reaching its peak in the winter and falling away again in the spring. The exact timing of that cycle, and the extent of its movement in any particular year, could be affected by unseasonably good or bad weather, by gales or snow which disrupted shipping in the Severn, or rail traffic, and by merchants who built up or reduced stocks with a view to manipulating the price. The markets for coal and the price of coal could also be affected by the competition of other districts. The Forest's masters had especially complained, from the early thirties, of the competition of Welsh and Staffordshire coal. That problem became greater after the Forest's local railway system had been linked in 1855 to the Great Western and Midlands systems. In that distribution network the Forest was puny. In 1873, for example, Gloucestershire as a whole shipped 293,069 tons on the Midland Railway, while Derbyshire shipped over 5 million tons, Yorkshire almost 2 million and Leicestershire and Nottinghamshire about 1 million tons each.[8] Alfred Goold complained of the competition to a Dean Forest Mining Commission in 1871. Asked if he could compete successfully with South Wales or the Midlands, he answered:

Certainly not. We are within 12 miles of Gloucester, or less, as the crow flies, and yet the Midlands can successfully compete with us. Thus, if you take Cheltenham, we are within twenty miles of that town, and the complement of coal supplied to Cheltenham is 120,000 tons a year, and the most that the Forest sends is 15,000 tons a year.[9]

Another master, James Sully, agreed with Goold. He complained that 'the north country coal has been sent down by railway to Exeter, and also that north country coal, having been discharged from vessels at Exeter, into trucks, has been sent by railway into Dorsetshire and Somersetshire'.[10] Markets which might once have belonged to the Forest had become more open, especially where, the masters complained, the railway companies charged freight rates which favoured the large producing districts and allowed them to bring coal to the south of England at prices which pressed the Forest hard.[11]

As a market force the Forest was plainly insignificant. As Arnold Thomas, another of the masters, put it in 1882: 'If the district were wiped off the slate tomorrow it would hardly make a bit of difference'.[12] The Forest, therefore, could never take the lead in setting prices. It was 'obliged to follow':

> Their experience had taught them, that, when they had taken a position which was untenable, and in opposition to more powerful people, they found their position a somewhat microscopic one. In other words, when they in the Forest had said, 'We will do this, or that, or we don't care about opponents', they had sorrowfully to confess afterwards they had made mistakes, as other districts had taken their trade, and the result was . . . they had to submit to months of reduced output, arising from the fact that they had attempted to do more than they had strength to do.[13]

The old model of the restricted trade of the free miners, able to set their price for coal through the 'bargainers', had given way to a vulnerability to market forces over which local producers had no control.

There had been other changes as well, for instance in the way in which the collier's work within the pit was organised. The basic skills required in the pit had not varied, of course.[14] The collier's basic task was to bring coal down from the working face and to take it out of the pit. The exact way in which that might be done varied a great deal from seam to seam, from working place to working place in the same pit and from time to time in the same working place. It was necessary not only that the coal was brought down but that it was in a saleable condition: large blocks of coal were required; the small and dust were separated at weighing and the miner paid little or nothing for them. Normally, perhaps one-third of the coal sent out would be small but the inexperienced man would send out more of it and since he was paid by the piece per ton of large coal he would suffer for it on payday. Dirt in the coal, bands of stone or shale, was also penalised if it became mixed with the coal in the skips. In the small seams of the Forest — the majority of them less than 2 feet in thickness — there were numerous dirt bands. Where seams were so thin, dirt bands imposed extraordinary demands on the skill of the miner. The relatively high 'thick Lowrey' seam, for example, which ran from 3 to 3.5 feet high, was made up of:

Roof: strong shale.
Dirt: 3 inches thick.
Top Coal: 20 inches thick.
Clod: nil to 3½ feet (where it becomes
   unworkable as one seam).
Bottom Coal: 22 inches thick.

From time to time a miner in this seam had to work in the bottom or top clod in order to free the coal, to work with dirt bands of varying size, and even, where the middle clod was particularly thick, to treat the coal as though it were two separate seams. At the same time the collier had to watch carefully the width of his stall. If he cut it a foot or two too wide the coal would fret, or run, at the sides of the stall. When that began to happen the pressures working through the roof and floor would gradually force them together so as, firstly, to make the stall unworkable and, finally, to shut it up altogether. Careless timbering too might lead to loss of control of the roof and floor pressures and the loss of the stall. All this had to be thought about and judged progressively as the collier worked: lying on his side, resting his hips and shoulder on a board, swinging his pick entirely with the forearms, using his knee as a pivot and pushing his body into the progressively narrower slit he drove into the clod.

There was no gas in the Forest's coal to cause the difficulties and disasters which plagued other fields and in general the Forest's accident rate was relatively low. There was though the problem of water. Shaped like a basin the field trapped water which worked through the porous sandstone strata overlaying the coal and into the workings or into abandoned pits, where it collected in reservoirs which could burst into the places of unsuspecting men cutting through the coal too close by. In his autobiography Timothy Mountjoy, the first miners' union agent in the Forest, described one such breaking through of the water from the 'old men's workings':

One day as my place had worked up too near some old workings full of water, and the underground Bailiff asked me to come with him, and make some preparations where the water should run if it broke in very suddenly, we went up to where this water was running through the cracks down into the horse road from there into some deep workings at the top of the road, we went up and we put some long sticks all across the road, and some planks up against the other sticks to prevent a quantity of rubbish coming down with the water into the road where our horses did work. We had just finished, and taking a whiff, when to our great surprise we saw the whole body of water heaving out; my partner got over the fence we had put up, and made his escape with a good wetting; our lights were both put out, there was nothing to be seen or heard but the rush of water. I stopped a moment to think what I had better do. If I stopped where I was the foul air would kill me, so I made a start, and was swept away with the flood and carried fourteen yards down into the horse road, covered with water and sludge. The rush of water shifted me, and I found an upright stick, and with the aid of the stick put up under a broken cap, I scrambled up on my feet in an exhausted condition . . . The first thing I saw was a dozen men with lights wading through the water to find me, believing I was drowned.[15]

Many of the smaller pits, without pumping machinery, could not work in periods of heavy rain.

The sorts of skills that were necessary in dealing with wet seams or in getting clean, large, block coal for the house trade, from 20-inch bands in 3-foot seams, were not to be learned quickly. A mines inspector, looking at the matter from the point of view of safety, wrote in 1883 that:

The circumstances of a mine are constantly changing. After every withdrawal of coal, as the working face advances, fresh danger may arise and the safety of each place depends on the individual care and attention of the collier in charge of it, and on him rests the responsibility of timbering and securing the place in the best possible manner . . . It is highly desirable that the best and most skilled men should be put in charge of working places. A collier's work cannot be learnt in a day; it is only after long experience that a man can master the difficulties of his occupation, and to the old hands we must look to initiate and instruct the younger men who are working with them.[16]

Colliers started as lads or as unskilled helpers to the face workers. Beginning with unskilled labourer's tasks, such as loading tubs and carting timber in to the face, the helper progressively learned the vagaries of floor and roof, how to set timber, how to undercut a face, how to separate the coal from roof and dirt bands and finally how to bring the coal cleanly down onto the floor of the working place. Eventually the helper, when he had gained enough knowledge, would take on the management of a stall himself. There was no apprenticeship system for the youth to negotiate. If he wished to have his own stall then of course he might have it. But there was another formidable barrier: colliers were paid by the piece and inexperience meant that at the end of the pay period instead of having tons of coal for which the master would pay, the collier had a valueless heap of dust and rubble. The skill which would allow the coal its natural fall and keep it in saleable blocks was what mattered:

> Go to the place of an unskilled collier, and you find it all confusion; you dare not trust yourself in it until you have made a personal examination. His props are set regardless of purpose; he does not prepare his coal for a natural fall, but hacks it to dust; he complains of having a bad place, and that his coal is more difficult to get than others, and he generally requires double the quantity of blasting powder his neighbour does; his roof is the very worst in the pit, and he gets the very worst timber sent him. In one sense the inexperience of a miner is its own punishment, where he is thrown upon his own resources, and he is dependent upon his own exertions. He is by no means so valuable a servant to his employer or the proprietor of a mine as another, for the force of his arm and that of his master's powder are expended with the least result, whilst the coal is reduced to slack.[17]

Because inexperience in a piecework system was its own punishment, the skilled miners did not attempt other forms of control of entry to their trade. Indeed, there was something boastful and extravagant about the way in which colliers declared from time to time that they were willing to let any man onto the coal who thought he could do the job:

> If you are an accomplished man as a collier, if you cannot prevail on your present employers to entrust you with a place, you shall come with me, and whether you are old or young, if you do the same work as myself, you shall fully share the profits. I have refused a great many of these public house slashers and have put them in stalls by asking the bailiff for them, and they have cut and mangled their work place to such an extent that in less than a fortnight they [the work places] have grown to such an enormous size that they were not able to get their body under the roof, and have come back to me acknowledging that they have not got 1s6d per day.[18]

This makes clear, too, the second barrier between the unskilled man and the coal face: the master or his bailiff had to agree to allow him to have a stall. Since a mangled workplace and coal reduced to dust gave the master no profit at all, he had no incentive to allow men at the face till he was certain of their competence.

The basic skills demanded of the collier in the nineteenth century were probably no different from those which had always been necessary. What was new in the nineteenth century was the way in which the masters at the large pits mobilised and organised the skills of their workmen. The new capitalists were not themselves working miners, nor did they spend their days in close supervision of the colliers. For the effective exploitation of their property, the masters relied, from the 1820s, on the 'little butty' system of contracting:

> The getting and haulage of the coal in large Collieries is done by contract. The contractor and his mate or marrow (here called 'Butty') undertake to get the coal and load it into tubs at the face of the stall, also to bring materials required from bank which are found by the Owners. In each stall the Contractor and his Butty, (who employ an additional man and boy), get and fill the coal: if two shifts are worked per day, the contractor takes charge of one and his partner the other.
>
>   . . . The coal from the face is taken by a contractor to the shaft; where another contractor onsets or 'hitches' the coal and delivers it to the loading place, where at some collieries the large coal is separated by screens and at others simply raked. In fact the whole of the getting of the coal is done by contract, very few men being employed directly by the owners.[19]

The masters employed some men on day wages, in order to maintain travelling and haulage roads in the pit (the master's daymen) but most of those whose pay came directly from the master were contract men, the butties.

The adult, experienced collier in the large pits of the Forest was not only a skilled workman: the butty system endowed him with other qualities. Firstly, it made of him an entrepreneur. In the development of a mine, tunnels were driven out through the main body of the coal and then working places were 'turned away' at intervals along these main roads. When the butty agreed to turn away a new place he could not know whether it would be easy or difficult to get the coal. A few yards in and there might be a fault or a broken roof or some other obstacle to producing coal:

> There was often great uncertainty in carrying out the work; because no man on being allocated a stall could say what difficulties might be met with: colliery work was not like some other work which a man could see what he had to do.[20]

Having made the best contract with the bailiff that experience and judgement could devise, the butty had then to develop the stall. That was not always a success, as a butty complained at a meeting in 1871:

> I have seen a good many 'places' in my time where the men after working ten or eleven days could not obtain their wages. At these times men have gone to their bailiffs and begged for a little more money, and at times 'it has been given'. At other times the bailiff would say 'go to the master'. They had gone and were told this, 'Your place don't pay me to work it you must shut it up, if you cannot make it pay for that money, let it stand'. Hoping it may turn out better men have toiled and toiled . . . and we have gone labouring and toiling on month after month hoping that the place would turn out better, and then at the last after long struggling have been obliged to give up the place altogether.[21]

While the butty was working these difficult places he still had to pay the wages of his daymen and his other expenses. For some butties that meant long periods of debt:

> After a butty has been working month after month, and no money to carry home to his wife, then the wife would say, 'What, no money this time?' 'No: I have had to borrow the money to pay the chaps'. Well, the wife goes to the Shopkeeper. Mr. 'so-and-so' I want you to trust me with another fortnight's things, my husband has brought me home no money again. The reply — oh, I can't let you go on any further, you must transfer your pig over to me for things you have had already. I know this to be the fact. I will not say this is the case with all in opening their stalls: It has been with more than one or two I have worked for.[22]

No wages books or company records have survived to allow a systematic analysis of the earnings pattern of buttymen in the Forest. Table 4.7, however, shows three sets of wages accounts which appeared as evidence in union disputes with the masters. The form and content of these accounts were not at issue. Table 4.7(A) shows the accounts of four butties for two fortnights in March 1874. Table 4.7(B) shows the accounts of a pair of butties in the two fortnights of December 1874. Even with this unacceptably small sample of accounts it is clear that the earnings of butties varied greatly. William Meek made £16 9s 9d, after expenses, for nine days in the first fortnight in March. Thomas Phillips made £4 0s 0d in the same period. Samuel Saysell and Jude Williams, on the other hand, worked a month for a total loss of £1 13s 10d. Perhaps it would not do to make too much of these losses. As a correspondent to the local newspaper observed in 1873: 'With regard to the buttyman's loss from month to month . . . I will ask why are these old buttymen, when they finish out a stall, so anxious to get another?'[23]

Table 4.7: Some Wages Sheets for Forest of Dean Colliers, 1874 — 1875

(A) March, 1874

(1) William Meek's account, *fortnight ending 7 March 1874*:

	£ s d	£ s d
		15 13 6
Paid to:		
Moses Meek, 9 days @ 3s 8d	1 13 0	
Richard Meek, 9 days @ 2s 6d	1 2 6	
James Pritchard, 9 days @ 3s 4d	1 10 0	
40 per cent	1 14 0	5 19 6

Equal to 21s 6d per day for Wm Meek working 9 days only   9 14 0

Fortnight ending 21 March 1874:   16 9 9

Paid to:		
Moses Meek, 10½ days @ 3s 8d	1 18 6	
Richard Meek, 10½ days @ 2s 6d	1 6 3	
James Pritchard, 10½ days @ 3s 4d	1 15 0	
40 per cent	2 0 0	6 19 9

Equal to over 18s per day on 10½ days   9 10 0

(2) Thomas Phillips' account *fortnight ending 7 March 1874*:   6 10 0

Paid to:		
Phillip Nichols, 5 days @ 5s	1 5 0	
G. Kear, 5 days @ 5c	1 5 0	2 10 0

Equal to 16s a day for Thomas Phillips at 5 days   4 0 0

Fortnight ending 21 March 1874:   6 12 3

Paid to:		
Phillip Nichols 9 days @ 5s		2 5 0

Equal to nearly 10s a day   4 7 3

(3) Elijah Mathews' account, *fortnight ending 7 March 1874*:   18 7 9

Paid to:		
Elijah Mathews, 9 days @ 3s 8d	1 13 0	
Jos. Roberts, 9 days @ 3s 4d	1 10 0	
Paid to:		
J. Baggs, 9 days @ 3s 8d	1 13 0	
S. Powell, 9 days @ 3s 8d	1 13 0	
Two boys, 9 days @ 3s 4d	1 10 0	
40 per cent	3 4 0	11 3 0

Table 4.7: Some Wages Sheets for Forest of Dean Colliers, 1874 — 1875 continued

	£ s d	
Carried forward	11 3 0	
Equal to 16s per day at 9 days for		
Elijah Mathews	7 4 9	

Fortnight ending 21 March 1874:

Paid to:	£ s d	
Elijah Mathews, 11 days @ 3s 8d	2 0 4	
J. Powell, 11 days @ 3s 8d	2 0 4	
S. Powell, 9 days @ 3s 8d	1 13 0	
J. Baggs, 9 days @ 3s 4d	1 10 0	
Jos. Roberts, 9 days @ 3s 4d	1 10 0	
Two boys, 9 days @ 3s 4d	1 10 0	
40 per cent	4 1 0	14 4 8

Equal to 18s per day		9 17 1

(4) Joseph Baldwin's account *fortnight ending 7 March 1874*:

Paid to:	£ s d	
1 man, 9 days @ 3s 8d	1 13 0	
Geo. Roberts, 9 days @ 3s 4d	1 10 0	
Two boys, 9 days @ 3s 4d	1 10 0	
40 per cent	1 17 0	7 12 0

Equal to 16s 9d per day on 10½ days		8 16 10

(B) Account of Samuel Saysell and Jude Williams for *first fortnight of December 1874*:

Earnings:	£ s d	
6 carts @ 10d	5 0	
293 carts @ 7½d	9 3 1	
for cleaning ginney road	1 0 0	
add 10 per cent		11 8 10

Paid to:		
George Evans 12 turns @ 5s 6d	3 6 0	
Thomas Wright 10 turns @ 5s	2 10 0	
Joseph Walden 8 turns @ 5s 6d	2 4 0	
Wm Hall 10 turns @ 5s 6d	2 15 0	
Thomas Fry 2 turns @ 5s 6d	11 0	
Henry Thomas 11 turns @ 2s 4d	1 5 8	12 11 8

Loss of		1 2 10

Second fortnight of December 1874:

Earnings:	£ s d	
15 carts @ 10d	12 6	
311 carts @ 7½d	9 14 4	
drawing 24 supports		
add 10 per cent	2 0	11 9 7

Table 4.7: Some Wages Sheets for Forest of Dean Colliers, 1874 — 1875 continued

		£ s d
Carried forward		11 9 7
Paid to:	£ s d	
Geo. Evans 10 turns @ 5s 6d	2 15 0	
Thomas Wright 11 turns @ 5s	2 15 0	
Jos. Walden 4 turns @ 5s 6d	1 2 0	
John Saysell 4 turns @ 5s 6d	1 2 0	
Thos. Fry 2½ turns @ 5s 6d	13 9	
Walter Hall 9 turns @ 5s 6d	2 9 6	
Henry Thomas 10 turns @ 2s 4d	1 3 4	12 0 7
Loss of		11 0

They had as well 5s a yard on the cross headings which they let to Saysell's brother, excepting a few yards, and having relet the heading work at 4s raised their net earnings by £2, which left them 6s 2d to divide between them. In the first fortnight, Saysell worked 6 turns and Williams, 11. In the second Saysell worked 8 and Williams, 7 turns.

(C) Account of Shellah Russell and Joseph Burris
January to May 1874:
Earnings:

	£ s d
Preparing the Lowery Brow at Waterloo Colliery	16 10 0
Sinking pit from the Lowery seam to the Starkey seam	83 0 6
Drove 16 yards and 2 feet of heading in the Regulator Colliery at 15s per yard	12 10 0
Worked Regulator Colliery engine 19 turns at 6s per turn	5 14 0
	117 14 6

Paid to:		
Charles Coleman 10½ turns @ 6s	3 3 0	
Edward Davis 11½ turns @ 5s	2 17 0	
William Morgan 9½ turns @ 6s	2 17 0	
James Hall 4 turns @ 6s	1 4 0	10 1 0
		107 13 6

Russell and Burris thus made an average of £5 7s 8d each per week, assuming that there were ten fortnights in the period.

Sources:
(A) *Forest of Dean Examiner*, 22 May 1874.
(B) *Forester*, 7 January 1875; *Forest of Dean Examiner*, 8 January 1875.
(C) *Forest of Dean Examiner*, 5 June 1874.

The butty was an entrepreneur in the sense that he undertook risk and also in the sense that he had to calculate ways of making money from a variety of opportunities within the pit. While the principal source of his earnings was the cutting of coal for sale, there were other jobs to be done. The pit had to be progressively developed: that is roads had to be driven away through the bulk of the coal so that new working places might be turned away and when the company worked more than one seam, or where a seam had been displaced by a geological fault, internal pits and drifts had to be made. If pillars had been extracted the space left, the goaf, had to be packed with supports; or perhaps supports left in an earlier goaf had to be removed so as to direct roof pressures away from roads or stalls. At some pits the master's daymen did this work. At others the colliers bargained for it along with other work. Shellah Russell and Joseph Burris, whose account for January to May 1874 is shown in Table 4.7(C), made most of their pay from this sort of work. They made ready a section of seam to be worked by other men, sank a pit from one seam to another, drove headings and worked the pumps at another pit owned by the same master. For that they made an average of £5 7s 8d each per week. Samuel Saysell and Jude Williams made part of their money in December 1874 for cleaning a travelling road and removing roof supports. They had also contracted to cut some cross-headings at 5s a yard. They sublet that work to Saysell's brother and also sublet some heading work at 4s to other men.

The butty system made the collier an employer as well as entrepreneur. He was not an employer on the scale of the 'charter masters' or 'big butties' of Staffordshire, who contracted to work a whole pit or seam within a pit, but they were employers none the less. The little butty and his mate employed perhaps three or four others, some of whom were boys and youths and some of whom might also be relatively experienced adults. The numbers of daymen in a stall probably varied a good deal. William Meek — in Table 4.7(A) — employed three men in both fortnights of March 1874, while Elijah Mathews employed four men and two boys in the first fortnight and five men and two boys in the second.

The butty had two important powers in relation to his daymen. Firstly, he could determine how many days they would work. The butties adjusted to fluctuations in the demand for coal by offering more or less turns to the daymen:

> Butty men . . . contract to get coal from a stipulated area at so much per ton, and in turn employ labourers. It is this latter class who make so little time when trade is slack; the buttymen, naturally enough as masters of the situation, can generally find enough to do while they can send their labourers home.[24]

The butty's power of employment and dismissal was the more important because of the seasonal nature of the principal markets for Forest coal. At the beginning of spring as trade slackened and the prices of house grades fell, the demand of the butties for labour also fell. Customarily, men left the pits and went into the countryside to look for work on the farms, returning to the coal as the weather cooled in the autumn.[25] Many men had a dual life over the course of the year as colliery daymen and agricultural labourers. The daymen seem to have been almost a casual labour force, experiencing all the uncertainties and the relationships of dependency with their immediate masters that afflict any casual workforce.

That dependency was the more marked because the butty also set the rate at which his men would be paid. Some of the daymen of Table 4.7 received 2s 6d per day, others 3s 4d, 3s 8d, 5s, 5s 6d and 6s. Some butties defended vigorously their power to discriminate among their daymen in the rates they paid them:

As regards day men's wages, here they are — some from the smith's shop, others from the shoemaker's bench, others from the plough tail, and so on. First they begin to have them to fill, then to pick up, and some of thèm both; and others are very neglectful, where others are more provident. Shall all these men have the same wages? How monstrous to talk of such a thing, when I, for one, know that some men are worth 1s per day more than others. Thirdly, as regards timberers in the road, these men are obliged to be kept on all coal works in the district, but these vary, both in steadyness and experience. Some of them will stay away from their work while others will be found at their work, and one man can make a pair of timber, while the other is turning the timber about. Again, one man will see which way to put the setting up, and do it, while another will be taping [sic] this and that, and sacking up his trousers. Shall these have the same wages? If the timberer is a steady and good workman and his wages will not do for him, let him ask for a stall.[26]

Men varied in their providence, work habits and mental and physical powers and should be paid accordingly. Not surprisingly, some daymen objected to this arrangement and resented the fact that 'they think that because they are buttymen they are all'.[27]

This then was part of the context in which controversy about rights and customs revived in 1870. The Forest had become, with railway development, part of a national system of coal production and distribution. A relatively few large collieries, producing principally for the seasonal house coal trade, had to compete with giant neighbours in markets which were no longer exclusively reserved for the Forest.

Free miners still worked little pits in the crop but they were economically of little significance either as sources of tonnage royalty to the Crown or in the work experience of the majority of miners. For most of them the butty system and the cyclical trade of the big pits was what mattered. Perhaps a quarter or a third of the men in those pits were little butties: small working masters, employers and entrepreneurs in their own right. The balance made up a casual force of daily paid labourers, more or less skilled and experienced as colliers, on whom the butties depended for their profits. In the early 1870s there was something else of importance which helped to shape discussion of the rights: the formation of a trade union among the colliers.

5. The New System II: The Little Buttymen and the Union

Oh! workmen awake for the strife is begun!
Be faithful and true, both father and son;
To vanquish oppression go, fearlessly go,
And stand like the brave with your face to the
foe!

Chorus
Stand like the brave,
Stand like the brave,
Stand like the brave, with your face to the foe!

For years that are passed asleep we have been
To our interests as men in the Forest of Dean;
To help in the conflict go, fearlessly go,
And stand like the brave with your face to the
foe!

AAM. Song for the Forest of Dean, Forester, 29 December 187!.

The Forest in the 1830s had not seen the sorts of quarrels between capital and labour which had begun to appear in other coal districts. The dispute about the rights and customs had set native against stranger, whether the native was an employer or an employee. It was true that the most important of those who were strangers were employers and that the grievances felt against them had been the consequence of the ways in which capital had reorganised the mining industry. There none the less had been no evidence of a conscious antipathy to employers as such. If only the strangers would go away all would be well. When a new controversy about the rights arose, however, that situation had altered. In 1871 the miners formed a trade union, whose values and behaviour changed the pattern of social relationships in the Forest and informed a new discussion about the ways in which the resources of the Forest should be used.

There had been some signs of discontent among the Forest colliers before 1871. In 1864 a number of letters of complaint about conditions in the mines had appeared in the *Miner and Workman's Advocate*. Some men, at the urging of a visiting Welsh miners' agent, had also attempted to form a union lodge. That venture failed: the landlord of the public house at which the meeting was to take place refused to allow it to begin and 'we have been disappointed in making a start yet'.[1] The Forest, after all, was a small place. If a man complained he had

> the sack, and cannot get work at another place, because the one master says to another, 'that is a troublesome man; he knows too much; the sooner we send him out of the country the better'. It is through such unjust acts as these that the men in the Forest of Dean are kept in subjection.[2]

Though there was no open union, some sort of covert activity continued. In December 1870 the *Forester* printed a letter from a 'Miners' Committee' at the small town of Cinderford which indicated that the Committee had been in correspondence with miners' unions in other coalfields.[3] It also became clear later that the Cinderford men had corresponded with foresters who were working in South Yorkshire, had discussed unionism with them and had from them copies of the South Yorkshire union's rules.[4]

The first open disputes between masters and men took place in 1871. A strike in July at the Trafalgar colliery was followed two months later by another at the Parkend Coal Company. In both strikes the men demanded higher tonnage rates, the weighing of coal at the pit mouth and the appointment of a checkweighman. They also wanted a reduction of winding hours and to be paid at two rather than five weekly intervals.[5] The masters complained on both occasions that they could not afford to make concessions. How could they pay for them unless they increased coal prices? If they did that they would lose the already slack summer trade and not be able to get customers back for the high prices of the winter season. This argument soon lost its force. The market was rising and there was a strong demand for colliers, a condition made clear by agents from pits in Durham and South Staffordshire who came to the Forest to recruit men for their own works and who made the prospect of moving 'up country' attractive with talk of the relatively high wages to be made there. On each day of the Parkend strike trains left for the north carrying colliers, as many as 100 of them on one day, all 'in their "very best", with bundles at back'.[6] Those sorts of pressures soon brought the masters to concede most of what the men had demanded.

More importantly, a meeting at the Cinderford Town Hall in the third week of the Parkend strike had decided that it was time to have a permanent miners' union in the Forest. Timothy Mountjoy, in the chair, argued thus:

> He would remark that his friends with him were of opinion that the demands of the Forest of Dean colliers were so moderate and reasonable that no dispassionate or thoughtful person could avoid being persuaded that a real want — and a real claim and simple justice underlay the spirit which had simultaneous possession of so large a section of the working classes. (Hear, hear). The time had come he believed when the working men must stand by each other and take united action. The time was come, he thought, when the class to which he referred should set at open defiance the tyranny and injustice of their employers.[7]

Their object, he said, was to bring all the colliers and mine workers in the Forest into a union to be built around an adaptation of the rules of the South Yorkshire miners. They wanted a hall of their own and a small subscription from every member so that they might establish a two-sheet newspaper — to be called the *Foresters' Friend and Miners' Advocate* — so that they might have the fair reporting which they believed the existing press denied them.

The union which they established was at first a 'union club' which had no formal connection with any wider organisation. In the month that the club was formed, however, Mountjoy attended a national conference of miners in Manchester from which he returned with news that the Amalgamated Association of Miners had allocated £50 to be spent 'to raise us Foresters out of the darkness in which our lots have been cast'.[8] Shortly afterwards, a deputation from the AAM's national executive came to speak to the Forest miners, who agreed that their club should become an AAM branch.[9]

The AAM branch in Dean prospered under the shelter of the national union and in the favourable conditions of the economic boom which occupied the first five years of the 1870s. By the time of the branch's annual demonstration in August 1873 there were thirteen lodges in the Forest proper and another five in the immediately adjoining parishes.[10] The lodges were scattered around the Forest but the town of Cinderford was especially important. The union had a financial membership of 4,500 at its peak in 1874 and about 1,000 of those were members of Cinderford no.1 lodge alone.[11]

District organisation was straightforward enough.[12] The members of each lodge met once a fortnight at the British Schoolroom or the committee room of the local inn. The members appointed a committee composed of a chairman, secretary and treasurer who looked after the collection of members' fees, called and conducted the fortnightly meetings and negotiated in the first instance with the masters on any matter in dispute. The lodges also elected delegates to the district delegate board, which met once a month to discuss those matters coming from the lodges which required the statement of a district-wide policy, which needed interpretation in the light of the rules of the AAM as a whole or which might have resulted in strike action. The district also administered the sick and accident fund which it set up early in its life in opposition to the 'ground clubs' which operated under the auspices of the masters at some of the collieries.

The delegate board was also the link in the hierarchy of union between the lodges and the national conference and executive. Conference made the overall policy statements for the union and, so far as the conduct of important strikes was concerned, the national executive administered it. Since the prior approval of the executive was necessary if the local union were to receive support for a strike, the district was very much in the hands of the executive on the larger issues between master and man which might provoke a strike or lockout. There was thus built into its structure the possibility of serious tensions within the AAM. The lodges and the districts were concerned with problems which arose in the context of local economy, local practice and local tradition. The national executive had to take an overall view of the mining industry and attempt to bring the districts to act in accordance with its analysis.

The man most immediately affected by that problem was the district miners' agent, arguably the most important man in the district union and the one who took the greatest part of the burden of the work of the union. Chosen by the men, he was responsible, as a full-time paid official, for the organisation of the district. He arranged, and was usually the chief speaker at, the series of meetings held around the forest when the men had to be informed of some decision, asked to make one or simply reminded to keep up their subscriptions. Whenever matters arose at individual pits which seemed likely to end in strikes or penalties on individuals, he attended with the lodge committee on the master or manager and often acted as its spokesman. If the problem were not solved on the spot, the agent took it to the delegate board where he had to report, to justify his actions to that point, to advise on union policy and to accept or suggest instructions for further work. The agent had to face in two directions at once. He had to be acceptable to the men in dispute. If they were truculent or aggressive they had to be brought to act in a disciplined manner and perhaps persuaded that they were acting unreasonably. And the master had to be listened to with every appearance of deference and respect. At some pits the masters refused to deal with him and would see only deputations of their own men or listen only to men who came as individuals to make a complaint. But the attempt to deal tactfully with the master of that sort might provoke from the men accusations of treachery and double dealing — especially if the agent recommended some form of compromise.

The new organisation, and its agent, won a number of easy victories within a short time of its formation. As prices had risen in the boom to over £1 per ton for best Forest block, wages had followed them upwards. By 1873 the butties had pushed their rates up by 40 per cent over those of mid-1870 and the daymen had the 1870 day rate plus 40 per cent. The collier's actual earnings, given the heavy demand and the regular work of the boom years, probably increased by more than that. It was complained indeed that the colliers were earning so much that they were sending out less coal: total output in the Forest actually fell from 170,611 tons in 1871 to 153,255 tons in 1872 (Table 4.4). In conformity with national policy the union had also been able to bring winding hours at the large pits down from ten to eight and had insisted that weighing machines were installed. Shorter hours, weighing machines and higher rates of pay — all signs that the colliers had come out of Egypt.[13]

The union made a clear difference in these matters but had it made a wider impact on the way in which people thought about the social relationship of master and man? The *Forester* summed up a widespread sense of unease about what union meant:

We refer to the breaking up of old ties. How many of these have existed in the Forest of Dean, as a consequence of its isolated character, and how strongly they have bound together masters and men will be acknowledged by all whose life has been spent here, or who have lengthened acquaintance with the district. The bond has been of a primitive, in many cases of a patriarchal, nature. Families whose names are as familiar to Forest ears as household words, have generation after generation continued in the same employ. Men have grown grey in the service and have been followed by their children in a like simplehearted, undeviating adherence to one firm. There are those who have spent more than half a century upon the Parkend Collieries, who have never worked a day elsewhere, and who, moreover, never meant to work elsewhere, until the present unhappy disturbance came. But a sudden, and, as is being proved, a very natural dislocation has taken place, and the old order of things is breaking up. Any man with eyes to see can perceive it. Not only has the 'foreign' element permeated the ranks of the employers; it has entered in amongst the workmen as well — not, indeed, to be seen in any serious addition to their number from without, but in far different influences operating upon native labour. It is patent now that the events which are happening in our day are exciting the minds of our colliers; that direct pressure is being brought to bear upon them by the workmen of other districts, who will not suffer this or any other hitherto quiet corner of the labour market to fail in contributing its quota to the general movement . . . The result is that the clannish relationship in which employers and employed have been bound together is perishing — dying, in fact — before our eyes. We shall never see it again as it has been, we may depend upon it. The conditions of its existence are being swallowed up by the advancing tide of a general agitation, and along with the conditions must go the bond itself — its rights, privileges, influence and all.[14]

Where there had been vertical divisions in the Forest community, in which the masters might count on the loyalty of their men — or so it was assumed — the divisions were coming to be horizontal: the working men were uniting against all the employers.

The first obstacle to that unity had been in the workforce itself. The organisers of the union thought that if it was to be a success it should be industrial in character and not just a union of butties. When Mountjoy took the chair at the founding meeting he shared the platform with 'representatives from the majority of the pits and mines around the neighbourhood, including several of the butty-men from the collieries at Parkend on strike'.[15] The butties had led both the Trafalgar and Parkend strikes and the matters at issue were tonnage rates and weights: these were buttymen's problems. But the butties could not afford to ignore the daymen who, more or less experienced, might welcome the chance to take up stalls of their own. The problem had become immediate because Edwin Crawshay, owner of the Bilson and Crumpmeadow pit, which employed about 800 men, had attempted to exploit the division between butty and dayman by offering an advance of 5 per cent to the former but not to the daymen he employed directly himself. A surer way, Mountjoy argued, of rousing animosity among the men could not have been conceived. The serpent of old could not have had a more designing purpose than this when he went into the Garden:

For this reason. When 20 or 30 of your young colliers go into a public house after their pay — and there is no denying the fact that they do go into such places — Bill says to Jack, 'Thee needn't swagger. If thee gets a shilling a week more than I, I be as good a man as thee beest any day'. They then wrangle amongst themselves about this percentage and then they will fight. I say that [Crawshay is] thus providing a cause to promote discord, and probably bloodshed.

He argued at length that the daymen and the banksmen had as hard, as dangerous and as unpleasant work to do as anyone in the pit and that both classes were necessary for the success of the union:

> Then I mean to say stick to one another. I will venture to tell the coal and mine cutters of the Forest of Dean that it is as much your duty to stick to the daymen as in your case, if you are dissatisfied with the price paid for cutting the coal, to expect the men to stick to you. (Loud Applause.) When the buttymen recently gave notice to their masters they wished all the daymen to turn out along [sic], and in some cases they have done so. Now if they stick to you, my advice is to stick to them. If we are to have a union let us have it. (Applause). The fact is, we have been frightened of one another — I repeat frightened, that if anything was said Tom would take Jim's place, and Jim would take somebody else's place. In this way we have been frightened, and have thus given our masters an advantage over us.

There was another good reason for his concern. The butties had won at Trafalgar but some of them had not passed on a proportionate pay increase to their daymen. John Hodges, a Trafalgar butty who had been a prominent spokesman in the strike, had reported that it 'was quite true there were a few of the butties who had not raised their under-men, and among those there were men who received their 8/- and 9/- a day, keeping the whole to themselves. The very men who did so were those whom the masters most encouraged'.[16] For the union the resolution of that early meeting to demand that all advances go in proportion to all pit and mine workers was as important as the capitulation of the Parkend masters.

Thus the union was an influence in favour of unity and co-operation among all grades of the colliery workforce in the face of the common opponent. So it was too in its dealings with other groups of workers: mechanics, enginemen, iron-workers and agricultural labourers. Their national or county organisers came to the Forest under the auspices of the miners' agent. He went to the meetings for the visitors, had in fact arranged them, took the chair and made the first speech of the evening, usually on the theme of the intellectual, social and moral benefits of union. This, preceded by the inevitable union melody, led into the more specialised appeal of the visiting speaker. The annual demonstrations were not for the colliers alone: John Kane of the iron-workers', Thomas of the enginemen's and Yeats of the agricultural labourers' unions addressed them as well as the miners' leaders, Halliday and MacDonald.[17] The mechanics, the iron-workers and even the bargemen of the Severn actually asked to be allowed to form lodges of the AAM but were encouraged to form unions of their own.[18]

The agricultural labourers were of some importance to the colliers. Over a few seasons the man who worked on the farm in summer and came to the pits in winter might pick up enough skill to become a strike-breaker. During the Parkend strike of 1871 a buttyman, John Beddis, spoke harshly at a meeting about a dayman who had been set to cut coal by the company. 'This man he designated as a clod-hopping collier and one who tried to take the bread out of the mouths of those on strike. A voice: he is a farm house collier (Laughter).'[19] It was men of that sort rather than the Irish who were the principal competitors for Dean colliers in the labour market. Thus Yeats, the secretary of the Gloucestershire labourers' union, expressed the hope at the demonstration of 1874 that he should see the 'day when all working men, no matter what their calling was, or who they were, should unite in one grand federation . . . and that when one part was assailed, the other part should rise and protect them'.[20] He explained the blessing that would be to the colliers:

He (the speaker) and those who, like himself, were in the habit of addressing the labouring classes in question, were endeavouring to make it worth their while to stop at home, to remain in their own village without entering the mineral districts and competing with their labour with the miner or collier. (Cheers.) He had some knowledge of the matter to which he was about to refer, and he would remark that he never knew an agricultural labourer go to a coal pit and ask for work because he liked it or because of any desire to leave the green fields and the plough, but because the poor men — probably having a large family — was [sic] tempted to leave his village home and old associations on account of earning more money. This was to the agricultural labourer a great temptation, and hence it arose that the agricultural labourers had found their way to the collieries and offered their labour. Well, then, if by the aid of their union they were able to make it worth the while of that class to stop at home the miner would be benefited, and, moreover, the miner would be enabled more effectually to fight their battles than before. (Cheers.)

As the only full-time resident union official in the region, it was logical that the miners' agent should be at the centre of this sort of activity. That he was and that the miners, iron-workers and labourers shared platforms gives us a strong sense of the development of a trade-union *movement* in the Forest in this period.

Part of that impression comes from the fact that the union brought a new newspaper for the working classes to the Forest: the *Forest of Dean Examiner*.[21] The *Examiner* was part of the first syndicated labour press in Britain. The *Examiner* syndicate had been promoted from the Potteries by William Owen, a former potter who had left his bench to become editor of the *Potteries Examiner* in 1868. Working from that base Owen had developed a number of regional newspapers which were designed to carry local trade and union news as well as material on the national labour movement. Each paper had the support of trade unions in its locality and was their 'official organ'. The relationship between the syndicate and branches of the AAM had been especially close after the national conference of the AAM had resolved in 1873 to adopt the 'system of labour newspapers now published under the name of the Examiner, as a medium of intercourse and general organ of the Association'.[22] William Owen addressed the foresters at their annual demonstration in 1873, arguing with the support of the union's officers the need for an alternative to a press which they believed served only the needs of the coal masters. The gathering, in response, resolved to adopt the *Examiner* as its official organ. The first issue of the *Forest of Dean Examiner* appeared the following week.[23]

The paper was in the first instance the colliers' book of record. Each issue carried full and often verbatim reports of miners' meetings. The delegate meetings were reported in full and the reports taken as the minutes of the meeting. Publicity for union events, local trade reports, reports of meetings of local institutions other than unions and the opportunity to comment on reports of miners' activities which appeared in other papers, were provided by the *Examiner*. As well, the paper served the important function of linking the colliers in Dean to other districts and to the labour movement at large. Other unions and other strikes than those of the colliers were reported. Parliamentary business was not neglected and editorial and other articles discussed problems ranging from education to the work carried on by Mr Plimsoll. All this was done on the assumption that working men as working men and not as foresters, Methodists or Odd Fellows had a point of view which required representation. We cannot say how far the paper was read or understood by its intended audience but the Dean branch of the AAM 'guaranteed' sales of 1,500 copies per week. Even after the union in 1875 had been soundly beaten by the masters and had lost most of its membership, the delegate board decided to keep up the *Examiner* subscription, which perhaps indicates the importance they thought it had for their work.

The consequence of the sense of the community of interest of all working men which the AAM branch and *Examiner* brought to Dean was a fracturing of other, older loyalties. For some Christians — as well as for supporters of the established press — the intrusion of union into the Forest caused doubt and confusion. It is difficult to estimate the religious affiliations of the foresters in the early seventies but it seems likely that the majority of them were Nonconformists of one sort or another. An inspection of the ordnance survey map gives the list of places of worship shown in Table 5.1. There were six Anglican churches, five Baptist, three Primitive Methodist, three other Methodist, two Bible Christian, two Independent and seventeen other chapels whose denominations were not recorded on the map: in all, 38 places of worship of which six were Anglican.

Table 5.1: Places of Worship Shown on the Ordnance Survey of the Forest of Dean, 1873

	Denomination	No.		Denomination	No.
1.	Anglican	6	5.	Methodist	
2.	Baptist	5		(Unspecified)	2
3.	Primitive		6.	Bible Christian	2
	Methodist	3	7.	Independent	2
4.	Wesleyan		8.	Chapels —	
	Methodist	1		denomination not	
				specified	17

Source: Six-inches-to-a-mile, Ordnance Survey of Gloucestershire, *County Series*, 1st edn (1873).

The strength of the Nonconformist presence is likewise suggested by the results of the first School Board elections in the Forest in April 1875.[24] Of the nine places on the Board, six were won by Nonconformists. The *Forester* thought that the polling supported 'the calculation that the Foresters are two thirds Nonconformists and one third churchmen'. Of a total of 19,593 votes, 5,498 went to churchmen and 14,095 to Nonconformists. A total of 2,177 ratepayers voted: 611 for churchmen and 1,566 for Nonconformists. At the head of the Nonconformist party stood the coal-owners. The successful Nonconformist candidates were W. B. Brain, colliery proprietor, S. J. Thomas, colliery proprietor, Alfred Goold, colliery proprietor, Joseph Thompson, colliery clerk, Cornelius Griffiths, Baptist minister and Thomas Nicholson, Baptist minister. Edwin Crawshay, coal and iron master, headed the Church party, along with Sir James Campbell, the deputy surveyor of the Forest, and W. H. Taylor, the vicar of Christchurch.

Some Christians thought it was a bad idea to have unions in the Forest. They expressed their disapproval in small gestures like that of the refusal of the Baptist chapel at Cinderford to allow its schoolroom to be used for an organising meeting early in the life of the union.[25] In the case of the lay preacher Henry Jones, a buttyman, union was synonymous with 'confusion, starvation and death'. He reminded the foresters of the fate of the Chartists in Wales who had followed Frost at Newport and of the bad end of Warren James. Mountjoy, like them, would only bring suffering:

If you establish a union at Cinderford Town Hall, and get a few pounds in it, there will soon be a strike or strikes which will prove more hurtful to the men in the Forest district than those in South or North. The man who has a pig in his pigscot must let the shopkeeper have it; the man who has a cottage may lose it; and thus confusion will be found between masters and men, and men and their wives and children. What else will strikes do? Clothe wife and children with rags, empty the cupboard, and send the children to bed with empty bellies. Consider this, brother foresters, and let him who stands connected with a Christian Church make peace instead of destroying it.[26]

Churchmen could be influential in ways that did not turn on their interpretation of the Book. Mindful of their responsibilities they might feel duty bound to attempt a more thorough-going critique of unionism. In the Forest of Dean the only attempt to confront union in any systematic way came from the minister of the Baptist Church, Thomas Nicholson. While the coal-owners kept their thoughts on political economy largely to themselves and demonstrated their attitudes in action rather than in print, Nicholson kept up throughout the life of the union in Dean, and long after, a stream of letters to the local newspapers, of sermons, of addresses to public meetings and pamphlets, which were designed to show that union was not only wicked but contrary to the laws of political economy.[27]

But these Christian admonitions seemed to have little effect, partly because it was possible to question the motives and understanding of some of those who offered them. Perhaps Mr Jones' God was one who smiled too exclusively on the buttymen:

Your correspondent can talk about the consequences of strikes, but I am one of those who believe that if he felt the hardship of low wages like some men, his theories would be at least slightly different. Now he is not thus placed, because, always having help from his sons, and invariably good places in the pits, he has not felt the shoe to pinch. But are his 'bowels of compassion' closed against the poor banksmen who have to toil far harder than himself to be ever closed! And will he condemn those who stand forward to point out the manner in which they are unfairly treated? I would ask Mr. Henry Jones this local divine how would he like to toil for 2/8 per day? Whether he could quiet his 'Christian brethren' in the same soft tones and with the same fine broadcloth he now dons? I think not. But, again, has he no word of correction to his master who makes fish of one class of his men and flesh of another? Can he look on and approve this injustice to the daymen? But sir, he is not a dayman, and therefore will not suffer neither will his cupboards be scanty in fare.[28]

More importantly, the AAM men were not merely defensive in their dealings with religion. They were frequently religious men themselves, taking justification for union, not condemnation of it, from their creed. Indeed, it was sometimes difficult to tell whether it was converts to union or converts to Christ that were wanted. After William Brown had been to the Forest on the first of the deputations from the AAM he wrote a newspaper account of the work there. He concluded his account of their meetings:

> On the Sunday we held our last and best meeting in the Baptist Chapel, Cinderford. The meeting should have been held in the schoolroom, but, it being far too small, the people assembled in the Chapel which was kindly lent to us. Let me venture to hope that good was done and God's name glorified. We had a fair chance to speak a few words of admonition to a number of poor outcasts who never attended a place of worship, or if so, on very rare occasions. The congregation was a very mixed one, and, as I thought, it would be my last day I should have come among the forest people for some time to come we could not separate in a better way than by asking the Almighty to bless our efforts in trying to benefit mankind, and more especially the mining population.[29]

For that sort of work by unionists the Baptist Chapel was available.

The Book provided them with the parable and metaphor which made effective their speeches about matters at issue between master and man. God was watching the masters, whether they liked it or not, and the day of judgement was bound to come:

> To a certain extent he held they were their brothers' keepers, and should be determined to work for each other not only in heart but in hand, and if their masters oppressed them they should remind them that it was wrong, for there was woe to the oppressor. Ungodly men would be dispersed like the chaff before the wind.[30]

The banner carried by the Lydbrook lodge to the annual demonstration of 1873 depicted a master and a man, the latter carrying a pick in his hand. Between them stood a female carrying a pair of scales. Beneath her was inscribed: 'A just weight is God's delight but a false balance is an abomination to the Lord.'[31] He had his eye on the buttyman as well: 'A poor man that oppresseth the poor is as a sweeping rain that leaveth no food.'[32] And while he watched sternly the enemies of the working man he lent his power to the miner's attempt to raise himself up:

> Now referring to the agitation in Dean Forest when it first commenced, there were some religionists who expressed themselves as surprised that I should take part in it; but at Manchester I met preachers of the Gospel, class-leaders, and circuit stewards, and I am happy to say that the gentleman present (Mr. Mitchard) is a member among the Primitive Methodists. I believe there is a hand superior to any human hand directing our movement. (Applause.) I honestly and candidly believe that a time favourable to the forester is come, and as I have said before, a power lies within us which we have not of late years been able to estimate.[33]

Their religion was important to these men but it was not for them a religion which neglected the need for a weighing machine on the pit bank or for better wages, in favour of a heaven to come in the after life.

Perhaps the surest sign that the old order was changing came in 1873 when, as it became clear that a general election was likely, the Forest miners began to agitate for a working man's candidate. Until then West Gloucestershire politics had been dominated by the contest between the Tory and Conservative Dukes of Beaufort and the Whig and Liberal Berkeley family. In the Forest division, in 1870 as in 1832, the leading liberals were mine and pit owners. In September 1870 the Liberals held a demonstration at the Speech House for Colonel Kingscote, landowner, and Mr Marling, a Stroud clothier, who had been returned in the Liberal interest in 1868. W. B. Brain of Trafalgar colliery, whom we have already met, arranged the marquee in which the assembled voters sat down to their cold meat and hot potatoes; William Crawshay, coal and iron master, brought the members from the station in his carriage; and Osman Barrett, Henry Crawshay and Mr Goold, coal and iron masters, waited with the MP for Stroud to receive the visitors. At three o'clock when they moved to the tables there were another 17 owners of coal and iron mines among the diners. The Liberal masters owned all the large- and medium-sized collieries, and iron mines and all the ironworks in the forest.[34]

Beneath the masters, in the order of things political in the Forest, came the mass of voters. What was the nature of the Forest electorate? Table 5.2 shows, so far as it has been possible to discover them, the occupations of the persons listed in the 1874 electoral register. Each voter was traced in the 1871 census enumerators' books and his occupation recorded where it was clear that the man listed as a voter and the man listed in the census were the same. A number of those listed in the register were not to be found in the census. More

Table 5.2: Occupations of Voters in the Forest of Dean, 1874

Occupational Category	Number	%
Clerical, non-mining professional	17	1.5
Shopkeepers, merchants	156	13.9
Industrial trades	61	5.4
Metal workers	28	2.5
General labourers	99	8.8
Colliers	427	38.1
Iron ore miners	105	9.4
Other mining	50	4.5
Stone and quarry	86	7.7
Agriculture	40	3.6
Wood and timber	36	3.2
Miscellaneous	16	1.4
	1,121	100

Source: *Census of England and Wales*, 2 April 1871, PRO RG 10/2, 596—2, 605/2, 686/5, 296—5,300; *Register of Persons entitled to vote at any election of a Member or Members to serve in Parliament for the Western Division of the County of Gloucester between the thirty first day of December 1873 and the first day of January 1875* (Gloucester, 1874).

importantly, in a number of the enumerators' districts, and even in smaller areas within those districts, there was a number of people having the same name but employed in different occupations. Where the number of people of a given name and address in the register did not correspond with that in the census, all the people of that name were taken as 'not known'. This problem arises in part because the enumerators' books are imprecise in their recording of addresses. Most people are simply listed as living at 'Viney Hill' or 'Yorkeley Slade'. The nature of the Forest settlements — with few streets set out and named — probably prevented closer identification. Fortunately, it is enough to know for most voters that they lived in such a sub-area and that no one else of that name lived there. Table 5.2 also excludes those who were on the Forest register but who were to vote elsewhere. There were 1,565 voters in the Forest polling divisions in 1874. Table 5.2 groups 1,121 of them according to the occupational categories used in Chapter 4. Clearly this was a plebeian division of the electorate. About four in ten of the voters were colliers. Seven in ten of the voters belonged in the categories which were unequivocally part of the working classes: colliers, iron miners, metal workers, stone and quarrymen, general labourers and the agricultural and wood workers. This was the constituency to which Mountjoy believed he might appeal in 1873 when the Bristol conference of the AAM called on its member districts in October to investigate the possibility of bringing forward their own parliamentary candidates.

In November, when the Forest colliers gathered at Cinderford to present a purse to the Reverend T. D. Mathias of Merthyr Tydfil for his services in a strike there, Mountjoy raised the question of parliamentary representation:

It is time for the workmen of England to share more largely in the privileges which others possess and use to a higher level. I hope . . . to see the working community of this and every other country represented in Parliament by men who have risen from their own ranks. In the borough of Wenlock, in Shropshire, the working men are trying to return one of their own class, Mr. Brown, to the House of Commons, and they also felt sure that two of their own rank would be made Town Councillors. And now let me ask what part the foresters intend playing at the coming election; my opinion is the working men can never be truly represented except by working men, Brother Foresters, never again send any man to represent you who contemptuously ignores the rights of farm labourers. Some have gone so far to say the present system of government does not need renovating, I say it needs abolishing or reversing. The more useful a man is to the community, the lower he is placed in the social and political scale. The farm labourer and miner, instead of being honoured are dishonoured. Is it not an outrage on justice that the least useful class of all should have a representative in Parliament for every family, while the most useful class, which produces all the wealth shall not have one representative for a million families. I hope the members of trade unions will at the forthcoming election, choose men to represent them who will do what is right, and which they should do. Let us no longer sit down in contented ignorance and fondle the chains that bind us.[35]

Colonel Kingscote had referred in a speech to a number of agricultural labourers and their families who had gone to Brazil and come back in rags. Their experience he had blamed on the labourers' union as organisers of the emigration. Their union and the colliers' union deployed that as evidence of a more general hostility to working men.

The delegates discussed the problem of choosing a candidate at their meeting a fortnight after this speech and decided to ask George Howell to contest the seat on behalf of the working men. They instructed the Secretary to write to Howell and his opponents and invite them to address the working men at Cinderford and Coleford 'on questions which the working classes deem of great importance to them'. They also resolved that:

The end and aim of a salutary legislation should be the enlarge-
ment and preservation of the right of the people in their individual
as well as their corporal capacity. We indignantly condemn the
Master and Servants Act, and the Criminal Law Amendment Act,
as oppression to the working men of the country, and demand such
reconstruction or abrogation as may remove the stigma they imply
and the wrong they inflict.[36]

Howell took some time to respond to the letter sent to him and in the
meantime the agitation continued.

The speeches in favour of working men's representation were of two
types. In the first place they offered a general criticism of the working
of the whole of the British political system:

What is wanted within the walls of Parliament as well as among the
people is a sound, healthy political morality. This will be a work of
time. We might ask the question as we pass along — how many of
the 658 members in the House who really understand the great
questions which will have to come before them for consideration
before long. As long as men are selected by private favour from
select circles rather than for public worth, we shall always, more or
less, have a corrupt Parliament, no matter what the extent of the
franchise may be. No matter what bad laws there might be, they
will not be abolished so long as the working men are without
Parliamentary representation.[37]

It was necessary, secondly, to preach against the established loyalties
of the Forest. In 1874 men still spoke of the agitation against the Corn
Laws and of how they had marched to vote for Colonel Kingscote.
They had paraded behind two poles, a large loaf of bread hanging
from the one and a small loaf and a herring from the other: they saw
the Tories then and in 1874 as the party which wanted the working
people to have the small loaf. Kingscote's campaign literature made
great play of that:

True-hearted KINGSCOTE, foremost he,
Who valiantly fought,
When Tories ruled a penny loaf
Was worth a poor man's groat.
We raised the Big Loaf flag on high,
'Cheap Bread and Kingscote' was our cry:
    He met the foe
    And straight they go
Off with their tax to Jericho.[38]

But the Liberals and the masters were one and it was against the masters that Mountjoy spoke:

> The *Forester* tells us that some time ago we were very well contented to act upon the advice of our masters in political questions, and now we should with equal confidence trust them. Yes, I admit that we were poor, blind, down-trodden, ignorant things, but now the dawn has come upon us. Our eyes are no longer shut, and we can ask ourselves the question, 'will this man serve us in Parliament?' Then it was true we did the bidding of our employers, but is that a virtue to be repeated? Then we went like little lambs saying 'Hurrah for the bonnets of yellow' and we are 'Jovial Foresters'. I say such doctrines as this neither reflect credit upon ourselves or our leaders. Was it not a 'screw' as much as anything ever was? We trusted and followed our masters — (laughter) — and did what they desired, whether it was right or wrong, wise or foolish. If we didn't do the wise or foolish thing, we were told that we 'might go' . . . Well our district committee have ventured to invite Mr. George Howell to come down, and I believe there is a good chance of success; but according to the *Forester* if he does it will be unwise. I will say to the men of Dean Forest, 'Don't be discouraged'. The *Forester* has estimated the Forest men as one-sixth of the constituency. Now, supposing that to be true, have we not a brave army of colliers in the Bristol district? Then have we no help to expect from the agricultural labourers of West Gloucester? Let me tell you that their interest is with us, and they will give us all the support in their power. Now I feel as much sympathy for the agricultural labourer as I do for my own more immediate brethren, and we, as colliers and miners generally, I venture to say, are not indifferent to their claims. We think that no men should have our sympathy like those men. We have the promise of their help.[39]

He thought that the masters would be showing good feeling if they were to rally behind the men in the way that the men had once rallied behind them. It would be more in the proper order of things if the 'minority were going up with the majority'. A score of meetings on this theme gave to West Gloucestershire politics an entirely new character.

In the event the effort was wasted. Howell had already compromised his independence and was not ever likely to have taken to the platform in Dean.[40] The union, once it was clear that Howell would not stand, attempted to persuade a coal-owner, Captain Heyworth, to come forward as their candidate.[41] This was a retreat from their resolve to have a working man as candidate but was none the less an attempt to demonstrate their importance and independence by choosing their own man. Heyworth, not surprisingly, declined to stand and Colonel Kingscote and the Hon. Charles Berkeley took the field against the Tory, Mr Plunkett. The union offered support to the Liberals but of a grudging sort:

> At the Gloucester meeting I had the unpleasant task of telling Colonel Kingscote what the forest men thought about him. (Laughter and cheers.) It was a very painful thing to do I assure you, nevertheless I had courage enough not to flinch from the duty I was instructed by the district working men to perform. Notwithstanding the plainness of my remarks, I am pleased to know they were taken in a good spirit as given by myself. (Hear, hear.) I need not go over the details of what I said yesterday, but I want him to understand distinctly that what I said to him had been previously said by Forest men to myself. I am very glad to see Col. Kingscote and the other gentlemen present, and also glad to see so large a number of the electors present, but this, continued the speaker, and addressing the hon. candidate, is only a handful of my constituency. (Cheers and laughter.) I want members to understand that in future the Forest of Dean men intend to keep their eyes open, for it is quite true that
> In years which are passed asleep we have been
> To our interests as men in the Forest of Dean.
> I trust this sudden dissolution of Parliament will teach the representatives of Dean Forest such a lesson as they never learnt before . . . I am sure that the little bit of schooling Colonel Kingscote has had in the Forest this week will do him a power of good.[42]

This disturbing election ended badly for the colliers. Several hundred of them did not turn out to vote at all, perhaps confused by the shifts in tactics of the leadership and by uncertainty over a number of purely local issues which arose in the second stage of the election and which we shall discuss in detail below. This, the agent and the *Forester* complained, was what gave the Tory the small margin by which he went ahead of Berkeley to take the second seat for West Gloucestershire.[43] Kingscote topped the poll to take the other.

At the other extreme from the apathetic or uncertain were the working men who congregated around the door of the Tory headquarters, in an inn owned by James White, and pelted the people entering and leaving with herrings, the symbol of Tory disregard for the interests of workers. Upset by this Mr White produced a revolver with which he threatened the crowd. They retaliated after the closing of the poll by ransacking White's inn along with two or three others — the publicans were plumping for the Tories — a butcher's and a pawnbroker's. Once again the Forest magistrates felt compelled to call on the military for assistance and again a squadron of dragoons came to the Forest to keep order. In what the miners' agent characterised as a spiteful act of revenge, the magistrates kept 20 men in custody for two weeks without having sufficient evidence to bring charges against them. Most were subsequently released.

In the workplace, in politics and through a working-class press the union was the vehicle of a notion of horizontal division in society to which the old distinction between native and stranger was irrelevant. A master was a master no matter where he had been born. This view of the union, however, must be qualified: with religious fervour there went a dour piety and an emphasis on discipline; with the demand for freedom from the tyranny of the masters went the rhetoric of an assumed identity of interest between capital and labour; and with the demand for better wages went an awareness of differences of skill and ability within the workforce and a concern that those differences should be reflected in pay differentials. Above all, this was a buttymen's union, designed first and foremost to serve their interests.

For Timothy Mountjoy, far and away the most loquacious and apparently influential of the local men, the union was to teach piety, respectability and sobriety. Mountjoy was born in 1824, the son of a lime burner who lived on Little Dean Hill.[44] Mountjoy remembered his father as a sober and industrious man who 'used to get those of us that could read around the table, and the old family Bible covered with green baize, each one of us reading his verse in his turn'.[45] Young Mountjoy attended the Sunday School at a Wesleyan Chapel near his father's house, later becoming a Sunday School teacher himself, and spent much of his time tramping the district to visit the sick and the dying and to distribute tracts. The Sunday School had a library:

> I read a great deal then, which has proved a blessing to me in after life. I read the 'Boy's Start in Life', so ought every thinking boy; Baxter's 'Saints' Rest'; 'Luther and Cromwell'; 'Pilgrim's Progress'; 'Come and Welcome to Jesus Christ', by Bunyan . . . 'The Jerusalem Sinner Saved', and 'The Holy War'. I read the 'Dialogue of Devils', which was the cause of my taking more heed to my ways.[46]

All this no doubt encouraged piety but it also made of Mountjoy an austere man, not fond of frivolity or disorder. Thus on his marriage he put himself to some inconvenience in 'order to avoid being tanged, that is, to undergo the old-established process, now thankfully dismissed, by neighbours beating pots and kettles and tins around you and about your door'.[47]

Some of his fellow colliers Mountjoy regarded as unregenerate, disorderly fellows whose influence was to be avoided, whether they were drunkards or sheep stealers:

> I did my best to keep my mouth as with a bridle while the ungodly were in my sight. My companions at the pit were always planning how to do mischief; several of them owned sheep, as they do now; they did not always kill their own, but another's. I will tell you how it was done then, and it may be now in some cases. One fine morning old Farmer Smith found that two dry ewes were missing out of the Fishpool orchard; he went riding round to ask if these other men who kept sheep had seen them in their walks; he was told by the very man who was taking the skins off their backs, that he did see them down in Badcox Bailey, marked like Smith's. The old farmer went off on the jog trot to find them, but he never did, for their flesh was eaten on the Hill. This is how unregenerate men will act towards the other. I hope that these dark days are for ever past, and that in the future everyone will kill only those that are his own.[48]

Much to be preferred was the sort of man who would join the East Dean Economic Benefit Society which Mountjoy helped to found in 1854 at the Old Baptist Chapel in Cinderford.[49] This society was to be strict in its behaviour, 'held in a schoolroom, and no beer, and no parade, and no music or feast days'. That was not to the liking of all the foresters. Some of the notices advertising the first sandwich and tea meeting were torn down and burnt. The society paid accident and death benefits, kept a good sum in reserve and, according to Mountjoy, was less expensive to run than the 'public-house club'. Within a year of its beginning, he asserted, the society had 365 paid-up members.

Not surprisingly, these sorts of values informed Mountjoy's unionism. Union was to:

> Extend the principle of self help, and spread the noble principles of our association around us . . . it is calculated to further improve our moral and social position, and our usefulness to society . . . And let us individually try to secure steadier habits among our fellow miners by removing all our benefit clubs and lodges to places where no intoxicating drinks is sold [sic].[50]

Steady habits were important, in part at least, because they helped to create reliable and useful workmen, and so far as the union was responsible for that, it was of as much benefit to the employers as to the men. Because they had not learned the habits of sobriety and thrift, non-union men were of no use to anyone:

He unhesitatingly said that masters were fighting against their own interests when they selected non union men to work in the place of others, for they were most assuredly cultivating the worst propensities of the worst class of men that were amongst them. The non union men in the present Staffordshire struggle were being bribed and petted to work, but those men as a rule, cared nothing of their master's interest or any other principle; they only wanted the treats the pays and less work. They were true Adulamites, seldom at work, not worth a day's pay, the most dissatisfied of men, and, as a rule, those who made the most mischief. They were often turned off for neglect of work and disorderly conduct, often having to flee from their creditors, and were well known to the police . . . To capitalists they were wholly unproductive, and to labour a disgrace, they did a world of evil and lowered their class, engendering hate, strife, disorder and crime. Such was his experience in Dean Forest as the most industrious and upright miners were union men and warm supporters of the organisation.[51]

The demand for steady habits and discipline brought the union into occasional conflict with the membership, who were not always as committed as Mountjoy or the delegates were to the worthy principles which Mountjoy preached. The night men in particular were prone to bad behaviour for which the delegate board chided them.[52] They sent out wildly varying numbers of carts, attended irregularly and displayed less than the correct earnestness to their work:

Mr. Mountjoy drew attention to a company of men who on a recent Monday night went into this colliery, and on reaching the bottom tossed up to see whether they should work or return to bank. He said that according as he was informed the toss went against the first time, when it was continued until it was decided to return to bank which was done. He urged that a vote of censure be passed on them, and also on those persons at the same colliery who had destroyed 365 admission tickets belonging to the company.[53]

The delegates censured these men and similar offenders, especially the 66 men out of 150 who failed to turn up for the most recent Monday night turn. The chairman thought it was part of their business to 'do all that could be done to prevent irregularities'.

Discipline was important to the union too, for its own purposes. If the union was to prosper its rules and regulations had to be obeyed and its procedures as laid down in the rule book closely adhered to. Men often became impatient with that. At Lightmoor colliery in August 1873 a group of men had taken action on their own account and then appealed to the union for support. Mountjoy complained to the next delegate meeting:

> It was unfortunate when men kept off without doing so in the right way. On Saturday he went up to Lightmoor, as he learnt there was a grievance there. He found that notice had been put up, calling a meeting to discuss a matter, viz., an advance of wages of 9d per day. On finding the notice up, he at once took it down and wrote another, to say that if the timber men had a grievance as to wages they should see the manager — see rule 32 — and if they could not come to terms with him, then they had according to rule, to see him (the speaker) in order that the matter might be brought before the district meeting — he reminded the men that if they intended to go against rule their case could not be heard.[54]

Again, at a delegate meeting in 1874, we find G. F. Goode, the chairman of the district union, making the same sort of complaint:

> When men acted independently like that, he did not think they should knock up a lot of bother . . . The fact was that their district had rules and regulations and these must be obeyed. In cases of dispute the agent was to be consulted, and steps taken before parties could come upon the union.[55]

Their need of order and discipline was only one of the ways in which the interests of masters and men were alleged to be identical. The general harmony of the interests of labour and capital was preached at the local as well as the national level. William Owen argued in the *Examiner* that working men 'are not likely to kill the goose that lays the golden eggs by impoverishing or driving out of the country those most useful allies of theirs, the capitalists who provide the resources necessary for carrying out large industrial operations'. For William Brown capital and labour were like the blades of scissors, 'unless there be the two blades there can be no cutting. (Cheers). Capital cannot succeed without labour, neither can labour succeed without capital.'[56] So too for Mountjoy. In August 1873 he went to the village of Clearwell to speak at the opening of a new lodge. He said to the men assembled for the occasion:

> I hope that the interests of employer and the employed will go hand in hand together and your lodge will bear fruit. Let Truth and justice, and not might rule, and strikes and lock outs cease to be. Combination is power, and I hope this gathering will be good and trade and commerce still improve on this side of the district. I also hope that moderation and equity will guide you. We desire for our

society the strength which intelligence and true unity can give; what we want is fair remuneration for masters and men — The united interests of both considered.[57]

Thus, Mr Brown told the demonstration of 1873, union would bring progress and respectability:

> You can talk a little better, you are clothed a little better, you are shod a little better, and generally look a little more respectable . . . You used to meet in this place I have been told, and were in the habit of pulling off your smock frocks; but it was not for the purpose of elevating yourselves or getting better wages. Your object then was to break one another's heads. Thank god those days are past, or at least, fast dying away, and I hope never to return.[58]

This vast condescension did not produce a riot but, if the *Examiner* is to be believed, applause.

Stern, pious, disciplined and respectable, this was not a union which confused the individual worth of one man with another or promoted — so far as its own membership was concerned — any foolish egalitarian ideal. We may discover this in the principles which underpinned the union's wage bargaining. Firstly, there was a recognition that the butties undertook risk. That made their earnings unpredictable and a matter, to some extent, of luck rather than skill. The union accepted that condition of the butty's work. Thus, in September 1873, when the district delegate board pondered the question 'What is a fair day's wage', it decided that no standard could be set for butty men.[59] The butty — not the union — made his contract and then did with it what he could. The union, moreover, accepted the fact that the butties, as entrepreneurs, were competitors in bidding for work. In October 1874, Mr Jones of Whitecroft appeared before the delegates to complain that another member had taken his work. Jones and another man had tendered for a job at £1 per yard but had lost the work to Mr Tyler who had offered to do it for 14s. This, Mr Jones thought, was contrary to the spirit of unionism but the delegate board disagreed:

> The Chairman reminded Mr. Jones that this work was to be estimated for, and he had the same opportunity as others to put in a tender for it. It was not a question as to the men but who was the lowest, at the same time it was scarcely creditable to Tyler who had another job, to estimate in this case. A delegate stated that . . . he (the Speaker) would have as much right to give in a price of 12s as

Tyler did at 14s, and Jones at 20s . . . He could not see how any censure could be passed on Tyler.[60]

Some mild disapproval of Tyler's greediness, perhaps, but none of the system of competitive contracting under which they all worked.

The union did wish to insist that the butties should be paid their fair 'market value'. What was market value and how was it to be known? Market value was the wage dictated by the labour market from time to time and it was to be known by watching the price of coal. As a matter of fact, Mountjoy argued, 'the prices of coal and iron are the only index to which either masters or men can refer for guidance as to the condition of the labour market and they form an infallible guide'.[61] The colliers, therefore, were entitled to rises in their wages in proportion to advances in the price of coal, 'and what is more, if they are wise they will insist on having it'. The butty and the master made their bargain given the price of coal in the market place at a particular time. If the price rose the amount of the advance should be passed back to master and butty in the proportions already established by the ratio of contract tonnage rates to coal prices. This was the principle of wage determination later formalised in the sliding scale.

Market value was not understood to be the same rate for all men. Market value reflected the distinction between skilled and unskilled, butty and dayman. By 1873 those men who were working on union rates received a pay made up of two components. The first part of it was the contract rate or the day rate ruling in 1871 and the second part was an increment of 40 per cent over the 1871 rates, which had been won by union negotiation. The master paid the butty at the advanced rate and the butty in turn was to pass on a proportionate rise to his daymen. That arrangement did not alter the basic relationship between butty and dayman. The delegate board made a gesture towards the daymen in 1873 when it suggested that 6s a day plus 40 per cent was a fair wage for skilled adults but nothing was said about the unskilled. On some occasions, indeed, the unskilled were explicitly excluded from bargains with management:

The Agent said he had had a conversation with the manager at Lightmoor, who told him that if there were any men working at the colliery not receiving marketable value for their labour — he was referring to the men who could do a day's work either in putting timber or beginning and finishing their work in a proper manner — they should be paid it.[62]

This was not at all unacceptable to the delegates. Even the 6s standard for the experienced men was suspect since no provision was made to enforce it, with predictable results:

Many believe that an average rate of wage throughout the district should be insisted upon by union men. Mind you, sir, I do not mean that . . . 'clod-hoppers' or 'Hodges' from the plough tail should receive as high wages as the experienced coal cutter. On the contrary, taking — if I may permitted — the Rocky men in Lightmoor pits. I object to the system of buttymen there making a distinction between practical hands of from 6d to 1s per day. I am one of those who believe that the time has come when the ordinary collier should speak plainly out, objecting to the present unsatisfactory method of paying the daymen.

I venture to say that every day collier able to do a fair eight hours work ought to have the same uniform standard wages together with his forty per cent. Having in general terms explained the grievance of our daymen — or at least many of them — I would affirm that in the Rocky vein, where I am a day collier, there are some butties who out of every five per cent pay their men at a reduced rate, instead of what is fair, just and honourable. The fact being they keep to their own check what is due to others.

Again, some of the butties object to pay the coal money, others pay none at all, and such is the state of things prevailing at the colliery named.

I would, in conclusion ask, is it right these men should be allowed to continue a system attended with so much injustice? I should like, sir, to see the day arrive when the butty men — if we are to have buttymen — and daymen combine in that which is right, instead of the former trying to rob the latter.[63]

For the butties the case was simple: mining was a skill which some men possessed to a greater degree than others. The unskilled should be grateful to think that the butty would help to raise them to a higher plane:

I am sorry to say that there are a great number of persons at Lightmoor who are not capable of being in a stall without the butty. I might say without hesitation, that a great many more lives would be sacrificed than at the present time, because there are a great number of persons who are not competent miners, and do not possess those capabilities which are requisite to enable them to carry on a stall either safely or beneficially . . . they ought to be thankful to think of the butty taking them from the plough tail, and for the instruction given them to try and bring them as financial as good as themselves. The butty does not scandalise any incompetent person, but is doing much good for him daily in trying to make them if possible, practical miners.[64]

No move for abolition of the butty system came from within the union and the dayman remained subordinate there as he was in the workplace.

This preoccupation with the problems of the butty was reinforced after the collapse of the AAM at the end of 1874 and in the subsequent period of union weakness in Dean Forest. In the course of 1874 the economic boom had faltered and then collapsed. As the coal markets began to fall the masters in all districts began to insist on wage reductions. In the Forest a wage reduction in November 1874 led to a strike which lasted until February 1875. Thoroughly beaten in the strike, the union's membership fell away to 1,000 and continued to fall to about 400 in 1877.[65] In 1877 the district council, unable to prevent further wage reductions, disbanded and discharged its agent. District organisation remained defunct from then until 1882. A new district union formed in November 1882 had some brief initial success in its dealings with the masters but within a few years it too had become ineffective.

During the strike of 1874 — 5 the union concerned itself narrowly with the wage problems of the butty. The union directed its bargaining, in accordance with its previous wages policy, at establishing the precise dimensions of the relationship between the market price of the product and the market value of the butty. In order to make that relationship clear and explicit the union demanded the institution of a formal sliding scale. A sliding scale was a formula which would stipulate by how much tonnage rates would vary with given percentage increases or decreases in coal prices. Variation was measured from an agreed base point. The base point might be, for example, a coal price of 15s a ton at pit mouth and a tonnage rate of 1s 6d per ton for best block. As the price rose and fell by agreed amounts the employer automatically varied the tonnage rate. This procedure effectively ruled out the need for continuous wage bargaining. Once a basis could be fixed for the scale, the *Examiner* prophesied, 'the great contention of wages need no longer be a bone of contention between master and men. And that evil removed, there is very little left to quarrel upon'.[66] The basis was the main obstacle to agreement between the Forest masters and their men. There was no disagreement about the assumption that coal prices and tonnage rates should move together. The colliers wanted the formal expression of a relationship between prices and rates which they already accepted: that for every rise or fall of 1s in the price of coal, rates should move by 5 per cent.[67] The fall in coal prices in 1874 and 1875, however, had created two difficulties. Firstly, there was disagreement about the point at which falling prices should provoke a cut in rates. The colliers believed that their rates had not increased during the boom in proportion to coal prices. There should not, therefore, the union argued, be wage reductions until prices had fallen to the same percentage margin over those of 1871 as rates were over those of 1871.[68] Secondly, it was difficult to tell when rates and prices had fallen into their pre-boom relationship because no one seemed able or willing to say whether coal sold at 14s or 16s the ton in the winter of 1874. In other words, this strike was about an apparently unfair advantage which the masters had obtained over the butties in the confused situation which came with the breaking of the boom.

The true conclusion to the strike came, not when the men were forced back to work in February 1875, but in July, after another two cuts in the rates. At that point the masters met the lodge representatives at the village of Littledean and agreed to the establishment of a formal sliding scale for the Forest. The basis for prices was taken to be 12s per ton at the pit mouth for best screened block and, for tonnage rates, 15 per cent over the rates of 1871. From that base, rates were to move 5 per cent for every movement of 1s in prices.[69]

There was nothing extraordinary about this arrangement, of course. There were sliding scales in other coalfields and in other industries.[70] What is of interest here is that the scale in Dean, by linking *contract rates* and prices, effected an agreement only between the masters and the butties. There was no provision for the daymen, who were left by default to the kindness of the buttymen. After all, if rates were to be settled by a formal mechanism strikes would be unnecessary, the daymen therefore would pose no threat and consequently there would be no point in organising them or providing for them.

The failure of district organisation after the strike left union in the Forest even more explicitly dependent on the butties. The masters were responsible for that. During the strike they had refused to negotiate with Timothy Mountjoy or the district officers who, the masters said, were inflammatory agitators, to be blamed for the fact that there was a strike at all. From that point each of the masters would meet his own men but not the officers or the agent. Where collective decisions were necessary — as at Littledean — individual pit deputations might congregate but, again, were not to speak through an agent. Thus, as the strength of the district union ebbed, the separate lodges became relatively more important. Now, as that happened, the checkweighmen came to assume a greater authority. The right to appoint their own checkweighmen had come to the miners from the Mines Act of 1872. Elected and paid by the butties, the checkweighman was perhaps the only person in the pit who was capable of surviving moments of vindictiveness on the part of the master. The checkweighman therefore became the focus of lodge organisation, keeping the books, calling and chairing meetings and leading deputations.[71] So far as union persisted in the Forest, in the bleak years after 1874, it did so in the hands of men who depended on the butties for their living.[72] When optimism returned in 1882 it was the checkweighmen who brought the lodges together in a new district organisation, whose first president was a checkweighman, John Ennis.[73]

As miners' agent the new council employed Edward Allen Rymer. He was an experienced agent and one whose recent history might have encouraged the butties and weighmen to imagine that his notions of unionism would coincide fairly well with their own. In Yorkshire, he had been an advocate of the sliding scale and a prophet of conciliation and arbitration.[74] His initial approach to the Forest masters was moderate and respectful in tone. The colliers did not wish to enter into strikes or lockouts, he told them, but would appeal to 'their sense of honour and Christian philanthropy' in asking for a wage advance.[75] Since the masters had fallen into price competition amongst themselves and had in practice abandoned the Littledean agreement in 1879, Rymer also appealed to them to establish a board of conciliation and a sliding scale.[76]

Within two months of his arrival, however, he had fallen into dispute with the weighmen. Rymer saw himself as the embodiment of the will of the colliers. He expected the weighmen to act as servants of the district union and to accept the policy which he formulated for the district, interpreting opposition to that policy as opposition to union.[77] Though protesting that they were good union men, the weighmen asserted that they had a first duty to the butties and were reluctant to subordinate themselves to Rymer, who denounced them as tools of the masters and moved, apparently unsuccessfully, a resolution at a mass meeting that the weighmen all undergo re-election.[78] He managed, however, to have all the checkweighmen excluded from membership of the district council.[79]

This was in part a quarrel about relative authority within the union but it was also a more fundamental dispute about the purposes of unionism. Rymer's cautious, moderate, market-conscious unionism had only come to him after the defeats and disasters which followed the collapse of the boom in 1874. Before that he had been an exponent of views which were basically at odds with those of the butties and their weighmen. In his earlier career he had not subscribed to any notion of the identity of interest of capital and labour whose measure was to be found in the fixed ratio of coal prices to tonnage rates.

> Whatever be the price of coal or iron, or whatever be the state of trade in the money market, we must have our position made secure and our labour protected from the wolves and vultures of a mean, selfish and brutal generation.[80]

Labour was the creator of value and that, not some mechanical 'law' of supply and demand, should determine labour's reward. 'We create annually over £12,000,000,000,' he wrote. 'We only get a third of the money in wages. We shall demand it all as our own property and hurl your dirty law from us with a philosophical disgust that has never penetrated your numskulls.'[81] Arbitration was 'but another means of concession to capital, for it allows them to use their organized knowledge in commercial matters against our ignorance'.[82] He was pugnacious and aggressive, cast in the mould of 'old unionism' and bred in the ways of mass radical agitation, favouring the rhetoric of the apocalypse and the challenge to tyranny and oppression broadcast to thousands massed on a moor or in a city square, rather than the prudent negotiations of the union and the union official.

To the disgust of the weighmen this older strain in Rymer's character came to the fore once he had arrived in Dean and established himself through the masters' concession of a wage advance. That success had won Rymer great popularity.[83] Membership of the union jumped from 1,000 shortly after its foundation to 3,000 in December 1882.[84] Since that represented three-quarters of the colliers in Dean it is clear that Rymer was not directing his attention exclusively to the butties but was making a wider, populist appeal to all the workmen in the mines.[85] Here was a champion for the 'ordinary' miner, one who disregarded petty hierarchies and was prepared to fight the weighmen. In appreciation of his services the Drybrook lodge presented him early in 1883 with a 'silver, keyless, chronometer watch with a gold chain'.[86]

At this point the masters became important. They had contributed to the fall of Timothy Mountjoy by ignoring him and the district council and dealing only with the separate lodges. They now proceeded to isolate Rymer in exactly the same way. Though conceding a wage advance they had refused to establish a conciliation board. Rymer's reported statements about what the colliers would *demand*, the masters said, made the idea of a conciliation board farcical.[87] Then, at the beginning of March 1883, as the spring slackening of the trade began, they took away the wage advance, announced that they would not talk to Rymer or the district officers and locked their men out.[88]

It was not the intention of the masters simply to crush the union, it was rather that they wanted to direct the form that union took. While Rymer raged against them at a mass meeting, the masters met a Staffordshire miners' agent, William Brown, a moderate, 'responsible' advocate of conciliation, arbitration and the sliding scale.[89] Brown obtained from them an agreement that half the proposed 10 per cent reduction should take effect immediately and the other half should go to the consideration of an arbitration board. Rymer denounced these terms and led a large proportion of the men into a strike. After five weeks, however, the money ran out as it had in 1875 and the men had to go back to work. While Rymer waited in an outside room the pit delegates met the masters and agreed to resume work on the terms which had been offered to Brown.[90] Thus the masters had not only beaten the union in an open struggle but had also destroyed Rymer's authority.

The masters consolidated their advantage when the board met to arbitrate on the 5 per cent which was still at issue. Again the district council and Rymer were excluded from the negotiations. Enoch Edwards, from North Staffordshire, and William Chappell, of Yorkshire, both men of exemplary moderation, acted as arbitrators for the colliers.[91] Having agreed to split the 5 per cent, the arbitrators then agreed on two further points. Firstly there was to be a sliding scale of the sort which had been arranged in 1875. Secondly the sliding scale was to run to spring 1884 without alteration, at which time it was to be renegotiated by the same arbitrators. For the central purpose of wage bargaining for the butties, the district union and the agent were now redundant. The re-signing of the sliding-scale agreement in 1885 and 1886 effectively broke the district union.[92] The scale, like its predecessor, satisfied the needs of the butties and ignored the daymen: both classes now had little to gain from the union whose numbers fell away rapidly. With great astuteness and a clear understanding of the divisions within their workforce, the masters had countered the threat of Rymer's populist and dangerous agitation, by accommodating the butty men.

Rymer raged against the employers and against 'pagan' political economy and its law of supply and demand. It was unjust that wages should fall when prices fell:

> It is simply absurd to ask the miners to submit to a reduction to give other people cheap coal, for this would cause *fresh and keener* competition all round, which would have soon brought wages down all through the Forest. The game is played out, and its blighting consequences have taught our men a bitter lesson all over the country, though experience and facts do not yet appear to enter into the calculations of some employers; time, however, will teach them a modern political economy, by which labour will demand a living price for all work done.[93]

He raised the old cry of the producer, that the price of his product be set at a level which would allow him a satisfactory standard of life, and condemned the employers and their economic system in some of the most effective language to come from the pen of a miner:

The miner seeks not to injure his honest employer — to do so would be a violation of all just principles — he seeks to claim from the country a fair reward for his labours, and, as the country employs her wealth, and possesses her power and influence through the manhood, skill and labour of the workmen, he sees no reason why he ought to toil and live in poverty, and a surplus of that wealth being hoarded up day by day, and he thinks that if the coal owners are unable to pay more wages, that a higher value should be put on the coal, and labour paid accordingly. The old economic laws (?) are with him a mockery. He sees around the order of nature being openly set at defiance by employers competing and underselling each other in every market, and forcing sales of cheap manufactured articles to the utter ruin of all the best and honest trades. He hears of bankruptcy and roguery and gigantic swindling going on every day in almost every town; he reads the wills of millionaires, sees mansions, churches, and temples rising over his head on every side, while pauperism, misery and crime disfigures the land. He beholds the land lying waste and thousands of hungry people seeking employment. He finds the true natural order economic arrangements of supply and demand arrested by selfish villainy and converted into a heartless man-made system called 'political economy', — a thing to be used and abused at the will of the worst in creation. He knows nobody cares of any political economy beyond what he can get out of it. No one ever attempts to regulate their business affairs on 'economic laws' but rush on planning and scheming wherever they can. All is chance, speculation and competition, and get what you can, though you 'beggar your neighbour' and bring him to ruin. This the miner sees, and determines not to allow his blood and life to be bartered away like dead metal, or as though he were a mere chattel.[94]

In Rymer's 'true natural order' there was no place for the sliding scale.

It was all to no purpose. The union had almost become defunct by the end of 1885 and the weighmen took the opportunity to reassert their authority. Each of the pit lodges sent representatives to a meeting called for the purpose of reorganising the district union.[95] They did not invite Rymer to attend. Rymer accepted the *fait accompli*, apologised for whatever offence he had given and attempted to carry on as agent. Within six months, however, there were not suffcient funds in the union to pay his wage. The council therefore tendered him a reference and, led by the weighmen, set about finding a replacement for him.[96]

It was indicative of the opinion the weighmen and their employers, the butties, had of Rymer that they turned first to William Chappell, advocate of the sliding scale, rather than to someone who might have shared Rymer's populism and his fundamental hostility to the employers.[97] As one of the weighmen had put it:

> I do not believe in men that call themselves Union men, who will call everyone who do not see things just in the same light, all sorts of bad names — calling them rotten, and traitorous, and black ball them in every way. I cannot see a fraction of unionism in that; it seems to me more like tyranny and selfishness. Then there are some men who call themselves union men, and they will act any artful dodge to cheat their master, and impose on him in any way they can, even if it were calculated to ruin him. I should not like to daub my hands, tongue or pen with such unionism as that.[98]

When Chappell showed no interest in the job it went to G. H. Rowlinson, who had been president of the AAM's South Staffordshire branch. His first meeting was not for the purpose of denouncing the masters as tyrants and robbers of the value which labour had created or to demand a wage increase. It was a tea meeting presided over by the Reverend W. Thomas, at which Rowlinson expounded his belief that the interests of masters and men were identical.[99]

The contrast between the social background to debate about the free miners' rights in the first and second halves of the nineteenth century is striking. In the first half the miners in Dean were self-consciously and aggressively parochial in their attitudes. The Forest was 'the country' and other places in England, especially the counties beyond Gloucestershire, were other 'countries'. People born outside of the Forest were 'foreigners'. That terminology contained a splendidly arrogant sense of election which, in the second half of the century, was not so conspicuous. The collier had been carried down into Egypt and lived in thraldom. The master was tyrant and oppressor, not a brother free miner. In all the exchanges and quarrels of union and coalmaster there was not a single reference to the heritage and traditions of the free miners. A trade union, a working-class newspaper and working-class intervention in politics changed the nature of social relationships in the Forest. The union was not, however, concerned in an even-handed way with the problems of all colliery workers. The influx of capital to the Forest in the 1820s had meant the development of large pits in which work was organised around small working masters, the butty contractors. The buttymen had started the union in the first place and their view of pit work governed the behaviour of the union, particularly in the key area of wage bargaining. The butty wanted a fair share of the fluctuating price of coal but had no ambition to set a minimum rate or standard for his labour: he accepted the fact of risk and its influence on his profits. Given a formal sliding scale which would distribute the price of coal equitably between master and butty there was no reason for them to quarrel. The dayman was, in the union as in the working place, subordinate to the butty. The union made no attempt to abolish the dayman's condition of dependency. For their part the masters chose to deal with the butties through the nexus of the sliding scale and to defend that selective relationship against the democratic threat of Rymer. The weighmen, the servants of the butties, were important as brokers in that relationship. In sum, the new system in the Forest divided the miners in the workplace and offered only a small, relatively privileged section of them the chance of an amelioration of their condition through collective action. All this was new in the nineteenth century; much of it was new in the third quarter of the nineteenth century. On the face of it, however, some things had not changed. Among the working men of the Forest there were still freeholders, free miners and commoners. Their experience needs to be assessed alongside that of the union men.

6. Commodities: the Land

Arouse ye, free miners, who delve in old Dean,
And all ye freeholders with rights o'er its green,
'Tis time to be stirring for danger is nigh;
And if ye bestir not, you'll find by and by,
That truth, and truth only, is this now I tell,
They'll suck out the egg if they once prick the
*   shell!*

Say will you surrender, or barter away,
Your father's old charter — Twelve months and
*   a day,*
While yours, the bad bargain, to take what they
*   please,*
In rents and in taxes, in fines, and in fees.
Remember, free miners, yea, ponder it well,
They'll suck out the egg if they once prick the
*   shell!*

Anon., the Foresters' Egg! A Timely Warning! Dean Forest Mercury,
23 May 1884.

In the first half of the nineteenth century the Crown and the foresters had been in dispute about three main matters: the use of the land, the free miners' rights and the rights of common. In the second half of the century the Crown took these matters up again and, in another series of Bills and Inquiries, attempted to extinguish whatever claims the miners had on the resources of the Forest. Once again the Crown found itself in alliance with the principal coal-owners and once again the move to eliminate rights provoked opposition. The first phase of the new struggle culminated in a Select Committee and the framing of a government bill, in 1874 and 1875. On the face of it this Bill represented a victory for the working men of the Forest, who had for some time been demanding improved sanitary conditions in the Forest villages and the sale of Crown wasteland for house building. The Bill proposed to satisfy both demands. None the less, a bitter opposition to the Bill arose and the free miners and foresters again rallied to defend their rights and privileges. What had gone wrong? The first, and perhaps the most important, problem was that the land

106

campaign had come from a small, relatively privileged section of the working classes of the Forest, who had lost touch with the traditions of the free miners.

As the population of the Forest had grown over the middle years of the century, pressure had increased on the stock of freehold land created by the sale or grant of the old encroachments. Where there were 7,014 people competing for living space in 1831, there were 20,555 in 1871 (Table 6.1). At the same time the number of inhabited houses had increased almost threefold, from 1,462 in 1834 to 4,244 in 1871. As the number of cottages had grown, the average area of freehold land per cottage had fallen from about one-and-one-quarter acres in 1834 to about half an acre in 1871 (Table 6.2). The pressure on the land was evident at the national land survey of 1871, which showed that the number of holdings of one acre or more in the Forest had been cut almost by half from 604 in 1834 to 316.

Table 6.1: Population of the Forest of Dean and the Hundred of St Briavels at Census Dates, 1801 — 1891

Census year	Forest of Dean		Balance of Hundred[b]		Hundred of St Briavels	
	No.	%[a]	No.	%[a]	No.	%[a]
1801	3,325		6,628		9,953	
1811	4,073	16.2	7,492	13.0	11,565	16.2
1821	5,535	19.3	8,255	10.2	13,790	19.3
1831	7,014	16.7	9,078	10.0	16,092	16.7
1841	10,692	26.4	9,654	6.4	20,346	26.4
1851	13,566	17.1	10,257	6.3	23,823	17.1
1861	17,466	20.3	11,181	9.0	28,647	20.3
1871	20,555	14.5	12,254	9.6	32,809	14.5
1881	23,556	3.3	10,347	−15.56	33,903	3.3
1891	23,752	1.3	9,725	− 6.0	33,477	− 1.3

Notes:
a. Inter-censal increase in population (per cent).
b. The parishes and tythings of: Abinghall, English Bricknor, St Briavels, Little Dean, Flaxley, Hewelsfield, Lea (part), Lea Bailey, Mitcheldean, Newland, Ruardean and Staunton.

Source: *Census of England and Wales*, 1801 — 91.

The other possible source of building space was the Forest wasteland but the Commissioners of Woods had kept that securely locked up. Sales of the old encroachments had finished in 1845. In the decade after that only a little over an acre of land passed from the hands of the Crown (Table 6.2). There were many more sales in the period 1856 — 71 but altogether they made up only about 86 acres and 39 of those had gone in a single sale to the South Wales Railway. Most of those sales were of slips and scraps of Crown land which were mixed in with the encroachments. Having no use for them, the Crown sold

Table 6.2: Sales of Crown Land in the Forest of Dean, 1840—1871

Year ending	Acreage a.r.p.	Purchase money £ s d	Price per perch
31 December 1840	10 3 25	30 16 9	4d
1841	210 2 39	584 16 5	4d
1842	79 3 15	216 0 4	4d
1843	194 3 7	534 15 7	4d
1844	19 1 8½	53 17 8	4d
1845	55 2 16^a	163 12 0	4d
1846	—	—	
1847	—	—	
1848	—	—	
1849	—	—	
1850	—	—	
31 March 1852^b	0 0 1	5 0	
1853	—	—	
1854	—	—	
1855	1 1 3½	51 5 0	
1856	0 1 33	87 10 0	
C/forward	572 3 28	1722 18 9	

Year ending	Acreage a.r.p.	Purchase money £ s d	Price per perch (s)
b/forward	572 3 28	1722 18 9	20
31 March 1857	2 0 19	330 10 0	20
1858	7 3 39	932 8 1	15
1859	38 3 21½^c	3878 11 6	13
1860	8 1 9¾	1438 15 0	22
1861	8 3 4½	1600 15 0	25
1862	3 3 33½	992 5 0	31
1863	2 3 20½	775 5 0	34
1864	0 3 11	103 0 0	16
1865	0 2 12½	352 0 0	76
1866	1 2 0	482 15 0	40
1867	4 3 18½	782 16 0	20
1868	1 — 36	350 0 0	36
1869	2 1 24½	635 0 0	33
1870	1 — 14½	369 5 0	42
1871	1 — 20	282 17 6	31
Total	659 1 32½^d	15029 1 10	

Notes:

a. Sales to the end of 1845 were principally of encroachments at prices fixed in accordance with the Act 1 and 2 Vict. c.42.

b. Fifteen months.

c. Includes 38 acres 22 perch sold to the South Wales Railway for £2,820.

d. There were 2,196 acres 2 roots 14 perch of freehold land in 1871, made up of 2,108 acres 1 rood 12 perch of old encroachment and 88 acres 1 rood 2 perch sold by the Crown from 1852—71.

Source: *Returns Relating to Dean Forest* (PP, XXXVI, 1872), p. 188.

some of those scraps to the owners of adjoining freeholds. In 1860, 65 conveyances were necessary to dispose of just over eight acres of such land. For the land they did sell, moreover, the Commissioners charged prohibitive prices. The encroachments had brought 4d per perch and small sales in 1852 and 1855 had brought 5s per perch. From 1856 to 1871, however, the annual average sale price ranged from 13s to 76s per perch: £124 to £608 per acre.

One result of this policy was that the struggle between the keepers and the foresters did not abate. The Verderers' Courts recorded a total of 451 convictions of foresters for offences between 1846 and 1871. Of those 258 were for encroachments of land alone: the hedges had not stopped rolling. The other 193 offences were building fern ricks, pigsties, goose cots and sheds on Forest land, taking stone, clay and sand illegally and, in one or two cases, the erection of cabins. Most convictions resulted in a fine, usually between 2s 6d and £1, and an order to abate the encroachment (Table 6.3).

Table 6.3: Convictions before the Court of Verderers in the Forest of Dean, 1846 — 1871

Year	Land encroachments	Other[a]	Total	Year	Land encroachments	Other	Total
1846	6	4	10	1859	10	33	43
1847	4	6	10	1860	5	8	13
1848	19	3	22	1861	2	1	3
1849	8	2	10	1862	8	3	11
1850	11	6	17	1863	—	—	—
1851	9	2	11	1864	8	16	24
1852	21	8	29	1865	6	3	9
1853	19	2	21	1866	10	3	13
1854	18	4	22	1867	12	5	17
1855	11	4	15	1868	5	3	8
1856	27	33	50	1869	4	5	9
1857	14	15	29	1870	11	—	11
1858	6	22	28	1871	4	2	6
				Totals	258	193	457

Note:
a. Includes erection of fern ricks, pigsties, goose cots, sheds, taking stone, clay and sand from the Forest and illegal cabin dwelling.
Source: *Proceedings of the Court of Verderers*, PRO, F.16/21.

The vigilance of the keepers, the limits on the supply of land and the growth in demand for it, had produced in some places the predictable unpleasant results. The small town which had grown up at Cinderford housed about a fifth of the Forest's population. Though it boasted a town hall, Cinderford made a poor impression on Arnold Taylor of the Local Government Board, who came to make an inspection of the sanitary condition of the Forest in 1869, after a complaint from the Westbury-on-Severn Poor Law Guardians. He found Cinderford to be 'worse, I think, than any place of the same size that I have had to inspect in England, in regard to the irregularity of the way it is laid out, and also as to the general sanitary shortcomings of the place'. There were no sanitary regulations, no drainage and no water supply except for a few natural wells. There were unformed tracks rather than roads among the houses and there was a great deal of overcrowding in the houses. The worst spots were Minty's Row, Long Row and Harris' Row, as Mr Taylor told the local Board of Health in a letter to it on 'the Neglect of their Duty as the Nuisance Authority of that District':

> You are aware that these had been stated at the enquiry, and on the authority of the medical officer, to be the seats of constant fever, or other filth engendered disease; and having seen the locality, my only wonder is, not that disease is always there, but that anyone living under such conditions escapes its ravages.
>
> Long Row consists of 12 houses, each having a small room and cupboard on the ground floor, and two sleeping rooms overhead. Only two of the rooms have windows to open, and none of the houses have either light or ventilation except in front. The total number of the inmates was given to me as 73, or, on an average, six to a house; now the total cubical area of the rooms available for habitation in each dwelling is less than 2,000 feet, so that no inmate has more than 300 cubic feet of space. This is an average; but three of the houses have eight occupants, three seven, and only one had three; hence you will see that in at least one half of Long row the overcrowding is far worse than I have made it . . . outside the houses, but one single privy in the row; no well, no means of drainage; whilst under the windows of the houses outside the stinking, filth-sodden ground is one mass of odour and offensive refuse. To all this abomination I might add the pigs and pigsties close to the houses only that it is a mockery to speak of these when the condition of the people and the cottages in Long row is so nearly on a level with that of the pigs and the sties in which they are housed. The above descriptions will apply, with the slightest possible alteration, to Minty's and Harris' row.[1]

In an earlier letter to the Home Office, Taylor had remarked that the Forest was 'undulating, and the ground broken most picturesquely into hill and dale' but he was not a romantic man.[2] Those picturesque hills and dales meant that the 'drainage of one set of houses quite commonly discharges upon a set below, and the latter upon another lower still'. In other places around the Forest where the smallholders' gardens had given way to colliers' rows, conditions were equally bad.

The first aspect of this problem to receive attention was sanitation, in a series of disputes and squabbles at the local Board of Health in 1870. These squabbles were an important prelude to the land campaign and establish the perspective in which that campaign should be seen.

There was no doubt good reason for a serious attempt to drain and sewer the district but who was to pay for it? The Commissioners of Woods would not. Neither in equity nor in law, they insisted, could they be held responsible for any such expense:

> The houses have not been erected by the Crown, nor does the Crown receive the rents of them, and it seems unreasonable, therefore, to hold the Crown responsible for the neglect of the freeholders who are alone interested in the proper sewerage and ventilation of their premises.[3]

It was up to the Health Board to deal with the matter. The majority of members of the Board, however, were masters of large collieries. They did not own large blocks of company houses, as the masters in other districts did, because the Crown would not sell them land for the purpose. Why then should they be called upon to make an onerous contribution to the development of the district. The ratepayers in their turn insisted that they should not bear a new rate burden and blamed the Crown and the coal-owners for their meanness.[4] In the course of these disputes the coal-owners resigned from the Board, which ceased to function in April 1870.

The 'anti-tax' protests of the ratepayers had a democratic, anti-employer character. The ratepayers had formed what they variously styled the 'Foresters' Protection Committee' and the 'Ratepayers and Voters' Protection Committee',[5] whose chief spokesman and chairman was Timothy Mountjoy. It is likely that he and the Protection Committee were the same 'Miners' Committee' which formed the union club at Cinderford in 1871. Mountjoy, as befitted a man about to form a union, thought that the masters on the Health Board had things too much their own way. He complained that the Board was undemocratic. Who had elected it? If all ratepayers were entitled to vote, had there been a sufficient and clear notice to the public that elections were to be held? Why did not Board meetings take place at a time when miners and colliers could attend them? He for one would pay no more rates until he knew more about the constitution and workings of the Board. He complained further that the sanitary and overcrowding problems were yet further evidence of the masters' neglect of their men's welfare. Where were the Mechanics' Institutes, the reading rooms and other signs that the masters wished to improve the men?[6] There was, in any case, a strong suspicion that the rates collected from the working men would go to improve the property of only a few wealthy men.

These democratic sentiments, however, were misleading. Mountjoy, after all, was leading an opposition to a rate which might have improved the condition of the working people who lived in the squalor of the rows. The fact was that there were significant numbers of property owners among the workers in the Forest and it was that group which Mountjoy represented. No rate books have survived to be compared with the census enumerators' books in order to show the extent of house or land ownership by working people, but some other evidence is available. The electoral register for 1874 listed the names, addresses and qualifications of voters for the Forest division. This document is in effect a list of foresters who held freehold houses and land (and who had also registered to vote). Of the 1,121 voters whose occupations could be discovered in the census books, 821, or 73.3 per cent, were in the 'working-class' categories: metal workers, general labourers, coal and iron miners and stone, wood and agricultural workers (Table 5.2). If each voter owned and lived in one house, then the 821 voters owned 19.4 per cent of the 4,244 inhabited houses in the Forest. This figure might be revised upwards by assuming, not unreasonably, that if the occupations of all the resident voters in the Forest division in 1874 were known, the pattern of occupational distribution would not change. That is, 73.3 per cent of the 1,565 resident voters would fall into the working-class occupational categories. In that case, 1,147 houses or about 27 per cent of the houses in the Forest belonged to working-class freeholders. The same data may be presented in another way. The 1,147 freeholders were about one-fifth of the total of 5,654 employed males in the working-class categories in 1871. These numbers give only a rough, minimum estimate of the proportion of houses owned by working men and the proportion of working men who owned houses: about one-quarter and one-fifth respectively. The true proportions were probably much higher: because there is no guarantee that all freeholders registered for the vote; because no account is taken of women freeholders; because some freeholders owned more than one house; and because the number of 'employed males' includes boys and youths still dependent on their fathers' households.

Within the larger category of working-class freeholders it is possible to identify another group: those who owned more than one acre of land. Of the 316 owners of one acre or more, six were coal or other companies and 66 were women. (The significance of women as property owners and the difficulty of discovering anything about them must seriously distort any statement about working-class property ownership.) The occupations of 139 others could be found in the census books. Of those, 99 or 46.9 per cent, were in the working-class categories (Table 6.4).

Table 6.4: Occupations of Owners of One Acre, or more, of Land in the Forest of Dean, 1871

Occupation	No.	%
Clerical, non-mining professional	3	1.4
Shops	23	10.9
Industrial trades	7	3.3
Metal workers	1	0.5
General labourers	10	4.7
Colliers	45	21.3
Iron ore miners	16	7.6
Other mining	6	2.8
Stone and quarry	7	3.3
Agriculture	13	6.2
Wood and timber	7	3.3
Miscellaneous	1	0.5
Women	66	31.3
Coal and iron companies	6	2.9
Total	211	100.00
Total in Return	316	

Source: *Return* for 1872—3, with respect to each county (exclusive of the metropolis), of name and address of every owner of one acre and upwards, with estimated acreage and annual gross estimated rental of the land, etc., of individual owners, and of the number of owners of less than one acre, with the estimated aggregate acreage, and the annual gross estimated rental of the land, etc., of such owners; together with the estimated extent of commons and waste lands (PP, LXXII, 1874).

Clearly, the experience of a significant proportion of working people in the Forest had little to do with Long Row and Minty's Row but instead had to do with ownership of property. It is not unlikely indeed that the transfer of the old encroachments freehold to their occupiers had given a generation of foresters and their heirs an experience of property ownership unparalleled elsewhere in the English coalfields. It is likely, too, that the growth of the Forest's population and the demand for freehold building land that went with it, gave those foresters an unparalleled experience of property dealing and of profit from it. Timothy Mountjoy at least had become a property owner. Thrift and his membership of the Economic Benefit Society had allowed him to purchase a block of ground, build a cottage and then to acquire a second block and build a second cottage.[7]

As well as defending the propertied working classes of the Forest against rate impositions by the coal-owners on the Health Board,

Mountjoy had begun a campaign against the Crown. He condemned
the Commissioners of Woods for their ungenerous land policies and,
raising up the old cry of 'Home Colonisation', demanded the cultivation of the Forest wastelands. Once again he employed a radical
rhetoric. Pauperism was evil but it should not be remedied by
shipping the poor to distant shores. Why could the poor not be given
the dignity of work at home:

> We think the time has come when the working men of the Forest
> and other districts should ask the question — how much longer
> shall our countrymen, high in power, help to swell the flood of
> emigration at the expense of our country, of thousands of the
> flower of our stalwart classes, to till the soil of the backwoods of
> America, while there are thousands and thousands of acres of
> uncultivated land at home that ought to be brought under
> cultivation.[8]

England's 'class legislators' should consider what would happen if
war should break out with America: fathers and sons would be thrown
into battle against each other. The words of Solomon, he thought,
were true: 'When the righteous are in authority the people rejoice, but
when the wicked beareth rule the people mourn.' Thousands of
employers of labour had amassed great fortunes, produced by the
industrial population for whom there was nothing but poverty and the
imigrant ship. The remedy for such social and political evils was for
the working men of the Forest to 'come out of their isolated indi-
vidualisms and organise themselves, and unite into one grand league
or body, and cooperate in all social and political matters'.[9] More
immediately, he thought the Members of Parliament for West
Gloucestershire should bring in a 'Bill to enclose the entire
unenclosed Crown lands in the Forest of Dean, with a view to sell out
when in a marketable condition'.[10]

What is striking about this is the complete absence of that sense
that enclosure was oppression, which had led Warren James into riot.
Mountjoy remembered the riot, though he was only seven years old at
the time it happened. In his autobiography, he recorded a version of
the event which reflected his strong antipathy to disorder and
violence. The rioters had not come out to resist a tyranny but were
merely 'mischievous foresters':

> Some forty-five or fifty years ago, many of the Foresters acted as
> though there was no law to be respected; they got it into their heads
> that the office of woods and forests had no right to enclose the
> forest lands and plant trees thereon, and, under this belief, they

banded themselves together, under the leadership of one called Warry Williams, to pull down and throw open again Her Majesty's enclosures. They did a great deal of mischief, and I do not know where the mischief would have ended, had not a cavalry regiment come upon the scene; it was useless for the woodsmen to attempt to stop them, they did get one hundred in a rank against a stone fence, or a turf fence, and sent it down like madmen. I saw them at work near the Latimore Lodge, but as soon as the soldiers came it was real fun to see the tall fir trees, with a bank-puller half way up it, hiding from the soldiers; others in cowsheds, taking the Sunday's meal, others in mine holes, many were taken and put to prison, others got clear away. Another mischievous band of Foresters.[11]

The Office of Woods had every right to enclose and presumably to sell what they had enclosed.

The local newspaper, the *Forester*, supported the Protection Committee, arguing that 'on public grounds it is undoubtedly advantageous that [the working man] should be bound up with the interests of his country by the possession of a stake in the soil'.[12] The Crown stood in the way because where it would sell land the price it charged, which was payable in full in cash along with the expense of the plan and the conveyance, was too much for working men and above what similar land would fetch in an open sale:

> In fact it was never meant by the Crown authorities to give the inhabitants of the Forest facilities for purchasing land within it. The prices were simply meant to be prohibitory; and for the most part they answer their end. Very few of the miners, colliers, and quarrymen of the Forest are in a position to buy Crown land, however much they stand in need of it.

The editor denounced the autocrats of the Woods and Forests, declaring that the foresters had shown a great forbearance, contrary to their 'ancient instincts and traditions'. What would their forefathers have thought of such prices for the land? He added in a later article: 'Crown prerogative is a fine bogie; but as it fared at Runnymede, so shall it fare in Dean Forest and everywhere else, if the people be but true to themselves as their forefathers were'.[13] At the same time the paper printed a series of articles on the 'Romance and Reality of Dean Forest', which 'rediscovered' and retold its history, emphasising the distinctiveness and independence of the foresters and the antiquity of their peculiar rights and privileges. That history was not without its lessons:

There may have been no political manoeuvres to accomplish in a wild and thinly populated region, where politics were almost unknown. But these antiquated Crown officers had their trials and crosses then as now. And if they were not as narrowly watched and as cleverly checkmated as they may be in these days of freely expressed opinion and popular Parliamentary government, they surely found that within the Forest of Dean lived a race of free spirited men, who would not bear the ruler's oppression, nor yield without a struggle the subject's right.

The Liberal Members of Parliament, at a demonstration in the Forest in September 1870, responded favourably to the plan to cultivate the waste but they were cautious.[14] The government should be called upon to do something, Colonel Kingscote agreed, but there might be difficulties. It was difficult enough to go through the formal stages which would lead to the introduction of a bill. It was more difficult to get the bill through. Members did not understand the locality 'until it is driven into them'. Mr Marling, unlike Mr Mountjoy, thought there might be other problems. There were many who had rights over the land and their claims had to be considered. It was easy, moreover, to raise a cry against enclosures: 'there is a popular feeling against them, as they say that the object of the enclosures is to make the rich richer and the poor poorer'. The MP for Stroud took the opportunity to point out that if every bit of land were enclosed their children would have nothing but the roads to walk upon. 'Taking the land in that way and using it as private property was practically robbing the people.' Mountjoy had no such reservations:

> He remarked on the long distances which some men had to go to and from their work, and said he felt sorry on wet mornings — their masters did not know what it was — to see the men dripping with wet go into the pits in their wet clothes and be obliged to work in them. Shame on the country, shame on the district in which they lived, shame on their masters. (Cheers.) He believed the important measure to which he referred might have been carried long ago if their masters had done what they ought to have done.

The meeting, which included all the leading masters of the Forest, then resolved to press the matter, asking the members to 'obtain the sanction of Parliament to the enclosure and sale of the Forest, portions of it in small allotments to suit the requirements of working men'.

Having thus moved successfully through its preliminary stages the land campaign came to a halt in 1871 as Mountjoy and the miners turned to the business of establishing and building up the district union. The *Forester* was distressed by that. 'Robin Gray', an anonymous but regular author of anti-union columns and correspondence in the paper, complained that the men had become obsessed with the 'One Idea', the idea of union:

> Are there no means by which this 'One Idea' can be induced to divide its sovereignty over the enslaved mind; or is its despotic rule so firmly fixed in prejudice and exclusiveness that no terms can be made with it? Is it possible that the 'Forest Land Question' shall have been ventilated in vain, and all through this tyrant task master, this 'One Idea'? Why not form a Forest Land Association as well as a Forest Trades Union?[15]

Marling and Kingscote took some initial steps for the working up of a Bill but 'they have not been supported by the Foresters as a whole in their appeal to the governing powers'.[16] At the end of 1873 the question re-emerged in a list of questions which Mountjoy proposed should be asked of Parliamentary candidates by the working men. There were eight questions, most of which concerned the national trade union legislative programme and only one of which referred to a bill to compel the Crown to sell the waste.[17] William Williams did bring the subject up at a union delegate meeting in February 1874, arguing that each working man in the district should have a quarter of an acre from the waste, but the meeting only 'decided to recommend the consideration of the subject to the various lodges'.[18]

The lack of concern apparently felt by the union and the Liberal MPs about the land question provided the Conservatives with their opportunity at the elections of 1874. The Conservatives had taken no part in the agitation in 1870 but they were seen to be active, none the less, in a different way. The Conservative Benefit Building Society, co-operating with the United Land Company, had purchased 23 acres on the border of the Forest and divided it into a building estate of 438 allotments.[19] Unlike the purchaser of Crown land, the customer of the Society could have credit, paying for the land by instalments and, after the payment of the first instalment, being able to obtain a mortgage from the Society for two-thirds of the cost of a cottage. Charles Gunnison, Secretary to the Society, argued that it was a commercial and not a political venture. When the Society began it had unquestionably a political purpose but that had been found to be unattainable and was therefore dropped. None the less, the Society carried a conspicuous political label and it did have a social purpose:

> He observed that where the working classes availed themselves of [building societies] as a rule they went to their work day by day and

year by year with far greater spirit, and returned with a far deeper interest and pleasure, because they felt that they had a comfortable home of their own, and that their wives and children were provided for in that respect. Unfortunately there were too many working men who were housed more like pigs than human beings should be, and it was, as he had said before, part of the Society's object to alter that state of things, and bring about a more social, elevating and comfortable change.

At the election of 1874 the Conservatives took the initiative on the land question. Led by the Crown officials in the Forest, the Conservatives held out the land as a bait for voters. The Conservative candidate, the Hon. Mr Plunkett, was an unlikely man to succeed in the Forest, not least because he was a foreigner and an Irishman to boot. He was, however, a relative of Sir James Campbell, deputy surveyor of the Forest and leader of the Church party.[20] Plunkett also had the support of the majority of the verderers. All this might in other circumstances have been something of a handicap but so far as the land question was concerned, Plunkett's official connections were most useful:

> He had at length, after consulting the Verderers and other gentlemen connected with the local administration of the Forest lands, thought of a plan which would meet the case. This was that the Verderers should present a memorial to the Office of Woods and Forests, when that Office would send back to them for a report, and the Verderers had undertaken to make this report; upon which a Bill would be introduced into Parliament dealing with the question. This Bill, if returned to Parliament, he should heartily support.[21]

This interesting manoeuvre produced the predictable rage among the Liberals. The chairman of the coal-owners' association and leader of the Forest Liberals, Mr Goold, took up the cudgel to belabour Plunkett. The Conservative land scheme was a 'mere sop in order to take you in':

> I may tell you that the Verderers of the Forest of Dean with one or two exceptions are all of them Blues . . . These Blue Verderers have known of the grievances for years, and why is it they have not talked of this before? Why is it they have not put it right before now? Why is it that 'This way out of the difficulty' has not been seen until the eve of the election? To my mind it looks a little bit suspicious. (Hear, hear.) I can recollect when the Forest land was sold at 10s a perch, who was it that altered it? I apprehend that the

baronet we support, and who lives in a fine house, to which is attached a park containing some 50 or 60 acres of land, has had something to do with it . . . who is it that rides about the Forest of Dean looking after little encroachments? Who is it, I ask, that rides about the Forest and makes people pull down their hedges and walls, should these happen to encroach a little on the Forest land? . . . That is the man then who we Foresters maintain out of our hard earnings, and who is doing all the mischief. I hesitate not to say that he has no business to ride about the Forest of Dean canvassing for Blue voters, and inducing men to vote for his relative against their consciences.[22]

All that was to no avail and Mr Plunkett, despite his Irish connections, took Mr Marling's seat.

Worried by their loss of support in the Forest, the Liberals began the work of recovery, spurred on by an announcement from the Conservatives soon after the election that next time they would also contest Colonel Kingscote's seat. Kingscote, therefore, threw himself vigorously into the search for a solution to the land problem. In March he presented a Memorial to the Treasury which summarised all the arguments which had been offered to that point about the waste and in April, as a consequence, a number of officials from the Woods and Forests paid a surprise visit to the Forest, wandering about it 'recording in their official pocket-books the multifarious minutiae which they came all the way from town to obtain for the use of the Department'.[23] In April, Kingscote moved in the Commons for a Select Committee

> To inquire into the laws and rights affecting Dean Forest, and the condition thereof, having especial regard to the social and sanitary wants of its increasing population, and further, to enquire whether it is expedient that any, and if so what, legislation should take place with respect to such Forest, and the future disposition or management.

Mr Plunkett seconded, pointing out that 'this was not a conventional appeal on behalf of oppressed working men' but a request for an inquiry into the sanitary condition of 'some 25,000 loyal subjects of Her Majesty'.[74]

The terms of reference of the Committee seemed to derive directly from the previous debate about sanitation and the land and it was in that spirit that public meetings in the Forest discussed proposals to be put to the Committee. Mountjoy repeated much the same sorts of ideas the Protection Committee had canvassed in 1870.[25] This time he also offered a concrete plan for the wasteland. The government should sell it at, say, £40 per acre, accepting a small deposit from purchasers and taking the balance in monthly instalments. He insisted, moreover, that there should be such restrictions in any bill which the Committee might propose 'as would prevent capitalists from coming in and buying up large quantities for their own individual interests, or . . . it would make the rich richer and the poor poorer'.[26] Mr Williams of Bream repeated the demand he had made at the Union delegate meeting in February, for a quarter of an acre for all working men in the Forest, offering a novel argument for the plan:

> It was this the young Forest of Dean Colliers and miners got along with the girls, then the children came, and then in many cases the young men were summoned before the Justices, ordered to pay 3s a week . . . That was the fact and nobody could deny it, and where the latter course was not resorted to the young miners married the young women and took them to their cottages, it was doing, comparatively speaking, the last thing first. Now he ventured to think if there were cottages and gardens in the district so that young men could look them out before hand comfortable little dwellings they would do the right thing first instead of as heretofore the last.

As aware as Mountjoy of the danger of the intervention of rich men, Williams wanted his quarter of an acre to be the upper limit on land purchases by any one person.

The land problem also took up much of the time of the Select Committee. In his evidence Mountjoy increased the amount he thought should be allowed to individuals to one acre but he repeated faithfully his insistence on a low price and the exclusion of speculators. This antipathy to speculators should not be seen as indicative of a generous wish to see all the members of his class benefit from ownership of land. Mountjoy now spoke for an even more limited range of people than he had as spokesman for the ratepayers. He asserted that the foresters, born and bred, should have first refusal of the land

> and if there was an overplus left they would have no objection to another ratepayer who had settled down in the Forest of Dean, and who had been working at the mines for three or four years, to come in and buy a piece separate and apart from theirs.[27]

Not just ratepayers but native-born ratepayers were to have first choice and if a man already had five acres there was no reason why he should not have another.[28] The people of the rows had no place in this scheme.

Some other witnesses, however, held markedly different opinions. While some of them agreed that the Crown should sell small plots to the working men at low prices, others — notably the Hon. J. K. Howard, the Commissioner of Woods and Forests in charge of Dean Forest — thought that there should not be a fixed, low price and that the Crown should attempt to realise the full market value of the land at public auction.[29] The coal masters thought, moreover, that it would be wise and profitable to the Crown to sell the whole Forest and not just the waste at its fringes. Had W. B. Brain not already indicated that he would be prepared to buy up the lot at £40 the acre: 'And he would ask, if that were so, would it not be infinitely better to do so, and put the Forest waste land under cultivation, by which employment could be given to the poor agricultural labourers, whose case was so ably championed by Mr Arch?'[30] A scheme based on public auction and unlimited right of purchase had as little to offer the poor as Mountjoy's plan.

To this point, at least, the evidence taken by the Committee was what might have been expected. The Committee did not, however, confine its inquiries to the problems of land supply and sanitation. Much of the evidence given had instead to do with the free miners' rights. The advocate for the Crown made it quite clear that the Commissioners of Woods wished to see the rights extinguished entirely. At that stage, of course, the miners' rights were not vague, ill-defined and based on an alleged customary practice. They had been given specific shape by the Mines Act of 1838 and had the authority of statute law. The Crown seemed to resent that and conveyed in its submissions a sense of having been cheated by the 1838 Act. Since the Act, Mr Justice Byles, in the *Attorney General* v. *Matthias*, had given it as his opinion that, but for the Act, the free miners' rights could not have been maintained in court against the Crown and had invoked in support of his opinion the notorious Gateward's case:

The claim of the Free Miners is to subvert the soil, and carry away the substratum of stone without stint or limit of any kind. This alleged right, if it ever existed, must have reposed on one of three foundations: custom, prescription, or lost grant. The right of the Free Miners is incapable of being established by custom, however ancient, uniform, and clear the exercise of custom may be. The alleged custom is to enter the soil of another, and carry away portions of it. The benefit to be enjoyed is not a mere easement; it is a *profit à prendre*. Now it is an elementary rule of law that a *profit à prendre* in another's soil cannot be claimed by custom, for this, among other reasons, that a man's soil might thus be subject to the most grievous burdens in the favour of successive multitudes of people, like the inhabitants of a parish or other district, who could not release the right. The leading case on the subject is *Gateward's Case*, which has been repeatedly followed and never overruled . . . The next question is: can such a right as this be claimed by prescription? I will assume, against the fact, that there is no evidence to negative prescription. The present is a claim not only to carry away the soil of another, but to carry it away without stint or limit; it is a claim which tends to the destruction of the inheritance, and which excludes the owner. A prescription to be good will be both reasonable and certain . . . and this alleged prescription seems to me to be neither . . . The only remaining question on this part of the case is this: can the claim be sustained by evidence of a lost grant? Prescription presupposes a grant; and if you cannot presume a grant of an unreasonable claim before legal memory, *a fortiori* can you not presume one since. The defendants have relied on statutes of limitation, but, as to that, a claim which is vicious and bad in itself cannot be substantiated by a user, however long.[31]

So far as those rights were confirmed and made safe against Gateward by the Act of 1838, the Crown argued — and the Committee in its report agreed — they 'are detrimental to the interests of the Crown and the public at large'.[32]

Most of the witnesses, including the coal masters Brain and Goold and the deputy surveyor Sir James Campbell, agreed that the rights were worthless. Mountjoy too thought that every gale worth applying for had been taken up and he would not give twopence-halfpenny for those that were left.[33] He also said that, if given a sovereign for them, he would surrender his rights and those of his children, so small did he think his chances were of getting a gale.[34] Only Richard Hewlett, free miner and commoner of Bream, gave clear evidence that he would not give up his rights for a sum of money, even though he had never had a gale.[35]

This line of questioning on the miners' rights was important, for when the Committee reported it made a satisfactory solution of the land problem depend on agreement to extinguish the rights. The Committee, which included Colonel Kingscote and Mr Plunkett, resolved that the government should bring in a bill in the next session to provide for the appointment of a new Commission to see to the detailed drafting of a bill:

(a) For ascertaining and commuting the right of common in Dean Forest.
(b) For making or contributing towards making roads in the Forest, where such roads will be beneficial to the development of Crown property.

(c) For setting out lands . . . for public recreation.

(d) For providing allotment gardens for the labouring classes.

(e) For selling land for houses and cottage sites and other purposes, so as to furnish a fund towards the compensation payable to commoners, the amount contributed for making roads, and the expense of the Commission.

(f) For inquiring into the sanitary condition of the town of Cinderford and other largely populated districts in the Forest and ascertaining what measures it is expedient to adopt for the improvement of the same.

They recommended a number of provisions for the Bill, two of which are important here:

(b) That the powers of sale, and of granting leases for terms exceeding 31 years, which the Commissioners of Woods possess as regards Crown land not being part of a Royal Forest, be extended to the Crown lands in Dean Forest . . .

(d) That no person to be born after the passing of the proposed Act shall be entitled to be registered as a free miner. But where the purchaser of any Crown land is a free miner, a drawback may be allowed on the price of the purchase, in consideration of the surrender of the purchaser's right as free miner.

And one other resolution of importance:

(4) That it is expedient that provision be made, that the interests of the holders of gales which can be from time to time obtained on reasonable terms should be bought up and assigned to a trustee for the Crown, in order that the mines may be let and worked on leases upon the terms which would be usually secured by a mineral owner.[36]

This was to be the programme: the abolition of common rights, abolition of the free miners' rights and the consolidation of the gales in the hands of the Crown, all to be paid for by the sale of the waste land. There was no mention, moreover, of any restriction on the quantity of land to be sold to individuals or on the price to be charged. The Commissioners of Woods might well have been pleased with this Report. They had been asked for land and in return had asked that all those things left undone in the 1830s should now be done. The Report and its minutes of evidence offered promise that all those interested in these matters — including the leader of the miners — would be equally pleased to see a bill embodying the Committee's recommendations.

Somewhere, though, there had been a miscalculation. Kingscote and Mountjoy did not return to the Forest as victors. They found themselves instead obliged almost immediately to defend themselves against a furious opposition. In September 1874, Kingscote held a series of meetings around the Forest at which he attempted to justify his part in the work of the Committee. At a particularly turbulent meeting at Coleford, Mountjoy insisted, in contradiction of rumours to the contrary, that he and Kingscote had gone to London to protect the interests of those who had rights in the Forest.[37] He defended the plan to sell the waste to the working men but, obviously in response to ill-feeling in the meeting, agreed that the free miners' rights were in danger of being swept away. He denied that he had really meant that he would sell his rights for a pittance and argued that he had been bamboozled and flummoxed by the Committee. Now he thought that the free miners should rouse themselves, form themselves into a body and establish a fund for fighting their case.

For the time being, however, Mountjoy had lost his authority. This gave the Reverend Nicholson, implacable opponent of Mountjoy's trade union, the opportunity for an attempt to assume leadership of the Forest working men. Making use of the principles of Mountjoy's campaign in 1870, Nicholson called a meeting of 'freeminers and free-holders, commoners and ratepayers' at Parkend. The meeting then elected a committee, headed by Nicholson, to watch the Bill.[38] The meeting still wanted reasonable improvements in sanitation and roads but it did not want

> any interference with the existing rights of the free miners, or with the rights of commoners, excepting so far as relates to the outlying waste lands of the Forest: and in respect to those pieces of waste land, this meeting is of opinion that commoners' rights may be waived, provided such waste land is sold in small lots at a reasonable price.

The Committee's petition against the Bill asked for four main amendments. Firstly, the foresters were to have the right to nominate one of the Commissioners to be appointed under the Bill. Secondly, the Commissioners were not to have power to extinguish or commute any of the foresters' rights. Thirdly, there was to be no sale of land by auction or otherwise to 'strangers who have no rights of common and no claims to local privileges'. Lastly, only the waste land on the outskirts of the Forest should be sold, in small lots and at moderate prices, 'to persons having already houses and land in the vicinity, to enlarge and improve their dwellings and gardens'.[39]

Mountjoy did not leave the field to Nicholson. He continued to attack the provisions of the Bill: 'I have failed to discover what advantage it will bring to the toilers of the Forest of Dean . . . it will, in my opinion, take away our rights and privileges, and give power to those who have got too much already'.[40] Instead of offering the miners small blocks of land at 5s a perch, the Bill allowed the Commissioners to sell by private contract or by auction at whatever prices they deemed fit. It was time for the foresters to 'gird on the armour of progress and courage as our fathers did before us' and to fight the Bill. Mountjoy formed an alliance with Henry Hoskold of London and the Forest, who had spent 16 years as the manager of an iron-mining company and who had an interest in the miners' rights as an agent, mediating between the free miners and the men to whom they sold their gales.[41]

In a series of letters to the *Forester* under the pseudonym 'Forest Mining Engineer', Hoskold too had been critical of the Select Committee and the Bill. The Crown officials, he thought, were envious of the profits which agents made: 'but if the Crown can take away the rights of the free miners the officials could of course bring in their friends and so add to their revenues'.[42] He went on to criticise the Select Committee's work and its recommendations, asserting that those who gave evidence were incompetent to do so, that all the coal was not granted and that the gales were not worthless. He thought it was clear, moreover, that the Committee had been 'thoroughly instructed' on the sort of information it was to obtain. He exhorted the free miners to set up a fighting fund and to petition against the Bill which the Commissioners of Woods were framing:

> The great question now is whether the Forest free miners will stand still and allow the Crown to take away their rights, which were so dear to their forefathers. I would therefore say, arouse yourselves Foresters, and strike for your liberties and rights. Of old you were celebrated for standing up with a stern front to impending danger, now, then, is the time to show your determination.[43]

Hoskold and Mountjoy consulted a solicitor and drew up a petition which they carried to meetings around the Forest and to which they obtained 1,348 signatures.[44] Hoskold also addressed a meeting called for the purpose of forming a new miners' union.[45] He spoke in favour of moderate, responsible unionism and the formation of a co-operative colliery in the Forest. The meeting then discussed the Dean Forest Bill and resolved that Mr Hoskold should be appointed a Commissioner under the Bill. Hoskold also took care to send in a petition to the Office of Woods to establish his claim to be noticed when appointments were made.[46]

Both the Nicholson and Mountjoy parties then turned to people outside the Forest for help. At that point the basic character of the opposition to the Bill changed. Nicholson and Mountjoy were competing for leadership of the same constituency: one which would not give away the free miners' and commoners' rights but which did wish to add portions of the Forest land to their own property. Alexander MacDonald MP had a different view of the matter. He prepared to oppose the Bill at Mountjoy's request. The people should not tolerate, he argued, 'that the land to which they were rightly entitled should be taken away from them by a few greedy persons whose property lay on their boundary lines'.[47] Perhaps MacDonald thought that the 'greedy persons' were coal-owners or landed gentry. Three Fellows of Christ's College, Cambridge expressed a similar disapproval of the conversion of the open spaces of England into private property, in a petition they sent against the Bill:

> The effect of the said Bill if passed into law, would be to enable the commissioners of her Majesty's Woods and Forests, or other persons having the care and management of her Majesty's Woods and Forests for the time being, to enclose and absolutely exclude your petitioners and all other her Majesty's subjects [sic] from the said lands, and to hold the same in severalty as private property.
>
> The lands of her Majesty in the said Forest of Dean consist of wastelands and woodlands of great extent, broken into numerous hills and valleys, and covered in parts with very fine and ornamental timber. The said lands, except where plantations have been formed thereon, are in fact ancient Forest lands, and possess all the attraction of wild natural beauty.
>
> At present all her Majesty's subjects have access to all the said lands, except for those which for the time being are enclosed for oak planting; such access your petitioners believe is highly valued by the inhabitants of the districts near the said forest, who often resort there to enjoy the beauties of the scenery and for purposes of recreation.
>
> The power of resorting to an ancient forest like the Forest of Dean for the enjoyment of its scenery is in your petitioners' view a great boon to all her Majesty's subjects, a large portion of whom are compelled to reside in towns or thickly populated neighbourhoods, and with whom the enjoyment of retired rural scenery is increasing every year. The vast majority of her Majesty's subjects have no land of their own, and your petitioners view with alarm the gradual conversion of so much of the open spaces into private property and the consequent approach of a day when persons, not themselves landowners, will be confined in their use of English soil to the public ways.[48]

The need for wild, natural beauty, ornamental trees and places of recreation which were not private property, had little to do with securing an extra acre or two for native freeholders.

The Reverend Nicholson also appealed to outsiders for help. He moved from supporting a campaign for amendments to the Bill to demanding its complete withdrawal and called upon the Commons Preservation Society for assistance.[49] The Society, which included the Archbishop of Canterbury and a number of Members of Parliament, was innocent of the minutiae of conflicting local claims and interests and saw the scheming of the Commissioners of Woods and Forests in much the same light as the three Fellows of Cambridge. The Society set Nicholson to work collecting signatures on petitions against the Bill. By mid-May 1875 he was able to present them with three petitions: from the free miners and commoners, with 903 names; from other inhabitants of the Forest, with 98 names; and from the inhabitants of Cardiff with 132 names.[50]

The weight of what was becoming a widespread and influential opposition embarrassed the Commissioners of Woods sufficiently for them to withdraw the Bill. They had intended to introduce it again in the next session of Parliament but let it lapse entirely because of the continued interest of the Commons Preservation Society. G. Shaw Lefevre has left the only account of the demise of the Dean Forest Bill and the Society's part in it:

> In the following autumn, notices were issued of the intention of the Government to introduce the Bill again in the ensuing Session. Thereupon, on behalf of the Commons Society, I entered into a correspondence with Mr. W. H. Smith (Secretary to the Treasury), in which I pointed out the objections on principle to the inclosure of the Forest. I contended that there were precisely the same reasons against adopting this course, as had been asserted by the Committee of the House of Commons in 1875, of which Mr. W. H. Smith himself had been chairman, against the inclosure of the New Forest; that the object and intention of that Committee was to preserve the New Forest open and uninclosed, for the benefit of the Commoners and the public enjoyment; that the Forest of Dean was not unworthy of the same treatment; and that, although there was less of ancient timber left in it, it had some natural advantages superior even to the New Forest.
>   . . . I also pointed out that there could be no reason why a different policy should be pursued in respect of the two Forests; that both of them in their present condition were valuable legacies to the nation; that if reduced into absolute ownership of the Crown, they could not be recovered; while, so long as they were subject to Commoners' rights, they could from time to time be adapted to every necessary want, such as that now existing in the Forest of Dean for sites for miners' houses and for allotments

without depriving them of their value for public enjoyment and recreation.

The effect of this correspondence was that the Government announced that they did not intend to proceed further with their measures for enclosing the Forest; and that they were advised by their law officers that they had, under an existing Act, power to sell limited parts of the waste from time to time, for the necessities of the population. It resulted therefore, that practically the same policy was laid down with respect to the New Forest and the Forest of Dean. They are both to be preserved henceforth in the interest of the public and of the commoners, while the Crown is secured in its long established right of making large but temporary inclosures for the planting and growth of timber.[51]

There was — for the foresters at least — an important new principle in that the 'public interest' had been redefined. As that term had been used by Commissioners of Woods since 1788 it had referred to the revenue of the Crown. Now it was given a wider social reference in which the interests of the Crown were not necessarily those of the people. To reduce the Forest to the absolute ownership of the Crown would serve the one public interest but not the other. Local rights and privileges were important, not because they protected, or promised to increment, the property of a privileged section of the local community but because they interposed a barrier between the two 'public interests', securing the one against the encroachment of the other. At the same time, the new definition of the 'public interest' was not compatible with the notion that native freeholders, any more than rich speculators, should be allowed to convert the Forest into private property. That effectively ruled out any revival and extension of the working men's land campaign in the form it had taken since 1870.

The land campaign of 1870 to 1875 ran parallel to the effective life of the first miners' union in Dean. The stern, pious figure of Timothy Mountjoy dominated both movements. His attitudes and values gave them something in common. In both he made use of the language of liberty. In both he identified the principal coal masters as enemies. They denied fair market value to workmen and threatened, through the power of money and speculation, to keep the land from the people. The Crown, of course, was even more important in locking up the land and it was guilty of the sin of class legislation. The land and the union campaigns had another quality in common. Though both used the language of liberty, neither was especially egalitarian in its aspirations. Where the one served the distinctive needs of the buttymen, the other aimed to add to the existing property of native, freeholder working men. Like the daymen, the landless and the row dwellers had no advocates.

The land question became an important, though muddled, local political issue. It became a focus of Liberal and Conservative competition for votes in the Forest division and it became the means by which the Crown hoped to strip away the vestiges of the foresters' rights. It proved, however, that the foresters would not give up the rights. Mountjoy, careless of the rights himself, misjudged the attachment of others to them.

7. Commodities: the Free Miners

Away with the Bill! 'tis not needed at all,
'Tis not what you asked for, it came without call;
Your 'bit of waste land, at five shillings a perch',
Is treated as nonsense, and left in the lurch;
Away with the Bill! sound forth its death knell!
They'll suck out the egg if they once prick the shell!

Be resolute, Foresters, honest and true,
Keep all that's your own, give Ceasar his due;
Heed not for a moment the men who deride,
And say that your egg has nothing inside;
For you know, and they know, only too well,
They'll suck out the egg if they once prick the shell!

Anon. The Foresters' Egg! A Timely Warning! Dean Forest Mercury,
23 May 1884.

In their resistance to the Dean Forest Bill the free miners contradicted the testimony of those who thought the rights were worthless. The miners were just as stubborn in the first half of the 1880s when the Crown organised yet another attempt to extinguish the rights. In 1884 and 1885 the defence of the free miners dominated local politics and gave strength to a successful campaign by the working men for a 'labour' candidate for the Forest of Dean. More than at any time since Warren James had levelled the enclosures, the invocation of the rights had the quality of a rallying cry for the poor in their war against the rich. Sentiment had something to do with that and there was no doubt that the rights had become an important symbol. There was, however, more than sentiment at stake. The policy which the Crown had pursued from the late 1860s onwards, though it aimed at the abolition of the rights, had paradoxically reinvested them with a potential commercial value.

However unimportant they were in the routine life of the mining industry, there remained significant numbers of free miners. The Dean Forest Commissioners in 1838 had registered 816 coal and iron free miners and 175 quarry free miners.[1] From 31 December 1838 to 31 December 1873, another 343 coal and ore free miners registered: about ten each year. By 1 April 1875, another 445 had registered, bringing the total to 1,604, of which the Commissioners of Woods and Forests estimated about 630 had died or left the district.[2] From 1837 to December 1873, an additional 241 quarry free miners had registered, making a total of 416 men who had registered as quarry miners. The number of them dead or away from the district is unknown but undoubtedly enough of them survived to bring the number of adult males interested in the rights up to over 1,000 in 1875: more than were in the union by the end of the year.

Though few of these men had ever had the chance to have a gale, the practice of galing had not died out. From 1845 to 1873 inclusive, free miners had registered 145 separate gales of coal and 50 of iron ore.[3] Altogether, 181 free miners had shares in the gales. Some of those gales were never worked and some of them had a fitful life, producing a few score tons now and then. A few, like those belonging to the masters of Trafalgar Colliery, were successful. Perhaps what mattered was not that the number of men who had actually found a worthwhile gale to work or sell was small but that there were some at all and there remained the chance of a find and a windfall from its sale. Thus, John Miles had not registered as a free miner even though he had been entitled to do so 20 years before he gave evidence to the Select Committee of 1874. Yet, when asked if he thought his rights were valuable, he answered: 'Yes, I have only to be registered, and if there was a chance I could gale as well as any other man.'[4]

In the early 1870s it might well have seemed to the free miners that the chance of galing had acquired a new value because of the tendency of recent Crown policy in dealing with the galees. In order to understand why that was so it is necessary to look at the rules for the working of the field which the Mining Commissioners drew up in 1841. Rules four, 13 and 14 were especially important. Rule four put a limit on the time which galees could take in beginning to open a mine. For those whose gales were registered under the Award of 1841, the limit was four years; for those whose gales were registered after 1841, the limit was five years. Unless the gaveller had granted an extension of time because the galee had shown reasonable cause of delay, the gale was liable to be forfeited.[5] Where rule four encouraged the opening of the gales, rules 13 and 14 encouraged their working. In summary, gale owners were assumed to produce a minimum number of tons of coal per annum and were obliged to pay the Crown a royalty, called the dead rent, on that tonnage, whether the coal had been raised or not. Where actual tonnage fell below the minimum royalty tonnage the difference was known as 'short workings'. Where actual tonnage exceeded royalty tonnage the difference was known as 'overworkings'. Shortworkings could be accumulated from year to year and deducted from subsequent overworkings.[6] One other matter needs to be understood. Under the Act of 1838, the dead rents once set were to stand for 21 years, at which point they were to be revised.

There was some ambiguity about rules 13 and 14. For what period of time should they run? If shortworkings might accumulate indefinitely there would be no limit on the amount which could be built up to the credit of an unworked gale. The Commissioners of Woods thought that shortworkings should accumulate only over the 21-year period for which the dead rents were set and that at the end of it the books should be wiped clean and a fresh start made. After the determination of new rents for the old gale holders in 1862, the Commissioners acted to establish their interpretation of the rule. In August 1863, they notified the galees that they were not entitled to any further allowances for shortworkings accumulated before the expiry of the old rent period.[7] As a 'matter of grace', however, the Crown would continue to allow shortworkings to be recouped for a further period of ten years. It was to be clearly understood that 'the concession thus made is altogether exceptional, and that no similar concession will be made or admitted in future'. The Commissioners sent another circular to the galees, in February 1869, reminding them that 'according to the most liberal interpretation' the period of grace would end at Midsummer 1873.[8] Those who had paid dead rents on unworked gales would lose their money. Worse than that, the Commissioners announced in another circular, in July 1867, that they would enforce rule four.[9] Holders of gales which had not been opened and who had not applied for extensions of time according to rule, were now required to show reasonable cause for the granting of an extension. The holders of unworked gales stood to lose their gales as well as their money.

Outraged by these proposals, the galees formed a Defence Association, whose opposition to the Commissioners forced the appointment of a Commission to examine the rules. The Commission, appointed under the Dean Forest (Mines) Act of 1871, had sweeping powers to make new rules 'in such manner in all respects as they in their absolute and unfettered discretion may think most fit, equitable and expedient, and as fully and effectually as could be done by act of parliament'.[10] The galees did not contest the legal construction of the rules but appealed to equity. In the first place, their advocate pointed out, there were many gales on which the five years had long since elapsed but for which the Crown had continued to receive dead rent. Acts of omission being as important as acts of commission, the Crown had, by not forfeiting the gales, waived its right to do so.[11] Some capitalists, because of the conduct of the Crown, had believed that no forfeitures would take place and had purchased gales on which the time limit had expired. They had believed themselves to be acquiring good title, had paid further dead rents and were now to be turned out of possession. Could this be equitable on the part of the Crown?

The Commissioners' judgement cannot have been entirely satisfactory to the Crown or the galees. The latter won the quarrel about rule 14. Galees were to be permitted to recoup shortworkings until the gale was surrendered or forfeited to the Crown. More importantly, the galees lost the quarrel over rule four. The only concession made to the galees was a new provision for the appointment of an arbitrator to decide whether 'reasonable cause' could be shown for the failure to work a gale.[12]

The judgement on rule four thus gave the free miners good reason to insist on the preservation of their rights in 1875. Of the 300 gales which had been granted at one time or another, almost 200 remained unopened, 171 of which had been granted more than five years.[13] Of those, 54 had been granted extensions of time. That left 117 unopened gales which were liable to be forfeited. A betting man among the free miners might have thought it likely that many of the unopened gales would be forfeited and that he might have one of them re-granted to himself. That, of course, could only happen so long as the basic right of the free miners to have the gales remained intact.

Why was it, though, that the Crown thought it necessary to take away what was left of the free miners' rights? There were two main difficulties. The Crown might be able to compel a galee to forfeit his coal if he had not begun to work it within the time limit but the gaveller was obliged to re-grant the gale to the first free miner who applied for it. There was nothing to prevent a succession of grants, forfeitures and re-grants stretching on forever without a block of coal being cut. The Crown would continue to receive its dead rents, of course, but would rather have a substantial income from active mines which produced more than the minimum royalty tonnage. The second difficulty was that the free miners stood in the way of the working of the 'deep gales'. It was clear by the 1870s that the upper coal measures would soon be worked out and that the revenue from them would cease. The future revenue depended on the deep seams and it was necessary that the Crown begin to encourage the coal masters to put their capital into new, deep mines.[14]

There were 45 deep gales, classified in four separate groups by the deputy gaveller in 1882: eight gales in group 1, at a depth of 500 yards; fifteen in group 2, at 250 to 350 yards; nine in 3 at 160 to 260 yards; and thirteen in 4, at about 150 yards. All told, the gales covered 10,800 acres and, in groups 1 to 3, included an estimated 971,900,000 tons of coal.[15] The workable coal in the deep gales included three narrow seams, ranging from 1 foot 10 inches high to

2 feet 10 inches, and the Coleford High Delf seam which ran at 4 feet 6 inches. These were rich gales on which substantial shortworkings had accumulated.

Though that was a strong inducement to work the coal, these gales had not been opened. The first attempt to sink through to the Coleford High Delf seam had taken place on the New Bowson gale in the 1860s. Up to 1867 the company had spent about £40,000 on two shafts which it drained by lifting the water up, by machine, in wooden containers.[16] It had taken three years to put the shafts down about 240 yards. At that point the sinkers met a 'current of water which now rushes through the stone like so many gas jets or springs'.[17] At 280 yards, when the sinkers broke into a fresh layer of rock, water came flooding in, driving the men from the shaft and rising at a rate of a yard an hour.[18] It took two years, the liquidation of the company, its reformation with new capital and the installation of new pumping machinery to clear the water.[19] By 1871, however, with £80,000 lost, the gale was abandoned, 'purely in consequence of the water'.[20] Clearly, an attempt to develop a deep gale was not to be undertaken lightly or without the expenditure of a large capital. That was a risk which the coal-owners asserted they would not take because of the regulations which governed the field. The regulations stipulated that each gale should be limited in size, that each gale should be worked separately and that substantial barriers of coal should be left between gales. All that effectively prevented the consolidation of a number of gales into a holding large enough to justify the capital outlay. But for the presence of the free miners, the Crown might have been able to offer the coal masters the large holdings and favourable terms that would induce them to venture their capital. In order to break the cycle of grants and re-grants and in order to give itself a completely free hand in developing the deep gales the Crown needed to dispose of the vestiges of the rights. That prospect, of course, faded with the defeat of the Dean Forest Bill in 1875.

How then, might the Commissioners of Woods bring about the development of the deep gales? Why not select a list of unopened gales and send a circular to their owners, pointing out that forfeitures were likely 'and this course may either compel the opening of these Gales or elicit from the Galees some suggestion or scheme which may be of value in dealing with the general question of the Lower Coal Seams'.[21] Thomas Forster Brown, the deputy surveyor, suggested an alternative scheme, in which the Crown would pay for the drainage of the whole coalfield. A note written across his memorandum ruled that plan out:

It would probably be decidedly preferable that the Galees should take up the matter themselves, independant [sic] of the Crown altogether and possibly pressure put upon the Galees may elicit from them some scheme which the Crown can acquiesce in.[22]

Accordingly, in 1878, the Commissioners issued a circular to gale owners reminding them of the possibility of forfeiture and the local Crown officials began to reiterate the need for a solution to the deep coal problem.[23] The villains in the piece, the great obstacles to commercial progress, were yet again the free miners:

> There were local causes which he believed greatly militated against the Forest proprietors and the Forest generally taking that position it ought amongst other districts in the United Kingdom. (Hear, hear.) Now he anticipated some of them would say, 'Mr. Francis is going to stalk his old hobby-horse again'. (A laugh.) Be it as it might, he believed that with regard to the free miners of the Forest; that every mine had been granted, and in his opinion the free miners stood in the way of the growth of their great Forest of Dean, and he feared none of them would ever again see men of capital launch out their money to open out the unworked collieries and iron mines. He would repeat his fears, they would never see this unless the free miners' question or rather their rights were taken in hand.[24]

This was Mr Francis, the Crown receiver of rents in Dean, speaking to the coal masters at the dinner he gave each half year to mark the audit of the gale rents.

Arnold Thomas, chairman of the coal masters' association, and Edwin Crawshay, coal and iron master, made the first response to these pressures in 1882. They made three proposals. Firstly, the dead rent on existing unopened deep gales was to be halved and the short-workings on them abolished. Secondly, once the coal had been reached, dead rents should continue for 21 years. Thirdly, when there had been an agreement among the owners of several gales to work them together, the opening of one of the gales should be deemed the opening of them all.[25] The deputy surveyor agreed that these were sound proposals. None the less, there would still be a problem with the free miners:

> Although the rights of the Free Miners, for all practicable purposes, are now, and likely henceforth to be, of little or no pecuniary value to the Free Miners as a Body, yet any attempt hitherto to interfere with these rights has always given rise to political agitation. In fact these rights have become in the District a question more of sentiment, and an excuse for a political cry than of any practical importance. Otherwise, but for this reason the question is probably more difficult to deal with, and I have been casting

about for some mode of evading as far as practicable any serious interference even with these sentimental interests consistent with accomplishing what is essential to the object of improving the Tenure of the deep Coal Measures.[26]

His solution was that, instead of abolishing all the rights at a stroke, the Act of Parliament which was necessary for the alteration of the rules, should enable the Commissioners to buy out the interests of the free miners in the deep gales only.

Up to about September 1883 all went reasonably well for the Commissioners. The Treasury gave permission for negotiations preparatory to a bill and, in an exchange of printed memoranda, the Commissioners, Thomas and Crawshay worked out and broadly agreed upon a detailed list of points for legislation.[27] Crawshay and Thomas had called a meeting of galees, that is to say, of coal-owners, which had elected a Committee to negotiate on their behalf.[28]

In August and early September, however, the free miners formed another Protection Committee, distinct from the galees' association, to defend their rights. At a public meeting at the Speech House it became clear that the mass of free miners thought that the new scheme for the Forest was an unjustifiable encroachment on their liberties. The meeting resolved, without reservation, that 'nothing be altered which would affect the interests of the free miners of the Forest of Dean'.[29] Arnold Thomas had addressed the meeting but the miners interrupted his speech with 'We will have no alteration' and 'We will consider our own rights and not other people's'. On the whole, the meeting agreed, there was a need to drain the deep coal and ensure that there was plenty of colliery work for years to come but why, they asked, did the free miners have to be dispossessed? There was a feeling that the free miners would be robbed: somebody wanted to buy the rights 'for a song'. Why should the gales not be forfeited according to rule and the poor and the rich be treated alike?

The agitation continued to the end of the year, with public meetings, resolutions and a petition against the Bill which the Commissioners had made public in 1883.[30] It was now clear from the form of the notice that the Crown intended to buy up and extinguish the rights affecting the deep gales.[31] Consequently, in December, the Protection Committee presented a petition bearing 1,700 names to the MPs for West Gloucestershire, to be passed on to the Commissioners.[32] At the heart of the free miners' complaint was the feeling that they were about to be deprived of a fair chance of having the 45 deep gales:

Now these gales were considered the most valuable in the Forest, and as the limit of holding, viz, five years for opening, had expired, they were forfeited to the Crown, and, in which case, could be claimed again by the free miners . . . if the gales were forfeited to the Crown, the free miners would be able to claim them again and sell to other capitalists, so that instead of the gales being shut down by men who were unable or unwilling to open them, they would be in full work.

Colonel Kingscote, though he wished not to act too precipitately in demanding the withdrawal of the Bill, agreed to pass the petition on to the Commissioner with responsibility for Dean Forest, Sir Henry Loch.

Sir Henry responded with an invitation to the free miners to send a deputation up to London to discuss the Bill. At this point W. B. Brain emerged as leader of the free miners and of the deputation.[33] Though Brain was far and away the wealthiest and, by that sort of measure, the most important of the free miners, neither he nor his brother had taken any part in the agitation against the Crown. Perhaps now his sense of local loyalty and of attachment to the rights had asserted themselves and become more important to him than his position as a large coal master? It was not so. Thomas Forster Brown, the deputy surveyor, had already written to his masters in London to report that he had spoken to Mr Brain, satisfied him that the Bill was a good one and discovered that 'he will be with us'.[34] Brain's role in the business was that of covert agent and manager for the Crown. Thus he wrote to Brown in May 1884:

> We had an important meeting last night the tone of which was much more to my satisfaction but during my absence the meeting held was unsatisfactory. I should be glad to see you to guide me in framing my reply to Sir Loch.[35]

Brain, no doubt, was anxious to develop the Holly Hill deep gale in which he and his brother had shares.[36]

The deputation, led by Mr Brain, duly attended upon Sir Henry in London. Sir Henry stressed again the importance of the commercial development of the Forest and proposed that the compensation to be paid to the free miners should be paid to elected trustees who might dispose of it as they chose. Most members of the deputation opposed any interference with the rights and insisted that the Crown's failure to forfeit unworked gales explained the lack of development of the deep gales. One of the members of the deputation, however, was Mr Dew, a barrister and 'small galee'. He concentrated on a discussion of the amount of compensation offered. Sir Henry thought £5,000 quite adequate recompense but Mr Dew, taking the dead rents as the annual value of the gales and assuming that 30 years' purchase was a fair basis for fixing the price, thought that about half a million pounds was nearer the mark. Mr Brain also argued that they 'would have been better pleased if a higher sum than £5,000 had been named'.[37] Mr Dew thought that 'it was their bounden duty to fight for as large a compensation as could be got'. These contributions distorted the discussion and persuaded Loch that the debate was not now to be about the preservation of the rights but instead about how much the compensation should be. Accordingly, he wrote to the Treasury to tell them that 'the Free miners are not likely to offer any very serious opposition to the principle of the Bill and that so far as they are concerned the main question will be the amount of the compensation'.[38] He asked that the Bill should be introduced into the Parliament as soon as possible.

Unfortunately for Loch, his optimism was entirely unjustified. When the deputation took its report of the meeting back to the Forest the free miners were not pleased by what had happened. Mr Brain did his best to persuade a meeting that the £5,000 was worth having and that it was of paramount importance that the trade of the Forest should be developed: 'The importance of this I hold as firmly as any statement I put forward in regard to the free miners' rights'.[39] The *Mercury*'s interpretation of his line was 'that the Chairman stated, in as plain terms as he dared, that the development of the Forest was of first consideration and if the free miners' rights stand in the way, these should be held as of secondary importance'.[40] His audience was not convinced. Their response on the whole was like that of Mr Barnett, a member of the deputation: 'My poor children shall never have cause to curse me, and say "My old grandfather sold my birthrights for me!" If they [the Commissioners] take it, let them do so.' Whether the Commissioners offered £5,000 or £50,000 the rights would not be sold.

Late in May Mr Brain tried once more to swing the free miners in the Commissioners' direction. This time he called upon the aid of James G. Wood, author of a volume on the Laws of the Forest and possibly the foremost living expert on the intricacies of mining operations in the Forest: a man whose opinions had weight. His preference was clear:

> The deep gales *must* be worked if the future of the Forest is to be secured. The working them [sic] will be the gain of the many; including the working free miners, the loss — or rather postponement — of the prospective right of re-grant will be the loss of very few.[41]

He proposed that the Crown and the miners should establish a sort of standing commission to administer the deep gales, perhaps offering long leases to galees and long periods for opening and the assessment of royalties. In the interests of some such plan, he advised, the miners should neither accept nor oppose the Bill but agitate instead for the appointment of a Commission.

Feeling against the Commissioners had built up too far to be so easily suppressed. The *Mercury* published the final text of the Bill on 20 June 1884. The same issue reported that the miners' Committee had read the Bill, discussed its clauses with a legal gentleman and decided unanimously to reject the whole measure.[42] A general meeting of the free miners then decided that they would accept no money consideration whatever for the rights.[43] The freeminers and commoners sent a petition to Parliament, on 27 June, bearing the signatures of 2,085 freeholders. Another, from the Protection Committee, followed a few days later. Both petitions asked for the withdrawal of the Bill. There were other petitions, in favour of the Bill: from the Gloucester Chamber of Commerce; from the mayor, aldermen and citizens of Gloucester; from the Severn and Wye and Severn Bridge Railway Companies; the Sharpness New Docks Company; and the Midland Railway Company.[44] Despite the formidable array of commercial and mine-owning companies in favour of the Bill the weight of local opinion was too great. The Commissioners, as in 1875 in a similar situation, withdrew the Bill.

The demise of the Bill marked the end of 20 years of striving by the Commissioners of Woods to extinguish the rights. Every effort the Crown had made ended in defeat. Pressure on the free miners did not work; pressure on the coal-owners and galees did not work; offers of land and offers of money did not work; Commissions, Select Committees and private dealings did not work. The Crown, in 1885, stood no closer to its goal of being able to deal with the coal masters 'as between landlord and tenant', than it had in 1838. By focusing new attention on the unopened gales in the 1860s and raising the real possibility of forfeiture of gales, the Crown had given the rights a potential value which made it unlikely that the miners would acquiesce in the various schemes of the Commissioners. What was at stake was not mere sentiment, nor even politically useful sentiment, but real property. The Act of 1838 had transformed the rights. They were not now use rights in the older sense. They now conferred a title in the nature of real estate: a gale was as fully marketable and mortgageable as the land the working men had wanted. It was true that the gales were speculative property but perhaps, in the buttymen's world of risk and competition, that made them all the more attractive. The only result of 20 years of effort, by the Commissioners of Woods and deputy surveyors, was an awareness on the miners' part of a persistent threat to their property. In 1884 and 1885, that awareness influenced the political life of the Forest.

A proper understanding of the political climate of the Forest in 1884 requires a digression for the purpose of reconsidering the role of the miners' agent, Edward Rymer. Rymer had never had a narrow vision of what trade unions were for: they were not only to deal with wages and working conditions but to be the vehicle for the complete realisation of what he called the 'social revolution'.[45] To enjoy a whole independence as citizens, to enthrone justice in every kingdom, the collier had to grasp 'every subject that belongs to social, commercial and political life'.[46] Monarchy and the Civil List, standing armies, war and the consequence of them all, the National Debt, were all anathema to Rymer. The remedies he proposed for the corruption of England were moral and social, to be achieved through education and temperance. To that would be added the dispossession of the robbers of the land: the 'proud, haughty, worthless, costly and idle aristocracy'.[47] In industry, co-operative production would sweep away the capitalist and the loathsome usurer. In politics, the extension of the franchise to all adult males and the flooding of working men into Parliament would make the English Revolution. He did from time to time indulge in the rhetoric of violent Revolution. He called upon the people of France to 'rise en masse' and to 'utterly exterminate every vile priest, or other scoundrels that stood in the way of peoples' liberty and France's redemption'.[48] He thought the English Tories were 'rank monsters of blood and plunder, your whole carcase is nothing but political carrion fit to be eaten up by the tigers and vultures of a bloody revolution'.[49] For the English working men, though, the vote would work the grand political transformation.

The miners had, under Rymer's leadership, agitated a number of political questions in the Forest. Thomas Burt MP came to the Speech House in April 1883, to talk on the county franchise, the land question, the Employers' Liability Act, the Mines Regulation Act and free education.[50] They also took up the cause of the republican Charles Bradlaugh, who had not been allowed to take his seat in the House of Commons because he refused to take a religious oath. At Rymer's urging, the District Council made the gesture of donating £1 to Bradlaugh's expenses and brought him along with Burt to address a miners' demonstration in July 1883.[51] The union sent Rymer to a great meeting of trade unionists at the Westminster Palace Hotel in London in February 1884. The delegates heard a speech from Mr Gladstone and then toured the Houses of Parliament under the guidance of Professor Thorold Rogers. In the Lords Rymer and the Welshman Abrahams, sat upon the woolsack: 'Mr Abrahams then spoke in Welsh and dismissed the Lords in the name of the democracy of the world, to which we both said *Amen*.'[52]

In 1884 and 1885 the miners in the Forest had their chance to realise a more limited ambition. A redistribution of electoral

boundaries which followed the Reform Act of 1884 created a separate
constituency of the Forest, giving the miners the opportunity to take
up again the agitation for a working man's candidate. The Trafalgar
Colliery men suggested that Thomas Blake, of Ross in the county of
Herefordshire, should be brought forward by the miners. Taking up
this resolution, Rymer and the Council, claiming the 'full right of
labour representation in Parliament', began a campaign to have
Blake adopted as Liberal candidate.[53] Blake was by no means a
working man but, as the 'first labour candidate chosen by the Dean
Forest workmen', his campaign forestalled and overwhelmed one
which had begun in support of Arnold Thomas, the chairman of the
coal-owners' association.[54] 'The peaceful revolution of democracy just
dawning,' Rymer wrote, 'affords you a chance of breaking every
feudal tie that binds you or threatens you.'[55] To that end Blake came
out as a 'thorough radical', offering a programme which included
reform of the House of Lords and the land laws, the separation of religion from state patronage and control, free education, the reduction
of the national debt and the extension of the franchise to women
householders. The new constituency included some areas of
Westbury-on-Severn and Newlands parishes but it was dominated by
the Forest. If the working men wanted a labour and liberal candidate
there was little the masters could do about it. Consequently, the newly
formed Liberal Association for the Forest voted to accept Blake as
candidate in April 1885.[56] With that and the full support of the
Liberal Party, Blake's victory over the Tory Mr Plunkett, at the election at the end of 1885, was assured.

In the course of this campaign, Rymer identified the needs of the
free miners with what he saw as the general oppression of the people
which the Tory landlord and the State priest imposed. The threat to
the free miners was more of that robbery and monopoly with which
the rhetoric of his unionism was concerned:

> Rise, ye Forest miners, rise,
> Maintain your ancient right;
> Let justice echo to the skies,
> Join in freedom's glorious fight.
>
> Let not priests and Tory lords
> Disturb our Liberal faith,
> We conquer by our moral swords!
> And create a nation's living breath.
> The Forest rights must be maintained,
> And freedom lost must be re-gained.[57]

The remedy for all the wrongs suffered by the people, including the
threat to the foresters' rights, was the social revolution, reform and in

particular the extension of the franchise to the counties and the greater representation of labour in Parliament.[58] The foresters might depend on it that the aristocracy would do nothing for working men, he argued at a meeting in support of franchise reform.[59] Had the deep gales been in the hands of poor men like themselves, they would have been forfeited years ago!

Rymer found an ally in Sydney J. Elsom, a collier, a preacher and the leader of the free miners. After Mr Brain had failed to persuade the free miners to accept compensation for the rights from the Commissioners of Woods he had stopped attending meetings of the Protection Committee. Free of his influence the Committee had re-organised itself in January 1885.[60] Adopting the model of the miners' trade union the free miners established lodges around the Forest: at Berry Hill, Drybrook, Cinderford, Blakeney, Whitecroft, Yorkeley, Land End, Lydbrook, Ruardean Hill, Clearwell and Bream. Their delegates elected a Committee of 23 and appointed Elsom as chairman.

The new leader of the free miners and freeholders had taken an uncompromising view of the plan to do away with the rights. What evidence was there, he insisted on asking, that it was the free miners who stood in the way of the commercial development of the Forest? He agreed with Rymer that if the Forest was stagnating and doomed to beggary, its land, labour and mineral property lying undeveloped, the fault was in the spirit of monopoly and privilege.[61] Had not King Charles given land to his bastards, ennobling them and endowing them with privileges? Would anyone now try to strip them of their land and privileges? The miners were threatened, he argued, not because they truly barred progress, but because they were poor.

There might have been some who labelled the miners, and men like them, as 'the residuum, the dregs, the scum' but the most 'striking distinction between ourselves and our "noble" calumniators is this — we have to toil day after day, year after year, work hard, live hard, and still remain poor, while they, as a rule, spend a life of idleness'.[62] Most disgusting to him were those who had pensions from the public revenue, men like the Dukes of Beaufort who, with their relations, had been paid over half a million pounds from the public purse over half a century. He developed this theme in a series of articles in the *Mercury* on 'Hereditary Pensions', the 'gigantic system of outdoor relief of the aristocracy'.[63] 'The roots of our greatest grievances,' he wrote, 'are traceable to the selfish actions, the *legal* despotism, the avarice and to the unreasonable and unreasoning opposition to all progressing and ameliorative proposals of our hereditary legislators — our old nobility'.[64] The descendants of King Charles' illegitimate progeny, those of the first Duke of Marlborough, the Churchills and the relatives of the hero of Trafalgar all had drained the public purse of large sums of money, to none of which they were morally entitled. The Pensions List above all else was evidence of the rule of avarice and privilege in England:

> We all believe, at least we all say that we believe it is righteousness that exalteth a nation. Righteousness as we understand it means *right doing*. When applied to a government it implies that justice is to be impartially administered to all classes, to characterise our actions towards all peoples, and, further but this appears to have been neglected to the most distant planots [sic] — the equitable and upright application and use of the nation's wealth, did in such a way as to procure the greatest good to the greatest number, and truest happiness to all. With our knowledge of some of the discreditable and disreputable transactions in reference to the use of our national financis [sic] can we truthfully say that Britain is a righteous nation? Certainly a highly exalted and much favoured land, but, as the pension list alone will show, no more worthy or entitled to be called a righteous nation than I am to be called a millionaire.[65]

At the other end of the social hierarchy, the history of the struggles of the foresters to maintain their rights and privileges led to much the same sort of conclusion:

> When the survey of our Forest was less complete than at present, some of our ancestors took in a bit of Crown land that may happen to be adjoining their gardens. In many instances, this would be waste land, and in every case it was absolutely unproductive. But by industry, the bit of waste and non-productive land became both cultivated, and produced food for man and beast.
>
> But in time, these audacious, these awfully wicked proceedings of the Foresters, were discovered by obsequious Crown officials. In some instances the fences were thrown down, and again the land became useless . . . If this is the right thing to be done when a working man apportions to himself a few perch of barren ground and makes it fruitful, what shall be done to the man who won't work, and robs the nation of thousands of acres of the finest and most productive land in Britain.[66]

Unlike Timothy Mountjoy, Elsom looked back on the doings of Warren James with pride:

> The Chairman, referring to the past history of the Forest, reminded the meeting that their old home had once been given right away bodily by the reigning monarch, and that it was fenced

in and enclosed; but so great and determined an onslaught was made at the time by the inhabitants that all the fences were torn down and destroyed. He also mentioned that fifty years ago, Warren James had immortalised his fame by a similar feat of daring, which secured to the present generation their privileges.[67]

Elsom, indeed, took a systematic interest in the history of the rights, preparing a paper on the subject which he delivered at the Lydney and Ayleburton Working Men's Club.[68] It was there that he met the only discomforting comment on his position: from men who were — with what Elsom thought was sarcasm — opposed to *all* hereditary privilege.[69] That category of course included the free miners' rights. That, however, was the only occasion on which that cavil arose and Elsom seems not to have long reflected upon its implications.

Elsom directed much of his attack at the Tory party, 'the friends of the aristocratic, the privileged and monied classes', but the free miners' problem also brought the Liberals under fire. James Birt, a collier and free miner, had, at a meeting in early 1884, expressed his disgust with the Liberals:

The Forest working men might have congratulated themselves that they were under a Liberal Government, but it should not be forgotten it was so-called Liberal men who were about making an onslaught upon the Forest rights. He was, for once, grieved that he was a Liberal.[70]

Colonel Kingscote had not seemed to be entirely of the same uncompromising opinion about the miners' rights as the Protection Committee. He had forwarded the various petitions from the Forest, to the Commissioners or to the Parliament, but he had taken no strong part in the campaign. Later, when the Commissioners had withdrawn their Bill, he incurred the disfavour of the foresters by giving support to a proposal emanating from the Westbury-upon-Severn Guardians that there should be a Commission — yet another inquiry — into the problems of the Forest.[71] Since the Commissioners' Bill was a government bill and since the government was Liberal, and perhaps because he anticipated the splitting-off of the Forest from his constituency, Kingscote's circumspect, perhaps even careless, behaviour was to be expected.

Kingscote, in any case, was not the real problem among the Liberals. Arnold Thomas had been Mr Crawshay's ally in taking up the deep-gale question in the first place and had with him conducted the galees' negotiations with the Crown. Arnold Thomas also proposed to stand as the Liberal candidate, with the support of the leading Liberal coalowners and the *Mercury*, at the first election in the new constituency of the Forest of Dean in 1884. What chance for the free miners' rights if Mr Thomas was to be the foresters' link with Parliament and Government?

Mr Thomas, Elsom agreed with the *Mercury*, was in many ways a suitable man to represent the Liberals of the Forest.[72] A highly esteemed employer, a reliable and loyal supporter of Gladstone, though not as advanced in his politics as he might have been, and with a good record for many years as the local leader of the party, Thomas was the natural candidate. But should not the foresters be sure that the man they sent to Parliament was prepared to guard their acknowledged rights and advocate their claims and interests? Thomas could not do that for two reasons. Firstly, he was a capitalist: 'Is it not a moral and a political impossibility for any capitalist, or large employer of labour, no matter how upright and just he may be; to fully and fairly, and satisfactorily represent a labour or working class constituency?' Since the working classes formed the majority of the constituency, it was right, in pursuit of the greatest happiness of the greatest number, that they should send one of their own men to Parliament. Secondly, Thomas was a galee. Never, Elsom argued, had the foresters been in such danger of having their birthright wrested from them and never had they so much required Parliamentary representation. But how could Thomas represent them honestly:

> Is it rational to expect that he would, that he could be for and against at one and the same time? Brothers, Foresters, freeminers, Liberals, and working men, we shall shortly have a glorious opportunity placed in our hands: shall we avail ourselves of it, and turn it to good account? or, with 'bated breath and whispering humbleness, say this:- Fair Sirs, altough [sic] in the past you have spurned us, and ignored our wants, and even now are endeavouring to rob us of our own; for these courtesies we will still meekly submit to, and cringingly and slavishly perform all that you may decree? Remember our interests are at stake, decisive action must at all costs be taken; let not feelings, age, sentiment, drown our sense of justice; but fearlessly and courageously do the right.[73]

Thus Elsom and other members of the Protection Committee joined Rymer in campaigning for a Labour candidate for the Forest. The alliance of unionists, free miners and freeholders helps to explain why it was that Mr Blake rather than Mr Thomas should have so easily and quickly won the Liberal nomination. The problem of the land and the rights had confused the campaign for a working-man's candidate in 1874: there was no such confusion in 1884.

As Mr Forster Brown had predicted in 1882 the attempt to interfere with the rights had raised a political cry and one which effectively prevented the Commissioners from having their way. From 1886 onwards, as a result, the Crown took an entirely new approach to the problem. Instead of attempting to extinguish the rights, and having failed in the strategy of putting the onus of development on the galees, they attempted to make the free miners directly responsible for it.[74] At the suggestion of Mr Forster Brown the Commissioners declared forfeit the four largest and richest of the deep gales, the Durham, the Northumberland, the Newcastle and the St Low, and announced that they would be amalgamated and re-granted as one gale. Until then the gales had been re-granted to the first miner who had applied for them. If more than one miner had applied on the first day after forfeiture, the successful applicant was chosen by lot. This time, however, the Commissioners suggested that the 179 men who had applied for the new gale — called the United Deep Gale — should work together: that one man should hold the gale on behalf of them all and that they should all share in any proceeds. In September 1886, the free miners having agreed to this new arrangement, the Commissioners granted the gale to Mr Elsom.

This was, in effect, the end of the free-miner question in the nineteenth century. As deep gales were forfeited from time to time the gaveller held them in reserve. He accepted applications for them from the free miners but did not actually grant the gales. Presumably the Commissioners wished to see what would happen to the United Deep Gale. Unfortunately for the free miners, nothing happened to it. For two decades Mr Elsom worked hard on behalf of the free miners in an attempt to attract capital to the gale but his efforts were fruitless. Even when he had reached the point at which he would almost have given the gale away to anyone who promised to work it, Elsom could not attract an investor. In 1903, at last defeated, the free miners forfeited their gale. The rights, after all, were worthless. By then there were ten groups of deep gales lying unworked, for which free miners had submitted 5,796 applications.[75] The Commissioners had no real difficulty at that point in framing and carrying through a new bill which, though it still left the free miners their nominal right to gale, gave the Crown the powers it needed to ensure the working of the deep coal.

8. Commodities: the Commoners

And ye who find pasture for sheep and for ass,
For pig and for pony, on good Forest grass,
Yield not your possessions, hold fast to your
* right,*
Or soon it will vanish, with more, from your
* sight,*
For easy enough it is to foretell,
They'll suck out the egg if they once prick the
* shell!*

Their Bill will delude you, will mock and ensnare,
Will do you some damage unless you beware;
It gives with one hand a scrap of a dole,
But takes with the other best part of the whole.
Oh yes, for an inch they will measure an ell,
And suck out the egg if they once prick the shell!

Anon., The Foresters Egg! A Timely Warning! Dean Forest Mercury,
23 May 1884.

With the land problem settled and the free miners' question temporarily in abeyance there remained only the problem of the commoners' rights to vex and trouble the Commissioners of Woods and their deputy surveyors. For some conscientious officials this was the most annoying problem of all. They did not believe that most of those who exercised the 'turn out' had any right to do so and were enraged by the failure of successive attempts to clear out the animals. The need to deal with the free miners first frustrated the deputy surveyors who wished to see the end of commoning. It was not until the 1890s and the affair of Walter Virgo and the Blakeney Gang that a campaign could be worked up against the commoners on a scale approaching those against the free miners.

After the riot of 1831, its authority confirmed and its rights in the Forest for the moment intact, the Crown had relaxed its control of commoning. Some such arrangement had been implicit in the bargaining around the Mines Act of 1838. In response to a petition from the inhabitants the Commissioners had agreed to discontinue clearing the animals from the Forest at the fence month and the winter heyning. The keepers were to drive occasionally 'in order to keep up the Crown's right'.[1] The effect of this policy was to encourage commoning and, because drifts were made now and then, to maintain a persistent ill-feeling between the Crown officials and the foresters.

It is difficult to discover just how many animals there were in the Forest and how many people made use of commoning. A drift in 1864 brought in 6,652 animals: 5,868 sheep, 246 donkeys, 233 horned cattle, 218 horses and colts, 86 pigs and one goat. It is possible that there were many more animals than this since once it was known that a drift was in progress, owners would have put their stock into temporary pens in order to avoid the fines levied by the keepers. Nor does this indicate how many commoners there were. Perhaps there were one or two large flock-masters who owned most of the animals? A census of the sheep made in 1898 suggests that this was not the case (Table 8.1). Then, there were 10,851 sheep owned by 236 people.

Table 8.1: Sheep and Sheep-Owners in the Forest of Dean, 1898

District	Size of flock					Sheep	Total sheep-owners
	0—50	51—100	101—300	301—500	500+		
Lea Bailey	21	1	—	—	—	554	22
Nags Head	16	—	—	—	—	255	16
Perch	6	4	—	—	—	475	10
Edge Hills	10	3	2	—	—	1,015	15
Chestnuts	13	—	—	—	—	295	13
Crabtree Hill	4	—	1	—	—	290	5
Church Hill	3	5	—	—	—	510	8
Ruardean	26	8	—	—	—	1,228	34
Blakeney	14	2	3	1	1	2,209	21
Russels	6	—	—	—	—	200	6
Serridge	16	1	—	—	—	560	17
Sallow Vallets	22	2	—	—	—	842	24
Park Hill	26	2	—	—	—	895	28
Stapledge	7	6	2	2	—	1,523	17
	190	34	8	3	1	10,851	236

Source: Deputy Surveyor to Commissioners of Woods, 7 June 1898, PRO, F.3/264.

Over three-quarters of them ,190, owned less than 50 sheep. Only 12 had flocks of over 100 sheep. Sheep pasturing did not exhaust the possibilities of commoning. Many comments suggest that the keeping of one or two other animals, and of fowls, was a widespread practice. At a meeting of commoners in 1898, for example, Amos Williams, a sheep-owner whose grandfather had helped Warren James pull down the enclosure fences, commented that:

The cottager may, for grazing purposes, turn on the common or in the open woods his cow, or horse, or sheep, or pig, and having in mind the fact that a vast majority of the Foresters usually keep one or the other of these domestic animals, it will be readily seen that the benefits thus derived are considerable.[2]

It was not only the freeholders who turned animals out in the woods. This was a matter of which the deputy surveyor complained in 1859. He asserted that only the residents of the parishes surrounding the Forest, and only the freeholders among them, had any rights to pasture their stock on the Crown land. Those who did so, he alleged, had no such rights. They were the occupiers of land *within* the Forest and people who owned no land at all but only rented their houses. He offered a list of examples of men who turned sheep out, instances which he might have multiplied 'to any extent'. All his cases but one owned or rented land in the Forest but not in the surrounding parishes (Table 8.2).

Table 8.2: Some Commoners in the Forest of Dean, 1859

Name	Place	Land[a]	Stock
1. James Jones	Brains Green	About 2 acres	At least 100 sheep
2. Richard Nelmes	Bradley Hill	About 3 acres	About 200 sheep
3. James Virgo	Loiterpin	About 7 acres[b]	From 80 to 150 sheep
4. John Virgo	Blakeney Hill	About 4 acres	From 80 to 150 sheep
5. John James	—	About ¼ acre	At least 80 sheep
6. James James	Tomblin	1½ acres	Perhaps 60 sheep
7. John Barker	Old Furnace Bottom	Rents small patch	At least 50 sheep
8. James Birt	Parkend Furnace	Rents cottage	From 70 to 100 sheep
9. Thos Hale	—	Rents land	Upwards of 30 sheep, 1 cow, 2 horses
10. Wm Smith	Howlers' Slade	?	From 90 to 130 sheep and 2 colts
11. Charles Teague	Hawsley	¾ acre	5 cattle
12. Joseph Hart	Gosty Knoll	¼ acre	At least 100 to 200 sheep
13. — Cooper	Lane End	½ acre	5 cows, 2 horses
14. Thos Bridge	Lane End	Lodger	30 to 40 sheep
15. James Jenkins	Lane End	Small patch	50 to 100 sheep

Note: a. All within the Forest and originally encroachments. b. Also had about five acres in Awre parish.

Source: Deputy Surveyor to Commissioners of Woods, 17 March 1859, PRO, F.3/263.

These people, the deputy surveyor reported, were most of them 'quarrymen, colliers or labourers of one sort of another'.[3] In his evidence before the Select Committee of 1874 however, Timothy Mountjoy said that the 50 colliers who, to his knowledge, turned out sheep 'do not work regularly at the pits and do not care about it'.[4] An 'Old Miner', complaining in the *Forester* in 1877 about the effects of the butty system, wrote of the buttymen that

> A good sprinkling of them have degenerated into a sort of 'half farmer' 'half collier' with perhaps a brood mare pony or two, and two or three score sheep running the Forest; half of their time is spent in the pit and the remainder on their ground or tending their flocks, whilst their 'day slaveys' are keeping a good 'tally' up, in which this quondam 'buttyman farmer' takes his whack on pay-day'.[5]

The vicar of English Bicknor had made a similar point in 1865 in correspondence with the Commissioners of Woods. Commoning was

> opposed to steady industry — the owner of stock instead of being engaged in his day labour, spending his time in locking up his stray animals; and his gains or hopes depending so much on the season both in winter and summer, that the business partakes somewhat of a gambling character from its uncertainty.[6]

But it is unlikely that many men were able to achieve the semifarmer status, gambling with their flocks and the seasons, though a couple of hundred butties, probably the most successful of those at the big pits, no doubt did so. Most men probably had only an animal or two or a few fowls to supplement their wages.

In the late 1850s Sir James Campbell had taken up the war against the commoners, as well as against the encroachers, with great vigour. Sir James had run into trouble soon after taking up office. He wrote to the Commissioners in 1856 to report that one of his keepers, William Wood, had been summonsed to the County Court at Newnham by parties whose sheep he had impounded.[7] William Mountjoy, Thomas Meredith, James Virgo and William Adams, who owned about 500 animals altogether, had been insisting for some time on their right to turn them out wherever and whenever they liked, which right of course the keepers had contested.[8] The commoners had opened gates, broken down fences and warned Wood not to interfere with them in any way. This was an addition to the difficulty the keepers already experienced in excluding from the enclosures the Welsh Mountain sheep which the foresters preferred. One of them, it had been demonstrated, could jump a five-feet high wall with one of its forelegs tied to its neck![9] The pounding of sheep by Wood on the occasion which led to his being summonsed had also produced two pound rescues: one by all the plaintiffs, for which they were fined 5s each, and one by Virgo alone, on which no action seems to have been taken. Clearly this was an unsatisfactory state of affairs:

I should be glad to know how it is possible to put a stop to such a state of things; because while the Forest is overstocked in this way it is scarcely possible to keep the enclosures free; the animals them- selves force their way over or through fences seeking for food enough to keep themselves alive . . . and the owners are more than suspect of making gaps for them to go through; only it is difficult to catch them in the fact; I am unwilling to take any active or extreme course, which might cause retaliation in some way; perhaps by setting fire to plantations or maliciously cutting or injuring trees; I would rather defeat a case, if possible, such as the present, leaving the parties to pay the costs etc. and should be glad to know, in furtherance of this view, whether such persons as Mountjoy and Adams could be prevented having redress, because of having no right of common at all.[10]

Campbell regarded these men as 'lawless and disreputable persons, who make no scruple as to any desperate Act to gain their ends'.[11] As to the keepers and woodmen, the commoners 'look upon them as their natural enemies and would lose no opportunity of injuring them if they could'.[12] It was difficult to catch the commoners in breaking down enclosures because they usually worked at night and, even if caught, it was difficult to obtain a conviction 'because there are very many of the persons implicated in these transactions who I am sorry to say, are as ready to take a false oath to defend each other, when brought to a court of justice, as they are to break down the fences'.[13] On this occasion, as Campbell had wished, the Crown won its point by preventing the plaintiffs from 'having redress': not by proving that they were not entitled to the right of common but by obtaining a stay of proceedings in the County Court and their removal to the Court of Exchequer. Faced with what would clearly be a long, ruinously expensive series of court actions, the plaintiffs decided not to proceed.[14]

This left the question of right unresolved, a point to which Campbell returned in 1859. In conversations with the Commissioners he made it clear that he thought that 'irregularities' ought to cease at once.[15] The main problem, he argued, was the damage to the young plantations which the sheep caused and the continual expense of repairing fences to keep them out. It was, he complained again, 'a regular practice all over the Forest, for the inhabitants to damage the Fences, for the purpose of enabling the sheep to enter the Enclosures'.[16] How could offenders be detected when the miners passed back and forth through the enclosures at all hours of the day and night with every opportunity to damage the fences without fear of detection? Something more substantial than occasional prosecution was necessary. His first line of attack was to be the regular driving of the Forest in the winter heyning, when the need of feed for stock was greatest. That would necessarily cut numbers down and result in the 'saving of a very considerable sum annually to the Crown'.[17]

A more fundamentally useful approach, he thought, would be to challenge the right of those who commoned in the Forest. Did those who lived within the borders of the Forest have any such rights at all? The reports of the Commissioners of 1788 and 1835 had indicated that the common rights belonged to parishes surrounding the Forest but not to those who had encroached on the Crown land. Few of those who had the right to turn out animals, he argued, actually did so, 'the Forest being entirely covered with the sheep of parties having no rights at all'. There were other problems with stock. Campbell wanted some sort of check on the number of donkeys which individuals should be allowed to keep. Properly speaking, he insisted, donkeys were not commonable animals and should not be in the Forest at all. It would be too harsh a measure to do away with them altogether, however, because some 'poor people' scrabbled for a living by carrying coal and charcoal on them.[18] Action should be taken, though, against those who had four or five donkeys but no use for more than one. Goats had not been such a nuisance because Mr Machen had not tolerated them but where they were kept they did serious damage, peeling the bark from the young oaks as high as they could reach.

Give notice of a drive in the winter heyning, Campbell advised, and in the meantime he would go quietly about and give advance warning to people to get rid of their animals so that there would be fewer people to deal with when the time for a reckoning came. In the meantime too he would set the keepers and woodmen to a closer watch on the enclosures. One woodman had already been busy. Observing that three donkeys appeared in a particular enclosure every morning, although he had left the fences secure in the previous evening, he watched and waited and finally caught some children pulling down the fences and driving their animals in. Campbell thought that, since the children obviously acted at the direction of their parents, he should not summons them. Instead he would levy a poundage fine of 6s — almost the whole value of one donkey — and give warning of heavier fines to come.[19]

The Solicitor to the Commissioners of Woods, John Gardiner, agreed that such irregularities should be eliminated but he had a larger policy in view, one which required Campbell and his staff to avoid upsetting the foresters and to see that nothing was done which would engender ill-feeling towards the Crown. It would be 'more advisable to deal with the various other matters in Dean Forest now awaiting investigation and settlement before proceeding to interfere as to deal with the question of Common Rights in the Forest'.[20] The free miners were to be settled first and then the commoners. Those among the miners who said that rights other than their own were in danger were not wrong in their judgement of the Crown's ambition.

In accordance with the Solicitor's advice the keepers did not drive the Forest in 1859. By 1864 there had been no drift for seven years. Apparently not finding that tolerable, Campbell did order a drift at the winter heyning of 1864, thereby incurring the displeasure of his superiors.[21] Mr Gardiner thought that the whole thing was to be regretted and advised the Commissioners that no drift should be made in future without their express instructions.[22]

In one sense the drift had been a success: the keepers impounded and levied fines on 5,868 sheep, 246 donkeys, 233 horned cattle, 218 horses and colts, 86 pigs and one goat. But the drift had raised a number of prickly problems. Several animals had died in the pound, whose owners were extremely angry and were threatening legal proceedings for compensation. Other animals had not been reclaimed by their owners. Campbell thought two of the horses in pound had been stolen and 'the animals are believed to be watched by people in the neighbourhood to see who takes them out of pound'.[23] What was to be done about these animals and how should a demand for compensation be met? There had, moreover, been two cases of pound rescue and what was to be done about them? On 9 June the keeper William Christie was driving in East Dean, assisted by three men. As they were taking a herd of 20 horses past the Holy Trinity Church, a man named Cook rushed in among them and seized an old mare and a colt which belonged to his mother. He then scattered the other horses so that the keeper and his helpers could not catch them:

They tried to keep the Horses together but could not and Cook threatened to hit (a woodman) and push his fist thro' him if he interfered with his taking his mother's horses saying they had no business to drive them when Christie saw what had happened he went up to Cook and asked what business he had to take the mare and colt away and he said that he (Christie) had no business to drive and he wanted him (Christie) to show his authority. Christie told him that Sir James Campbell and the Verderers had given him authority to do so — he said he did not care for any of them — he said if he (Christie) was not satisfied he could go to Law to which Christie replied he would as soon settle it that way as any way — whereupon Cook said that he could get as much Law for a shilling as Christie could.[24]

The second incident took place in West Dean. John Jones, a keeper, and several woodmen were driving a herd made up of two cows, a flock of sheep, several donkeys and a pig, past Mr Mushet's works on 22 June. William Williams and James Charles, owners of the pig, left their work and rescued it from the keepers, who warned them that the Forest was being driven on Her Majesty's behalf and that they would rescue the pig at their peril:

> Williams and Charles said they (meaning the keepers) should not take the Pig — he Jones demanded 4d for the pig Williams said he would not pay anything for they had no right to drive the Forest and they were all 'Robbers' and that neither they nor Her Majesty had any right to drive the Forest and he pulled a handful of silver out of his picket and showed it to Jones but said he would not pay one penny for the pig nor should they impound it — then he (Williams) took hold of his (Jones) horse's bridle and kicked the horse and picked up a stone and swore several times he would throw it through his head — and he knocked and pulled the horse about for some time to try and throw him (Jones) down — a stone that was thrown stuck the horse but he did not see it thrown another stone struck Edward Jones his son on the Jawbone — he then called to Mr. Gaudern to come to him for he thought that some of them should have been killed. When Gaudern came up William Williams went from him (Jones) to Gaudern and took hold of his horse's bridle and insulted him. Afterwards they went after the animals that were left and Williams and Charles followed them and rescued other people's animals and said they should not impound them.[25]

The statements of the keepers involved indicate that these were not the first such incidents. Williams had said to Gaudern: 'Look how Powell and Fox served that other keeper (referring to Gorey a late woodman who had impounded cattle which Powell and Fox had taken out of the pound)'. He also referred to a case of pig rescue three or four years previously, for which the keepers had not been able to obtain a conviction. Part of the hostility between some of the foresters and the keepers and woodmen was probably attributable to the fact that the latter benefited from the drifts, retaining for themselves fines on pounding which ranged from 2d for each sheep taken, to 1s for unshod horses, donkeys and mules.[26]

The Solicitor to the Commissioners much regretted that Campbell had made the drift. But though he advised that the offenders in these particular cases should not be proceeded against, something important was at stake. Cook, Williams and Charles had denied the Crown's right to drive the Forest, had asserted that their claims to commonage were good against the Crown, and that they could defend themselves with a shilling's worth of law. To allow that assertion to go unchallenged would be to forfeit the Crown's position.

An outbreak of disease among cattle in the neighbourhood of the Forest in 1865 gave the Commissioners a chance to establish the Crown's right against the foresters. The appearance of rinderpest among cattle at Coleford caused a minor panic. The magistrates closed all markets and fairs for the sale of stock and blaming the cattle turned out by the foresters for the disease, petitioned the Commissioners to have the winter heyning enforced.[27] This was an attempt on the part of the magistrates to get only the horned cattle out of the Forest but the Commissioners, having taken the advice of Mr Gardiner, gave notice that the heyning would be enforced against animals of all descriptions.[28]

Mr Campbell, acting properly in accordance with instructions from London, had the forest placarded with notices warning of a drift and advertised it in the newspapers.[29] Between 23 December and 6 January the keepers took in 2,794 sheep, 144 pigs, 57 donkeys and mules, 38 horses and 18 horned cattle.[30] Campbell thought that the reduced numbers of stock impounded, compared to 1864, reflected the greater notice given. People had penned their animals up temporarily and turned them out again when the drift was over: 'there were probably more than double the number of sheep and donkeys on the Forest yesterday, than were found on it during the drift'.[31] Since no cattle had been seen since those impounded were taken away, Campbell hoped the drift would at least be successful in removing a source of rinderpest.

But it was not so clear that any other purpose had been served. The notices had stirred up great excitement in the Forest. During the actual drift there had been an awkward incident when some women had attempted to rescue their sheep, assisted by a number of men 'who had nothing to do with the matter but only happened to be passing'.[32] Two policemen appeared, however, putting an end to the interruption of the drift. There had been rescues before this, as we have seen. What was different about the excitement in 1865 was that people other than commoners had complained.

Most interesting was the letter of the vicar of English Bicknor, for what it tells us about his attitude to commoning as well as his appeal for leniency on the part of the Commissioners. He thought that the privilege of turning out stock was of very questionable benefit and that:

> ... it would probably be advantageous to all parties if such rights or privileges could be extinguished altogether. The sheep are half starved during the winter months — 100's of them actually die if

there happen [sic] to be a continuance of severe weather. Sheep cattle and horses (especially the first) are constantly stolen; and the temptation to this when the animals are thus suffered to range at large is so strong that it cannot be prevented, and the effect is demoralizing to the population generally.[33]

But though he obviously disapproved of this situation, the vicar did not think the Commissioners should too abruptly end it — though he at least acknowledged the right of the Crown to enforce the heyning should they wish to. What would be the consequences? 'There may be no ground for apprehending a recurrence of what occurred 33 years ago, when the forest was enclosed', but none the less a strong sense of grievance at the possible loss of their privileges was 'fermenting in the minds of the people' and some of the poorest people, indeed, would suffer hardship:

It should be borne in mind that though this suffering may not manifest itself *openly*; the discontent which is come to be bred by it, may vent itself in mischief done by evil disposed people to the Crown property *by firing the young plantations*. It is only a very few years since this did actually occur in consequence of the discontent in Mr. Brown's time.[34]

If the Crown were to act it should do so *gradually* giving the foresters plenty of time to reduce the numbers in their flocks or to make arrangements to pen and feed them. This winter the Crown should leave well enough alone, limiting the absolute ban in the heyning to the horned cattle. That was after all what the petitioners of Coleford had wanted.

The vicar of Christchurch also wrote to say that if carried out with full vigour the Commissioners' order would 'lead to disturbance'.[35] He had objected to signing the memorial asking for the enforcement of the heyning because the effect of closing the fairs and markets 'would fall with very great harshness upon the Foresters, who would thus find great difficulty in disposing of their sheep'. It was finally agreed at Coleford that the memorial should only extend to horned cattle: that the Commissioners had acted against all animals was 'harsh and unfair'. He was particularly concerned about the exclusion of donkeys:

There are many poor widows and infirm persons on the Forest who add to their scanty subsistence by fetching coal for their neighbours, and for this purpose keep a donkey — and of course the winter season is their harvest. If the donkey is to be excluded from commonage on the Forest during the winter, all their little additional gains will have to be appropriated towards providing provender for the donkey, and thus when most needed their own means would be lessened.[36]

Alfred Goold, coal-owner and magistrate, also concerned about the livelihoods of the donkey women, took an even firmer line:

> You can have no idea whatever of the great excitement no mischief has yet been done but I assure you I believe it is only out of hope that you will rescind the order, I have had the freeholders with me by dozens. I have held out to them that I believe you would see justice was done, and I most sincerely hope that you will do so. If not I cannot in anyway be answerable for the consequences.[37]

Five years later the author of the series of newspaper articles 'The Romance and Reality of Dean Forest', confirmed that there had been much ill-will against the Crown and, though there had not been the riot which the clergymen and Mr Goold anticipated, there had been some retaliation against the enclosures:

> Some five years ago there was a wondrous panic amongst the donkey-keeping, sheep owning, pig-feeding, and geese-loving Foresters at a threatened heyning. Loud roared the Forester against this invasion of his rights. Here and there 'twas said the enclosure banks would be thrown down and the hedgerows uprooted to show the Foresters' mettle and to give the supercilious officials of Woods and Forests — 'a taste of Dean's despair, Proving by deeds, in some wild hour, how much the outraged dare'. Yet the wild hour never came, the despair was untasted, and perhaps the only result that followed the notice of this intended 'Forest driving', beyond the turmoil of talk and feeling it occasioned, was this, that some few trees in unprotected places were mutilated. The writer remembers that one dark night, when the agitation was at its height, he had to walk through the 'Bushes' towards Hoarthorns. Beside him journeyed a friendly collier, whose talk ran on the heyning grievance. Suddenly, a crash was heard in one of the neighbouring dingles; then, a long harsh rustle as of shivering foliage and snapping twigs. The writer was startled, and asked his companion for an explanation, which, when given, was to this effect — that the notice of the deputy surveyor from Whitemead, in reference to the driving of open Forest, had so angered the people that they did not mind what trespasses they committed.[38]

Such manifestations of discontent implied a challenge to the Crown's right to enforce the heyning. Some commoners had challenged that right more explicitly, employing the solicitors Carter and Goold of Newnham to send a protest to the Commissioners.[39] Other commoners, on removing their animals from the pound after the drift, had turned them out into the Forest again, declaring 'that they would certainly not remove them from it'.[40] Thus not only had questions of equity and hardship arisen, along with the threat of disturbance, but the question of right had been raised in a most provocative manner.

Campbell and Gardiner hoped that one problem, that of hardship, might be used to solve the other, that of right. Certainly, let the notices of endorcement of the heyning be modified and postpone its rigorous enforcement until next winter in order to deal leniently with the poorest of foresters.[41] But they argued this should not be done in a way which suggested that the Crown was afraid to do as it had intended. Before any concessions were made, those who had opposed the Commissioners, especially Carter and Goold, should send along a memorial clearly acknowledging the Crown's right. The Commissioners did decide not to enforce the heyning in 1865, though there is no evidence that any memorial ever came from the commoners or that Campbell cleared the Forest in 1866. It is much more likely that, given their plans for the deep gales, they allowed the matter to drop so that hostility to the Crown might die down. By the time of the appointment of the Select Committee of 1874 at least, the situation of the commoners was still as Gardiner had described it in 1865, one of 'confusion, uncertainty and apparent irregularity'.[42]

There can be no doubt that the Select Committee of 1874 wanted to solve the problem by extinguishing the rights of the commoners — along with those of the free miners — altogether. As we have already seen, the Report of the Committee had recommended the appointment of a Commission whose first task should be to determine what common rights there were in the Forest and to commute them.[43] This reflected, of course, the express wish of the Commissioners of Woods, who had gone beyond merely wishing to enforce the ban on animals in the Forest during the heyning: 'we think it very desirable that the commonable rights should be comprised in some general arrangement for the purpose of a commutation'.[44] Not just a commutation on small parcels of land that might be sold to the foresters but on the whole of the Forest: it was necessary, as well as convenient, that the common rights should be dealt with. If the land was to be used in persuading the free miners to give up their rights, it had to be freed from all encumbrances.

The evidence it heard from witnesses certainly encouraged the Committee to optimism. The Crown's witnesses were not at all uncertain about the question of right. Mr Watson, successor to Mr Gardiner as solicitor to the Commissioners, argued that any rights of Common which did exist were subject to the paramount right of the Crown: that is, in the terms of the old Forest Law, the king's deer took priority over the animals of the commoners. During the fence month the deer were fawning and not to be disturbed; in the winter heyning there was food enough only, if there was enough, for the deer. The commoners might graze their animals only from 4 May to 20 June and from 20 July to 22 November: about six months, all told.[45] None of the other witnesses challenged this view. Nor did any of them disagree that the right of common lay in the parishes outside the Forest and that those who held freehold land within it had none. Sheep, moreover, were not forestal animals: they were not permitted to be pastured in the Forest by anyone.

There was, indeed, a remarkable unanimity of evidence that the Crown would meet no opposition in doing away with commoning. That was so to the point at which the Commissioners felt justified in reporting that 'the general feeling of the locality is strongly in favour of a commutation of legal rights of common by which they should be released to the Crown on proper compensation being made'.[46] 'Proper compensation' was understood to mean either a payment of money or, better, some sort of advantage in acquiring land. Thus, Edmund Probyn, a verderer, had assured the Committee that 'I do not believe there would be any difficulty in doing away with the common rights in the Forest, provided that the commoners were quite certain by so doing they would have a fair chance of buying land'.[47] He agreed with the Committee that it would be best to allot a certain amount of land to commoners in lieu of their rights and to make the rest of the Forest 'the freehold of the Crown'. Mr Crawshay, Mr Goold, Sir James Campbell and other local men of importance all agreed that there would be no difficulty.[48] Mr Crawshay had some experience in the matter, having recently purchased the Abbott's Wood Estate on the edge of the Forest and successfully bargained with neighbouring commoners for the purchase of their rights.[49] The Crown had taken hope from Crawshay's success, believing that it could use the principle on a larger scale.[50] Thus, Mr Watson said, 'If Parliament approves, I see no difficulty in working out a measure for ascertaining and making compensation to the commoners in a similar way to that which has been adopted in the case of Abbott's Wood, which has been quoted by many of the witnesses.'[51]

As with those concerning the free miners' rights, the proposals of the Committee dealing with commoners found advocates in the Forest. Rather more explicitly than in the hearings of the Committee on its report, it was argued that the commoners should be prepared to exchange their rights for land. At a series of meetings in September

1874 to discuss the report, Colonel Kingscote had explained what were 'commonable cattle' and said 'the sheep did not come within the act as a commonable animal, and this was a matter worthy of consideration by those who now turned out sheep upon the Forest'.[52] The Reverend Nicholson also added his weight:

> Now he would give it as his opinion that the commoners should be entitled to purchase the waste land at a very moderate price in consideration of their relinquishing the right of common . . . He thought that the commoners should likewise have the right to purchase the land adjoining what they now held at a reasonable price; and having it at a moderate price would be some compensation for taking away the right of common.[53]

At an earlier meeting Captain Goold, playing on the foresters' dislike of strangers, had appealed for the same sort of solution on the grounds that, as things stood, 'it mattered not what stranger came to the district if he had sheep or cattle or pigs, he could turn them out'. Would it not be better for foresters to obtain a piece of land, rather than that 'the rights should be thrown open and shared by everybody whoever they might be or from wheresoever they might come'.[54]

But the witnesses at the Select Committee, and those who advocated in the Forest the extinction of commoning, were coal-owners, magistrates, verderers and clergymen: not the working people who actually turned out animals. These gentlemen, moreover, gave thought only to the situation of those who were *legally* entitled to common and not to those working people who turned animals out and who had done so for decades. Their voices were not heard. It was true that Timothy Mountjoy had held a number of meetings during the hearings of the Committee and, at its request, had asked his audiences if there were commoners among them who objected to giving up their rights.[55] No one had objected then but his listeners were thinking about the limited scheme to sell small patches of land to the working men. Thus a meeting in the Forest in March 1875 had resolved that it

> especially deprecated any interference with the existing rights of free miners, or with the rights of commoners, excepting so far as relates to the outlying waste lands of the Forest, and in respect to those pieces of waste land, this meeting is of opinion that commoners' rights may be waived; provided such waste land is sold in small lots at a reasonable price.[56]

There was no agreement that the commoners' rights might go altogether, despite what the Select Committee had been led to believe, or had persuaded themselves to believe was the general feeling of the district.

Indeed the commoners joined the free miners in opposing the Bill. Where action against the galees in 1871 or against the commoners in 1865 had produced a response only from those directly interested, the Bill of 1875 provoked united action among the foresters. From early in March 1875 to the decision of the Committee to allow their Bill to lapse quietly, the opposition came from a Committee which represented both free miners and commoners.[57] There had been some feeling that, though the two groups clearly overlapped in their membership, the distinction between their claims should not be lost.[58] That awkwardness soon disappeared, however, and the petitions and memorials which went to Parliament and to the Commissioners argued the case for the preservation of both sets of rights. Hence, the principal petition sent against the Bill submitted:

> That as respects the rights of common over the said Forest we further submit that the same were fully enquired into by the Dean Forest Commissioners of Inquiry, appointed by a commission dated 21st January 1832, and fully set out in [their] . . . several reports . . . and although we admit that from the vast increase of the population of the said Forest since that period, and the consequent necessity for the erection of new dwelling-houses and allotments for gardens, it is desirable certain portions of the said Forest should be sold for such purposes; yet we submit that no sale of Forest land should be made to any parties other than free miners, freeholders, and other residents within the said Forest and Hundred, and then only for the express purpose of building thereupon, and for garden ground; and that in each case the quantity should be limited to an acre, and that our commonable rights over the remainder of the said Forest should be left intact and not interfered with.[59]

Those who were merely turning animals out on the Forest, without any agreed, legal right to do so were not entirely defenceless. Such rights could derive from custom, from the fact that they had been exercised for a long time without being challenged. Tom Goold, the solicitor of Newnham, who had objected to the enforcement of the heyning in 1865, had argued to the Select Committee that testimony of an exercise of the turn-out for 60 years would be enough to establish its foundation in custom.[60] That might easily have been established: both Sir James Campbell and Mr Gardiner had recognised that in the 1860s. Campbell, indeed, had been told by his predecessor, Mr Machen, that he could remember the sheep being in the forest well over 70 years before.[61] Mr Gardiner, while willing to move cautiously for the enforcement of the winter heyning, had not been at all certain about the Crown's ability to exclude the sheep altogether.[62] The advantage of the Commissioners' scheme in 1875 was that the common rights would disappear, the sheep would go, without the question of right actually having been brought to trial in a court. The disadvantage of course was that when the Bill failed the problem of the commoners' rights, like that of the free miners' rights, remained unresolved.

The new initiatives of the Crown on the deep gales in the late seventies and the early eighties did not directly concern the commoners. The free miners' rights always had priority in the Commissioners' list of jobs to be done in the Forest. Presumably, while the gale question was still to be settled, the Commissioners did not want a continuing struggle with the sheep and donkey owners and all the ill-feeling that would go with it. Whatever the reason, there were not, in this period, any further drifts of the Forest and no major controversies about commoning.

None the less, the comprehensiveness of the Commissioners' intention to extinguish privileges in 1874 and 1875 was not forgotten and the memory of it played an important part in the opposition of Elsom and the free miners to the deep gale scheme of the 1880s. Edward Rymer had insisted on the importance of the right of common:

> On Saturday last, I was attending a mass meeting in a wood in Yorkshire, on the Fitzwilliam Estate . . . while I stood gazing into that wood, my mind leaped home to the Forest, and the contrast I saw before me caused many serious thoughts to flow through my mind. Here the Forest is open and free to the citizens, there we were hemmed in by hedges, rails, walls and statutes that the people never sanctioned. A few children seeking blackberries there were doing so in fear of the police, here they wander through the open Forest without fear at all. When I wander through this beautiful old wood, and see the numerous pigs, sheep, goats, cows, horses, asses and poultry, grazing freely on the external produce found therein, I feel thankful that our men are at liberty to run their cattle free of cost or taxes, to help them to meet the battle of life. I believe in the sacred principle, that God gave the earth to the human race for an eternal inheritance, not to be taken away by man-made laws; and the man or men who would attempt to rob us of our God-given natural rights, must incur the danger of revolution, or other modes of popular resistance.[63]

The foresters, he argued, needed their pigs and sheep to supplement their meagre wages: that was their 'natural free-born right'. This was a proper concern for a union leader, he argued, because 'the very principals [sic] of trades unions is to defend the social, political and land rights of the people in every direction'.

The free miners' committees which Elsom took over after the withdrawal of Mr Brain in 1885 took a rather broader view of its function than had the old one under Brain's chairmanship. It was not only concerned with the free miners' rights but was 'a society for the protection of the interests of the Forest inhabitants generally'; a 'Freeminers', Freeholders' and Ratepayers' Protection Society'.[64] It was argued then, as it had been in the 1870s, that all the foresters, excepting of course the large coal-owners, were threatened by the manoeuvrings of the Crown. As one speaker put it at a meeting at Blakeney in 1884:

> So far it was a question for the free miners — in other words it was the free miners first . . . The free miners regard the attack upon their rights as one which threatened the freeholders and householders. At present most of them know the great advantage in turning out upon the Forest their sheep, their horse, pigs, or donkey. It had been stated by Sir Henry Loch that there was no intention in the present Bill to interfere with the rights of common. But the free miners were of opinion that as they (the free miners) were the first to be 'charged' the Crown may some day bring their forces to bear against the free holders, and do away with the turnout, and unless the Forest forces were able to resist those of the stronger power, they must fall.[65]

All the people of the Forest had to unite: that included the butchers, the bakers and the drapers. With the deep gales locked up, the Crown refusing to forfeit and re-grant, were the shopkeepers not suffering from an artificial retardation of trade? Some evidently thought so, as the Commissioners discovered when an agent employed by them to go into the Forest to work up a campaign and petition in favour of the Bill from the tradespeople, reported that he could not do it: the shopkeepers and tradesmen had not believed that the Crown had the welfare of the Forest at heart.[66]

Thus the alliance of the free miners with the commoners and the freeholders, presented a broad, united front to the Crown. From 1885 onwards it had to deal with a committee which represented all those who stood to lose if the Crown had its way and whose attitudes and responses were informed by Elsom's sense of the difference between the privileges of the rich and the privileges of the poor. That alliance too confronted the *Mercury* and the Liberal coal-owners who wished Arnold Thomas to be the candidate for the new Forest constituency. That wider alliance in the eighties, formed in opposition to the Crown and the large coal-owners, ensured that Mr Blake would be the Liberal candidate.

The failure of the Commissioners' Bill in 1885 produced an entirely new departure in dealing with the problem of the free miners' rights. No such experiment was made with the commoners' rights. What then had been happening to the commoners while the debate about policy and right had been going on? Was the inactivity of the Commissioners perhaps due to the fact that the commoners had read the signs of discouragement from the government and quietly disposed of their animals? Unfortunately, since there was little official activity about the sheep there is simply no evidence which might allow an answer to this question. It is necessary, therefore, to move forward to the 1890s, to the case of Walter Virgo and the Blakeney gang. An examination of the activities of this gang and the attitude of the authorities to it will help to establish the continuity of both commoning and the Crown's policy towards it.

Walter Virgo came to the attention of the public in December 1893, as the defendant in a petition brought by Mrs Anne Adams for damages caused by his sheep in her vegetable garden.[67] Whatever some other foresters thought, Mrs Adams was far from convinced that the grazing of these fence-leaping animals in the forest was a good thing. 'I have not interfered with Forest rights or customs,' she wrote to the *Mercury*, '. . . but being only an humble cottager I have no right to speak for my own rights; I must keep silent, and have my garden overrun by a flock of sheep, 20 or 30 at a time, I suppose I must allow them to come and go as they choose, without interfering with them.'[68] At the same time Virgo was in disfavour with the recently appointed deputy surveyor, Phillip Bayliss. While Mrs Adams's action was pending, his keepers had impounded some of Virgo's sheep: which someone — Bayliss alleged that it was Virgo but couldn't prove it — had promptly rescued in a night raid on the pound. Bayliss ordered more of his sheep taken and a fine of 3s levied on each of them, with the result that Virgo uttered threats against one of the woodmen, who was so terrified by them that he would not discuss the incident with Bayliss.[69]

According to Bayliss, Virgo and his relatives were altogether a bad lot:

This man Walter Virgo is one of a family that has a most notoriously bad character in the Forest — and I am informed that Walter Virgo has been convicted of sheep stealing and has also on two other occasions been tried at Glos'ter for offences but acquitted — and at present he and other members of his family exercise a system of terrorism over the inhabitants of the Forest and it is commonly stated that if other people incur their displeasure or turn animals out on the Forest by which the pasturage used by the Virgos would be lessened the animals are either driven over quarries — or killed or injured or some other injury inflicted.[70]

Bayliss's allegations against Virgo found support from the Reverend A. D. Pringle of Blakeney, whose parish adjoined Virgo territory in Blakeney Hill. He wrote to the Commissioners in April 1895 to inform them of an outrage on two horses belonging to Mr Butler, draper and grocer, which Pringle alleged had been committed by the Virgos. He reported that the gang had grown in size in recent months and that their brutal deeds — fowl stealing, robbing clothes, poisoning dogs, maiming sheep and destroying dogs and horses — which had gone on for years, were growing worse. It would surprise no one, he wrote, if acts of violence 'in defence of property' were to be committed.[71]

The gang had taken to going about at night in groups of twelve or thirteen, armed with bludgeons, according to Bayliss. They were so numerous and well-organised that they could keep a complete watch on the police, day and night.[72] No sooner had the police left off watching some place than the gang moved in to commit some crime. Walter Virgo, moreover, was reported to have purchased two revolvers in Gloucester and the 'general opinion is that there will be serious murders as the outcome of the present state of things'.[73] The Chief Constable of Gloucestershire, Henry Christian, did not go so far as Mr Bayliss, who thought that an overwhelming display of force, preferably a troop of cavalry patrolling day and night, was necessary but he did draft in an extra eight men for the night watching.[74] Some such action was necessary, since Sir W. Wedderburn had asked in the House of Commons what the Home Office was doing about affairs in Blakeney.[75]

Predictably, the increased surveillance produced clashes between the police and the local men. In May 1895 the brothers Aaron and Moses Virgo, colliers, in the company of Evan Davis, labourer, were walking towards the Swan Temperance Hotel in Blakeney near to midnight when they encountered PC Newport, who thought he had reasonable grounds to believe that they were about to commit a felony. There followed a brawl between the members of the gang and a number of police in which PC Newport was hurt. Convicted of assaulting Newport, the Virgo brothers received a month's prison sentence each and Davis a 10s fine.[76] Bayliss alleged that if there had not been other constables present Newport would have died in the assault.[77]

Police Sergeant Morris was not so fortunate later in the year. In November he was one of a party of police watching for the Blakeney gang, three of whom they surprised in a poaching expedition. Two of the poachers were caught, but a third, James James, made his escape. The police surrounded James' house at Old Furnace Bottom end, and not finding him there split into two parties, one of which, including Sergeant Morris, went to Viney Hill. There they encountered three rowdy men who, after an exchange of words, began to throw stones. One of the stones caught Sergeant Morris behind the ear and killed him instantly.[78] Things quietened down for a time after that, to flare up again in 1897 and 1898. Trouble began in 1897 with the conviction of Walter Virgo's son Albert, a collier, for stealing a fowl worth 2s, the property of Henry Griffiths, a miner of Bradley Hill. For that the magistrates fined Albert 5s and costs. After the hearing, according to Bayliss' informant, Virgo had said: 'Well it will cost money, but we will make the B — s sit up for it'.[79] Shortly after that the houses belonging to Griffiths and his mother-in-law were attacked in the early hours of the morning. The windows were smashed, the window sashes and frames were broken and the fowls stolen from the yard.[80] Not long after that the Blakeney gang were blamed again when five sheep were mutilated and killed at Bush Hill.[81]

Much more serious incidents happened in 1898. About nine o'clock on 9 February, residents in the area of Blackpool Bridge heard three distinct explosions.[82] The following morning, workmen employed by Messrs Williams of Cinderford discovered that the firm's steam sawing machine had been dynamited. There was no evidence at all to suggest who had taken such extreme and disturbing action but Mr Bayliss had no doubt the Virgos were to blame.[83] Mr Bayliss was perturbed, having been warned several times by the police about danger to himself, and sent Mrs Bayliss out of the Forest for the time being. On the advice of Mr Christian the Commissioners offered a reward of £100, hoping thereby to exploit divisions within the gang which had sprung up when one of the brothers had run away to the north of England with the wife of another.[84] But before the announcement of the reward had time to take effect, another black deed had outraged the district.

On the morning of Sunday, 3 April, at about half past one, one of the men on night duty at the New Fancy pit noticed a fire near the lodge in Russell's enclosures. Thinking that the lodge was burning he went to help Hatton, the keeper, but found instead that the woods near the lodge were alight. Hatton and a gang of keepers and woodmen set to work to beat out the fire with branches:

> It appears that the outbreak occurred at several places simultaneously, and no sooner had the men put out one blaze, than their attention was attracted to another, and this went on for hours, and in the opinion of one authority, somewhere before mid-night on Saturday somebody deliberately made at least thirty fires in the district referred to.[85]

Mr Bayliss examined the burnt-out areas and decided that no less than 50 separate fires had been started in the enclosures, most probably 'by some person or persons carrying a small lamp such as miners use and just pushing it into the dry Fern where there happened to be a suitable place'.[86] The fires extended over a line from two-and-a-half to three miles long, on the windward side of the Forest, and must have been lighted by someone — by probably more than one person — who knew the paths of the Forest well. This was, the Commissioners wrote to their Solicitor 'a very determined attempt to burn the Forest'.[87] If the wind had not died away and a light rain begun, Bayliss thought, the attempt would certainly have succeeded. Needless to say, Mr Bayliss thought this was the work of the Blakeney gang.

The gang was nothing if not versatile: poisoning, maiming, stealing, midnight raids, dynamiting and arson. But what was it all about? Was it perhaps that the Blakeney Hill men had altogether missed the progress of civilisation, and this was all mere barbarism and brutishness?

Perhaps the fact was that Bayliss's attention to the Virgos had been deliberate, had something to do with policy on commoning? Crown policy and the sense of frustration which pervaded it, had not altered by 1893 when Bayliss took office. Memoranda written at that time rehearsed the history of drifts and the failure of the Crown to resolve the question of right.[88] Far from having decreased, the 'number of sheep turned onto the forest has increased enormously during the past few years'.[89] As always, their owners were not believed to have any legal right to the turn out. And again the alternative lines of action open to the Commissioners were to seek an Act of Parliament to commute the rights; to challenge the exercise of the right in a court of law; or to find some indirect way of forcing the sheep out, such as enforcing the winter heyning. Another useful measure might be to enclose the full 11,000 acres which the Commissioners were entitled to exclude from commoning. The plantations made in the early nineteenth century in due course had reached the point at which they were judged to be safe from damage by browsing animals and had gradually been thrown open. New enclosures had been made but not to the same extent, so that only about 4,665 acres were enclosed at the beginning of the nineties.[90] To re-enclose 6,000 acres would put a great pressure on the sheep-owners and force many of them out.

One of the memoranda had contained the observation that the 'case of the Virgos seems to be a favourable one to act upon since as they have established a reign of terror in this district there would be no sympathy extended to them by their neighbours'.[91] Someone in the Office of Woods, possibly the Commissioner responsible for Dean, Mr Howard, made a marginal note next to this: 'I do not agree'. There is no evidence of a policy decision in London to pursue the Virgos but none the less Mr Bayliss seems to have kept up his attention to Virgo and to have used the Blakeney outrages in order to put pressure on the Commissioners to do something about the sheep.

Thus Bayliss was involved in Mrs Adams's action for damages against Virgo. Mrs Adams's first action had in fact failed, on the grounds that she had not fenced adequately against the sheep. But Mrs Adams had spoken to Bayliss, who 'told her that the sheep were trespassing in The Forest of Dean, and no one was under an obligation to fence against sheep'.[92] With that support she asked for a new trial. Bayliss' intervention caused great anxiety. A 'Suffering Forester' wrote to the *Mercury*:

> Now, Sir, have the Foresters any common rights or the free miners any rights? Can they turn out their stock — sheep, pigs, horses, cattle or fowls — on the forest without leave from anyone or, must they keep such stock inside their own fences. Government men take our sheep and levy a charge of 2/- per head on them if they happen to get in certain woods now enclosed; which woods we say should now be thrown open to the public — as they were 40 years ago.[93]

Mr Elsom argued that the new deputy surveyor was 'the most deadly foe Foresters have, as regards their local customs'.[94] Distrusted and disliked, he had created a strong opposition in a short time. Who, Elsom wanted to know, was providing the cash for Mrs Adams's action? Virgo's case came to be seen as a test, for which some £50 or £60 was subscribed by the foresters.[95] Virgo, however, did not allow the matter to go ahead, stopping the action by paying Mrs Adams the damages she wanted. Perhaps Bayliss's intervention, the opportunity the case presented for a decision in law about the question of right and the possibility of a long and expensive litigation from which the Crown might turn out to be the principal beneficiary made resistance unattractive.[96]

Bayliss certainly attempted to persuade the Commissioners of Woods that the Virgos were a bad lot. His reports of incidents painted a ghastly picture: 'On another occasion a woman owned two heifers which she turned into Stapledge these beasts had their bellies cut open and their entrails let out and they were left lying kicking their own entrails to pieces in their agonies.'[97] If the attacks on beasts were horrible, the effect on the people was to create a great reign of fear in which the victims of outrages would not give Bayliss or the police any help because they were so terrified of retaliation. Bayliss also minimised as much as possible the extent of sheep-owning. The turn out, he reported, had become the monopoly of a few people. The outrages were the product of attempts by those few, especially the Virgos, to keep others off the Forest.[98] All this was tendentious. The point of all Bayliss's reports was that there would be no trouble if the sheep were cleared out; the sheep had no right to be there and the Commissioners should do something:

> I cannot too strongly or emphatically point out that a judicial enquiry into the question of common rights in the Forest is of urgent and vital importance to the interests of the Crown. Large tracts of land in the Forest which might easily be converted into a source of considerable revenue to the Crown by growing timber thereon are rendered entirely valueless by being overrun at all times of the year by thousands of sheep which are not commonable animals on the Forest.[99]

Since the outrageous Virgos had so cowed the district, since they had monopolised the turn out, it was implied that the foresters in general, would only be too glad to see commoning disappear altogether. Thus the Reverend Pringle wrote, 'I have no reason to believe that those Foresters who have sheep running in the Forest, would not gladly forgo from using the privilege, if it was entirely withdrawn, so as to deter this family from having any sheep running in the Forest'.[100]

Thus too, in June 1895, a petition bearing the names of 26 people complained of the gang to the Commissioners and argued that the closure of the Forest permanently, or for a long period such as the autumn and the winter, was necessary if there was to be order.[101] Some thoughtful civil servant has marked the occupations of ten of the signatories alongside their names. One was an inland revenue officer, one a clerk in orders, two were drapers and grocers, two farmers, a beer retailer, a gardener, a surgeon and a 'private resident'. These were residents of Blakeney and the parish of Awre. Two other signatories whose occupations are not given also lived in Awre.

The Commissioners of Woods, however, had acted cautiously, not focusing their policy on the Virgos. The matter, after all, was not so clear as Mr Bayliss made it seem. On the whole, opinion within the Forest was that the good Reverend was exaggerating the problem. R. J. Kerr, verderer and magistrate, agreed that the Virgos were something of a nuisance but he also thought that 'a great deal has been said and written upon the subject which I can only consider as being irrelevant, injudicious and unnecessary'.[102] He did not think that the source of the trouble was to be found in sheep keeping:

> Whether legal or not, the custom has obtained for so long a time as to be recognised as a *quasi* right, and for my own part I could not

recommend the adoption of such a course as getting rid of the sheep.

I believe that Petty jealousies, neighbourly annoyances, trespasses, breaking down fences, County Court, and Petty Sessional Summonses and other small irritations are the means of creating ill feeling to a much greater extent than rights of common however much those rights may be abused.

Mr Elsom, in the chair at a meeting called by the Forest of Dean Labour Association, prefaced his introduction of the miners' agent with a few remarks in which he deplored outrages and denied that the whole district should be blamed for the stealing of a few fowls near Blakeney: the district 'is as free from crime as any place in the kingdom'.[103] Mr Rawlinson, the agent, observed that it 'was not the first time the Vicar had made wild statements about the Forest and Foresters'. At another meeting Rawlinson took umbrage on behalf of the whole body of forest miners: 'They were held up to the public as being an extraordinary class of the community and hardly fit to associate with the rest of the citizens of the country'. What about the black deeds of medical men, legal gentlemen and even of men of the cloth? Besides if there were wicked men in Pringle's parish, wasn't it his job to lead them to the truth?[104] The *Mercury* thought that the vicar had become 'hysterical'.[105]

Why were the Blakeney people hostile to Virgo? The policy that the Commissioners *did* decide to follow helps explain that. Taking up one of the suggestions of the memoranda of 1893, they had decided to re-enclose the full 11,000 acres to which they were entitled. This was a procedure which the foresters could hardly have hoped to resist and though there was some discontent the first fences had gone up by 1897.[106] The difference which Bayliss's persistent reports about the Virgos had made was that the Commissioners believed that they could enclose substantial portions of Blakeney Hill with the full support of most of the populace. This they had decided to do, after a meeting with the local magistrates, thereby provoking an 'agitation' against the enclosures in the Blakeney Hill district.[107]

At this point the role of the farmers and tradesmen of Blakeney and Awre becomes intelligible: there was something more at stake than a few fowls or sheep. So long as forest land was open to common it was not rateable. As soon as it was enclosed the Crown became liable for rates. The substantial ratepayers of the area stood to have their own rates substantially reduced by new levies on the Crown: if only commoning could be put aside. Whereas current rates stood at 8s in the pound they were liable to fall to 2s if the Forest were enclosed.[108]

In the context of the Commissioners' policy the dynamiting and the firing of the plantations makes sense too, as something more than viciousness. The sawing machine belonged to the timber merchant who had the contract for fencing Blakeney Hill. In the week in which the explosions took place the machine had been moved to Cinderford Bridge to start the job.[109] The fires were most probably a protest against the enclosing policy, a type of protest often seen in the Forest before. Bayliss indeed had seriously misled the Commissioners: there was, after all, strong opposition to the enclosures. Nor was it true, as it also became clear in 1898, that commoning was confined to a few gangsters. It was at this point that the census of sheep, which was discussed at the beginning of this chapter, took place. There were not one or two large flock-masters but a relatively large number of owners of small flocks. A memorandum of the Commissioner for Dean recorded his surprise and marked the end of Bayliss' ambition to have all the sheep out:

> The number of persons keeping sheep as well as the number of the sheep themselves is very much larger than I had been led to expect, so that the matter will have to be dealt with very carefully and by degrees, no wholesale prohibition being in my opinion possible.
>
> It will be desirable to take means to let the owners of sheep know that their animals have no legal right in the forest but are only there on sufference . . . Apart from this, and so long as the rightful commoners do not step in to prevent it, the Crown will not interfere with the sheep.[110]

Thus at the turn of the century matters rested for the Crown in no substantially better condition than they had been in 1831. The sheep-owners had not been successfully challenged and commoning had not been abolished. As the century closed the sound of voices raised in dispute continued. A faction among the ratepayers wanted the complete extinction of commoning while Mr Elsom, at the head of the commoners, insisted that the rights should be preserved. The sheep are still on the Forest.

An Overview

Suitable though it might have been for antiquarian comment in a *Notes and Queries* or the *Gentlemen's Magazine*, the Forest was not separate, in the nineteenth century, from the forces which were at work in British society at large. Some things, it was true, had been detached by time and circumstances from everyday concern. There was a Roman road and a church or two, which had the age and the impartiality necessary for an acceptable tourist attraction in a place of ornamental beauty. Even some of the old iron mines, the 'old mens' workings' attracted attention, though they too expressed no opinion about the life and work of iron miners: the artefacts of Roman and Silurian had more of what passed for dignity than that. The customary rights were not so aloof. Until the end of the century they remained a focus of the interests of the State, capital and working men.

With hindsight, it seems doubtful that any of the alleged rights of the miners could have been sustained under any strict application of the tests of law. Perhaps the right of the miners to dig for coal and ore, to make roads from the mine to the nearest king's highway and to have timber from the Crown plantations for use in the mine, had the strongest claim to consideration. The versions of the Book of Dennis, the records of the Mine Law Court and the memory of the oldest living miners, could all testify that what was said to have been done, had been done. None the less, as the judge pointed out in *Attorney General* v. *Matthias*, the custom could not have been defended against the principles of the notorious Gateward's Case. No more secure, much less so, indeed, were the uses that the colonists of the Forest had come to make of the land and the forage. The cottages and the gardens of the miners were simply encroachments on the property of the Crown and little in the way of law could be offered to defend them. When Henry and Richard Dobbs turned their cow into Cockshoot's enclosure in 1831, they might have believed that they were exercising their rights in a perfectly proper manner but it is unlikely that they could have defended the right successfully. There is no evidence that anyone but the inhabitants of the parishes surrounding the Forest proper had any right to turn animals into the plantations to graze and even their right was limited by the prior claim of the King's deer in the fence month and the winter heyning. Other matters, such as the right to glean bark at the stripping of the birch trees, to take ferns and undergrowth and to burn off the undergrowth from time to time in order to improve the pasture, had even less reason to expect

172

the approval of the law. The gap was wide between the law of custom and the practice of custom.

None the less, the practice did not succumb in a contest with law. There were three reasons for that. Firstly, the vulnerability of the custom remained only potential, until someone actually chose to invoke the law. Secondly, no one used the law because no one at any stage was at all clear that the custom was truly vulnerable. There was always some sort of case to be made for preserving the rights. After 1838, of course, there was no question that the miners' rights had the sanction of statute. After the 1840s those who lived on the old encroachments did so under the protection of a perfectly acceptable freehold title. Even the sheep-owners had some sort of case. A great deal of caution was therefore necessary. That uncertainty meant, thirdly, that the possibility of going to law on a particular matter had to be judged in the context of larger strategy.

As much as it is a set of statements about what is right or wrong, defined as legal or illegal, the law is a tactical device. Its provisions and precedents may be brought to bear on an opponent so as to lead him to behave in the ways that expediency demands. That device, though, must be used selectively and prudently. The small victory may preclude a larger. The establishment of the application of one principle may require the sacrifice of another. Goodwill may be lost. People may refuse to be agreeable and accommodating across a whole range of informal arrangements and may insist upon a stuffy observance of the terms of law-determined relationship. People may even become rude or violent. There is the worse possibility of decisive defeat in court. If the opponent is of no consequence and has no resources or friends and the case that can be made against him is clear, perhaps those considerations have little weight. Where there is some doubt about any of that, it is as well to use other means. What matters is not whether this or that is illegal but whether going to law is the best means to a particular end.

Sensible people, of course, use political and legal devices simultaneously. Some abstract principle can be found in science or morality to justify the main purpose; opinion can be created and spread about; friends can be made and other enemies temporarily placated. Information may be released or suppressed as circumstance demands. The opponent and his case may be made to seem unacceptable in all their aspects: so long as no hope remains that, through persuasion or purchase, an amicable settlement can be obtained. At the same time it is necessary to make the cautious supposition that matters just might go to court. The opponent's case must be anticipated in detail. The things he has done and not done must be understood and related in detail to all the finest points of law that might be brought to bear. Everything should be done which is necessary to bring him in his ignorance to do or write or sign things which will undermine any case he might attempt to construct. He must not be allowed the same advantage.

The State was the maker of strategy and the planner of tactics in the Forest of Dean. There are three main formal elements in any State action: the assumptions about State, economy and society which inform policy and which are manifest in Royal Commissions, Select Committees and Parliamentary Debates; the policy itself, manifest in legislation, rules, regulations and the behaviour and decisions of ministers and cabinet; and the common law and the courts, interpreting and supplementing the statutes. These, at least, are the main components of the public State. The private State needs to be considered as well. The civil servants are an independent variable. They intrude their assumptions into State action through internal memoranda and working papers and informal understandings about what might and might not be done. They make independent submissions to committees and commissions. In their choice of the wording of rules and regulations and their selective attention to them, and especially in their selective neglect, they make policy de facto. They can act more directly too, as the Commissioners of Woods did when they employed a man from Cardiff to go into the Forest to work up feeling and a petition against the free miners' rights. The private State, moreover, has its own lawyers. Every administrative act has potential legal consequences. In matters of any importance it is the lawyers within the State, the Solicitors to the Treasury in the case of the Forest, who structure the detail of administrative action, who use the law as a tactical device within the framework of administrative purpose. Perhaps more importantly, they decide to refrain from using the law. Thus the insistence of his masters that Deputy Surveyor Campbell should leave the commoners alone for the sake of the campaign on the free miners' rights, despite the fact that all the opinion available suggested that the sheep-owners were acting illegally. Thus the attempt to bring the encroachers to pay a nominal rent for their land in the early part of the century. If they had done so, the act of payment of a trivial sum would have constituted an acknowledgement of the Crown's title to the land. The State may use and abuse the law, manipulate it as a means to some end, in the same way as any private person. And thus, the mere fact of the illegality of the foresters' rights was of itself of no consequence or interest but was important only in the context of State policy and the administrative and legal strategems it had in hand from time to time.

The overall policy to be pursued by the Crown had been laid down in the late eighteenth century when it had been decided that customary rights were a threat to the public interest. Customary rights, therefore, were to be defined and separated from those of the Crown.

In practice that meant a persistent attempt to extinguish the rights altogether. The object was not to grab other people's property for the use and profit of the Crown: there was never any question that the Crown contemplated dispossession of that kind. What did matter was that one form of title to property, one set of legal relationships, should be replaced by another. By replacing a relationship in which the language and notions of mutuality and reciprocity bound it to a tolerance of loose and ill-defined claims on its own property, with the ordinary, clear, rational relationships of private property, the Crown would be unhindered in dealing with its properties through sale, lease or any other form of use for profit. 'Profit', obtained through market relationships, became the public interest.

The Crown's strategy fell into two phases. In the first the objective was to change the basis of property ownership in the Forest. Most importantly, the Crown was to be able to hold and use its coal as any other coal-owner did. The Act of 1838, by which the Crown achieved the substantial destruction of the custom, was a brilliant tactic. Custom cannot stand against statute. An Act of the Parliament may extinguish or alter custom in any way whatever. Even if on the face of it the custom is not extinguished, if it survives in a form defined in detail by a statute, the custom has none the less ceased to operate. The law is statute law and subject to change and repeal by Parliament. Any caveats about who may exercise the privilege in question may be varied or waived without limit. As the Act of 1838 demonstrated, a statute can separate from community the rights conferred by custom, making them alienable, marketable, by individuals. The Act apparently preserved the exclusive custom but destroyed its essential character as a form of property.

The land and the sheep were of lesser importance than the miners' rights. It was desirable, of course, that tenure of the land was regularised. The casual occupation of Crown land had to stop and those who were already in occupation had to be given normal freehold or leasehold titles, so that no peculiarity would remain to blur the boundary between the Crown's property and other property. Where the Crown had a clear statutory right to fence its timber against animals and thieves, the fences should go up and be defended. There was latitude for bargaining there, though. If the foresters were afraid of losing their land or having their animals driven off the Forest altogether, that could be used to bring them to look favourably upon the Mines Bill and to moderate their political activity. Strict tests of law were less important than the administrative priorities.

Later in the century the demands of the Revenue again made it necessary to attack the rights. If the deep coal were to be developed, and large royalties taken from it, the vestiges of the rights would have to go. This was not now strictly an attack on custom but an attempt by the civil service to alter statute law through a government bill. In a model exercise in the creation of pressure from without, the Crown subjected the Forest to selective pressures designed to bring about that apparent public enthusiasm for change which would see a government bill through. If some of the foresters wished to have more land, they might be persuaded to promote change. The owners of gales might be threatened with the loss of their dead rents, and even of the gales, if change did not come about. Failing that, the onus for developing a successful scheme might be placed on the leading mine owners. In the meantime the roaming of the sheep and some of the transgressions of sheep and landowners could be overlooked.

All this is to insist on the autonomy of the State as an actor in these events. It would be misleading to see the process of change in the Forest as one in which a capitalist class of coal-owners, or a State servile to them, unilaterally, re-ordered affairs to their own advantage. The State had its own properties and interests to defend and they were separate from those of the Crawshays and Arnolds. If the Crown wished to encourage the coal-owners in the pursuit of profit, it was because that would serve to augment the Crown's own profit. It was a sense of that separateness and narrowness of the 'public interest' which led so eminently constituted a body as the Commons Preservation Society to oppose the making over of the Forest into Crown or private property, unencumbered by rights of any sort. The Society had a notion of the 'public interest' to defend which had little to do with cash returns or the discounted future value of land, considered as an investment.

None the less, the Forest had passed through a period in which the ownership and use of resources had been fundamentally transformed, in ways which favoured private property, the exchange of properties for profit and accumulation for the few at the expense of the labouring many. The Forest had come to be dominated by a consensus between State and capital on these matters. Against the background of disappearing customary right, the community of assumption about property, which joined the coal-owners and the officers of the Crown, is evident.

The miners might have been expected to provide an alternative set of assumptions and a resistance to the pressure on the rights. It was, after all, the community and the work of the ordinary miners which was under threat. The miners did indeed resist; all through the century there were movements of opposition to attempts to alter the arrangements concerning the land, the animals and the coal. That opposition, moreover, was successful at a number of points in frustrating the Crown. There were, however, important differences among the miners and important changes in their attitudes and purposes over the century.

Up to about 1838, a case may be made that many of the free miners understood the likely consequences of change and were 'backward looking' in wanting to preserve and revive the old days. Those men wanted to re-establish the Mine Law Court and drive away the foreigners. There was a sense of the way in which customary rights supported a community defined by birthplace and work. Even in that period, though, there were some free miners who saw only good in change. They acted as compradors to the great houses of the Protheroes and Crawshays. When the native system had broken down sufficiently for the newcomers not to need free-miner partners, some miners still acted as middlemen to the extent that they sold and leased their gales to men with capital. The rights were sold from within as well as purchased from without.

In the second half of the century the element of 'backward-looking' social conservatism had disappeared almost entirely. There was no demand for a Mine Law Court and no suggestion that the foreigners should go away. What mattered was the possibility of cash benefit for individuals from the deep gales from an extra few acres of land as from a successful season with the sheep. The miners were more than happy to sell the gales to anyone who wanted to buy them or to have the Forest turned into private property. Notions of the collective ownership of resources in their old form had gone. So had the principle of co-operative work. In the new order, work centred on the small working master and entrepreneur, the little butty. For him competition, the employment of other men and the ethics of individual work and reward, were part of the daily routine. His job gave him some of the attributes of the coal master with whom he made his contract bargain. There was not much room in the hard and selfish world of the little butty for sentimental collectivism.

But though private property and individualism had the upper hand and though the free miners had come to see the vestiges of their old rights as the source of cash benefits to a chosen few, there was not a clear consensus between the coal-owners and the Crown, on the one hand, and the miners on the other. There were tensions in the new order, which informed the miners' opposition to the Crown and gave it a meaning different from that of the movements of the 1830s and 1840s. The earlier quarrel was about which *principles* should govern the ownership and exchange of properties. The later was about the *distribution* of property and profits, given an accepted principle. Living within a set of social and economic arrangements vastly different from those their grandfathers had known, the miners were at once sensible of the possibilities of individual opportunity and aware that they might be stripped of everything but their function as the producers of wealth for other men.

In the work place there was the opportunity of reward for skill and effort. There was also the reality of false weights, unfair deductions and unjust manipulations of the contract hewing rate in relation to the market price for coal. That denial helped sustain the urge to union and to the separate representation of working men in Parliament: not in order to change the system, just to make it honour its promise.

The same sense of frustrated expectation was there in the opposition to the Crown. The land, the deep gales and the animals promised property and profit to the miners. But there were difficulties here too. The miners wanted an amicable arrangement in which they, and only a limited group of them at that, would have first pick of the land at a set price. The Crown and the coal-owners wanted a public auction with no restriction on who might bid or how much might be bid. How could the miners hope to compete in that sort of open market? That sort of scheme could only be designed to make the rich a bit richer. So too with the gales. Some adjustment of the conditions of galing might well be necessary for the working of the deep coal but if that adjustment gave a new value to the deep gales, why should the miners not have their share of it? And though it was true that no coal-owner stood to gain anything in particular from the abolition of commoning there was none the less the feeling that the poor, or the relatively poor, were to be robbed. That gave a force to talk about working-mens' representation and about the inequalities of British society which might not otherwise have been made. If the land, the coal and the pasture of the Forest were to yield anything to the working men, the masters must not have control of affairs. In this the survival of notions of customary right has a radicalising influence which went beyond the tea-meeting temporising of the buttyman's union.

Notes

Abbreviations

AAM	Amalgamated Association of Miners
Crest	Crown Estate Commissioners
DFC	Dean Forest Commission
GRO	Gloucestershire County Record Office
LRC (1788)	Report of the Select Committee on Dean Forest, 1788
LRRO	Land Revenue and Record Office
MNA	Miners' National Association
PRO	Public Record Office
SC (1874)	Report of the Select Committee on Dean Forest, 1874
SCW (1849)	Report of the Select Committee on Woods and Forests, 1849

Introduction

1. J. Stephens, *Commentaries on the Laws of England* (1874), vol. I p. 648.
2. For a modern summary of the law of custom see J. W. Wellwood, 'Custom and Usage' in *Halsbury's Laws of England*, 4th edn (Butterworths, London, 1975), vol. 12. Other useful summary material may be found in Stephens' *Commentaries*, Ch. XXIII; G. T. Sadler, *The Relation of Custom to Law* (1919), pp. 59—72; W. B. and W. B. Odgers, *The Common Law of England* (1911), vol. I, Chs. 10, 13; and Co. Litt., L.Z.C.10.S.170.
3. G. Rude, *The Crowd in History* (Wiley, New York, 1964), p. 224.
4. E. P. Thompson, 'The Moral Economy of the English Crowd in the Eighteenth Century', *Past and Present*, no. 50 (1971); see also his 'English Trade Unionism and Other Labour Movements before 1790', Society for the Study of Labour History, *Bulletin* (Autumn, 1968).
5. D. Jones, *Before Rebecca* (Allen Lane, London, 1973), p. 198.
6. See for example, R. G. Galloway, *Annals of Coal Mining and the Coal Trade* (David and Charles, Newton Abbot, reprint, 1971), vol. 2, pp. 146—8.
7. The question of skill and the collier is discussed in R. Harrison (ed.), *The Independent Collier* (Harvester Press, Hassocks, 1978). Harrison raises in his introduction the question of the butty system.
8. E. J. Hobsbawm, *Labouring Men*, 3rd edn (Weidenfeld and Nicolson, London, 1968).
9. E. P. Thompson, 'The Grid of Inheritance: a Comment' in J. Goody, J. Thirsk and E. P. Thompson, *Family and Inheritance* (Cambridge University Press, Cambridge, 1976), p. 348.

Chapter 1

1. This account is based on the *Third Report of the Commissioners appointed to enquire into the State and Condition of the Woods, Forests, and Land Revenues of the Crown, and to sell or alienate Fee Farm and other Unimproveable Rents* (1788) (hereafter *LRC* (1788), pp. 26—7.
2. *LRC* (1788), p. 20. The Act was 20 Chas 11 c.3.
3. *LRC* (1788), pp. 21—2. The Act was 1 Anne c.5.

4. *LRC* (1788), p. 562.

5. Commissioners of Woods to Treasury, 29 April 1879, PRO Crest 40/62.

6. Ibid.

7. See C. E. Hart, *The Free Miners of the Forest of Dean* (London, 1953), Ch. 11.

8. 'The Laws and Customs of the Miners in the Forest of Dean, In the County of Gloucester' in *The Compleat Miner* (issued by W. Cooper 'at the Pellican in Little Britain', 1688). A copy is held in the Gloucestershire Collection of the Gloucester Public Library (G.C.16,655) with an earlier manuscript copy of the Laws and Customs. C. E. Hart has it reprinted in its entirety in his *Free Miners*, and annotated, a 1673 transcript of the Laws. Clause numbers given here correspond to Hart's paragraph numbers. Further references will be to L. and C., followed by the relevant clause number.

9. Hart, *Free Miners*, p. 96.

10. H. G. Nicholls, *Iron Making in the Olden Times* (new edn, David and Charles, Newton Abbot, 1966; 1st edn, 1866); and see Hart, *Free Miners*, p. 96.

11. L. and C., 12.

12. L. and C., 30.

13. See the surviving records of the 'orders', or decisions and regulations, of the Court, which are among the Deputy Surveyor's Office, Records, PRO F.16/1. See also Hart, *Free Miners*, in which he reprints the records. References which follow will cite the order number and its date. Order no. 16, 2 March 1741.

14. Order no. 3, 9 March 1675 and no. 16, 2 March 1741.

15. M. Dobb, *Studies in the Development of Capitalism*, rev. edn (Routledge and Kegan Paul, London, 1949), p. 244.

16. The Fourth Report of the Dean Forest Commissioners (1835), Appendix no. 1, pp. 17, 32—3, 44, 57. On the Commission see pp. 29-30. Further references to this Commission will be to *DFC* followed by a report number.

17. Ibid., pp. 32—3.

18. Ibid., p. 7.

19. Ibid., p. 33.

20. Ibid., p. 7.

21. F. M. Trotter, *Geology of the Forest of Dean Coal and Iron-ore Field* (Memoirs of the Geological Survey of Great Britain, England and Wales, London, 1942) Chs. V and VII.

22. H. G. Nicholls, *The Forest of Dean* (new edn David and Charles, Newton Abbot, 1966; 1st edn 1858), pp. 238—9.

23. Trotter, *Geology of the Forest of Dean*, p. 21.

24. A. and W. Driver, *Particulars of a Survey of the Forest of Dean in the County of Gloucester* (1787), PRO F.16/31.

25. *DFC*, 4, p. 8.

26. *LRC* (1788), Appendix no. 25.

27. Nicholls, *The Forest of Dean*, pp. 84—6.

28. Mining Claims and Disputes; details of encroachments, depredations and abuses in the Forest. Representation to the Treasury, from the Office of Woods (hereafter, *Mining Claims and Disputes*), Appendix 5, PRO F.20/2; *LRC* (1788), Appendix 39.

29. Ibid., pp. 22—3.

30. Ibid., Appendix no. 37.

31. *Mining Claims and Disputes*, p. 1.

32. Ibid., p. 64.

33. *Gloucester Journal*, 22 July 1735.

34. *LRC* (1788), Appendix 37.

35. *Mining Claims and Disputes*, p. 291.

36. Ibid., p. 319.

Chapter 2

1. T. Sopwith, *The Award of the Dean Forest Mining Commissioners as to the Coal and Iron Mines in Her Majesty's Forest of Dean: and the Rules and Regulations for working the same: with Preliminary Observations* (1841) (hereafter *Award*, 1841), pp. 21—2.
2. Ibid., Third Schedule.
3. *DFC*, 4, p. 25.
4. Ibid., p. 22.
5. Ibid., p. 23; and H. W. Paar, *The Great Western Railway in Dean*, 2nd edn (David and Charles, Newton Abbot, 1971), Ch. 2.
6. C. E. Hart, *The Industrial History of Dean* (David and Charles, Newton Abbot, 1971) Ch. 3; Nicholls, *The Forest of Dean*, Chs. XII, XIV and XV.
7. *Award*, 1841.
8. *DFC*, 4, p. 10.
9. Ibid., p. 8.
10. *DFC*, 2, Appendix 3.
11. *Reports of the Commissioners appointed to enquire into the state and condition of the Woods, Forests and Land Revenues of the Crown*, I—XVII (1787—93).
12. *Report of the Commissioners appointed to examine, take and state the Public Accounts of the Kingdom*, XI (1783), printed in part in H. Roseveare, *The Treasury, 1660—1780* (Allen Lane, London, 1969), pp. 149—50.
13. *LRC* (1788), p. 560.
14. Ibid., pp. 40—8.
15. Ibid., p. 6.
16. Ibid., p. 48.
17. *Thirtieth Report of the Commissioners of Woods* (1852), p. 223.
18. Surveyor General to Treasury, 15 January 1804, PRO Crest 8/1.
19. Ibid., 7 April 1803; and Report on Salaries in the Office of Woods, PRO Crest 8/2.
20. 48 Geo. III c. 72.
21. *Third Report of the Commissioners of Woods, Forests and Land Revenues* (1819), p. 20.
22. *Report from the Commissioners of Woods, Forests and Land Revenues to the Lords of the Treasury, recommending measures for ascertaining the Boundaries of Dean Forest, and for inquiring into the Rights or Claims of persons calling themselves Free Miners* (hereafter *Boundaries Report* (1829)) (PP, XXIX, 1830).
23. The Act 50 Geo. III c. 65 of 1810 vested the functions of the Surveyor General of Land Revenues and of the Surveyor General of Woods and Forests in the Commissioners.
24. This account of Teague's tramway is based on the Appendices to *Mining Claims and Disputes*.
25. Ibid., Appendix I, Verderers to Surveyor General, November 1801.
26. Ibid., Acting Deputy Surveyor to Verderers, 1800.
27. Ibid., Verderers to Surveyor General, November 1801.
28. Ibid., Appendix II, Attorney General to Surveyor General, November 1803.
29. Ibid.
30. *Gloucester Journal*, 17 November 1800.
31. *Mining Claims and Disputes*, Appendix II, Acting Deputy Surveyor to Surveyor General, April 1802.
32. Ibid., Acting Deputy Surveyor to Verderers, 1800.
33. Ibid.
34. Ibid., Surveyor General to Treasury, 18 January 1804.
35. Surveyor General to Treasury, 15 July 1807, PRO Crest 8/3; and 5 March 1809, PRO Crest 8/4.

36. Surveyor General to Treasury, 20 March 1807, PRO Crest 8/3.
37. Surveyor General to Treasury, 5 March 1809, PRO Crest 8/4.
38. Ibid.
39. Ibid.
40. *DFC*, 4, p. 52.
41. Ibid., p. 23.
42. *LRC* (1788), pp. 1—34.
43. *DFC*, 4, p. 26.
44. *Award*, 1841, pp. 21—2.
45. Treasury to Commissioners of Woods, 15 December 1828, PRO Crest 8/16.
46. *Boundaries Report* (1829), p. 3.
47. Ibid.
48. *Returns respecting the Mines in Dean Forest* (PP, XV, 1818), p. 99.
49. *A Bill for Ascertaining the Boundaries of the Forest of Dean, and for inquiring into the Rights and Privileges claimed by the Free Miners of the Hundred of St. Briavels and for other purposes* (PP, II, 1830).
50. *DFC*, 1—5 (PP, XXXVI, 1835).
51. 1 and 2 Vict. c. 43.
52. *DFC*, 4, p. 10.
53. T. Sopwith, *Observations addressed to a Public Meeting of the Free Miners* (1838), p. 30.
54. Ibid., pp. 4—5.
55. Alexander Milne to Edward Protheroe, 9 February 1838, PRO F.3/837.
56. *DFC*, 3, pp. 23—4.
57. 1 and 2 Vict. c. 42.
58. 5 and 6 Vict. c. 83.
59. P. M. Procter, *A brief and authentic statement of the origin of an established Church and National day school in his Majesty's Forest of Dean, Gloucestershire* (1819), p. 28. Gloucester Public Library, Gloucestershire Collection, 3055.
60. Ibid., p. 2.
61. 'The Church in the Royal Forest of Dean', *Churchman's Family Magazine* (August, 1865), p. 137.
62. T. Bright, *Nonconformity in the Forest of Dean* (Coleford, 1953), pp. 4—5.
63. Procter, *A brief and authentic statement*, p. 40.
64. R. Morse, *Lays of the Forest and Other Poems* (Newport, 1836). Gloucester Public Library, Gloucestershire Collection, 3067.
65. 'The petition of the Methodist Society of Colliers in his Majesty's Forest of Dean, to the Methodist Ministers in Conference assembled', *Wesleyan-Methodist Magazine* (XLVII, 1824), quoted in Bright, *Nonconformity in the Forest of Dean*, p. 35.
66. See Nicholls, *The Forest of Dean*, Ch X; G. Hainton, 'The Development of Elementary Education in Gloucestershire, 1698—1846' (Bristol MA, 1953); D. R. A. Williams, 'Elementary Education in the Forest of Dean, 1698—1870' (Bristol MA, 1963).
67. Bright, *Nonconformity in the Forest of Dean*, p. 33.
68. 5 and 6 Vict. c. 65 and c. 48.

Chapter 3

1. *Mining Claims and Disputes*, Appendix I, Surveyor General to Treasury, 18 January 1804.
2. Ibid.
3. *The Third Report of the Commissioners of Woods, Forests and Land Revenues* (1819), p. 20; and the *Fourth Report* (1823), p. 29.

4. *Report from the Select Committee on the Woods, Forests and Land Revenues of the Crown* (PP, 1849, XX) (hereafter *SCW* (1849)), p. 239.

5. Ibid., Appendix 35; and Verderers' Courts, Notes of Proceedings (1846—65), PRO F.16/21.

6. *Miscellaneous Papers*, PRO F.16/53.

7. *SCW* (1849), Appendix 42; and Papers on the Stocking and Control of Deer in Dean, PRO F.16/52.

8. *SCW* (1889), p. 31.

9. *SCW* (1849), p. 182, evidence of the coal-owner Thomas Nicholson.

10. Machen to Commissioners of Woods, 12 May 1848, 27 September 1850, PRO F.16/52.

11. *Boundaries Report* (1829), p. 2.

12. House of Commons, *Journal* (1831, 85), 23 June 1831.

13. *Gloucester Journal*, 25 June 1831.

14. An 'explanation' of the riot, which is discussed below, referred to a 'Fellowship'. *Forester*, 4 August 1831. The reference to a 'Committee' appears at the foot of the manuscript copy of the notice which James posted in the Forest which is among the depositions and evidence for the trial of Warren James. PRO Assizes 6/2.

15. Deputy Surveyor to the Chief Commissioner of Woods, 31 March 1838. PRO F.3/837.

16. *Monmouthshire Merlin*, 11 June 1831.

17. Ibid.

18. Depositions in the Trial of Warren James, PRO Assizes 6/2.

19. Anon., *The Life of Warren James. By a Resident Forester* (Monmouth, 1831), p. 5.

20. Depositions in the trial of Warren James, PRO Assizes 6/2.

21. *The Life of Warren James*, pp. 4—6.

22. *Monmouthshire Merlin*, 11 June 1831.

23. Ibid.

24. Magistrates to Home Office, 11 June 1831, PRO HO 52/12.

25. *Gloucester Journal*, 11 June 1831.

26. *Life of Warren James*, p. 6.

27. Duke of Beaufort to Home Office, 15 June 1831, PRO HO 52/12.

28. No more precise account than this may be offered of the composition of the crowd. The reports of the riot which appeared in newspapers used only such general terms as 'workmen' or 'cottagers'. Newspaper reports of the Quarter Sessions and Assizes trials of some of the rioters did not identify the occupations of those tried. The depositions and other official papers of trials other than those for capital charges or treason have been destroyed. *Monmouthshire Merlin*, 11 June 1831; *Gloucester Journal*, 11 June and 20 August, 1831; Beaufort to Home Office, 15 June 1831, PRO HO 52/12.

29. *Gloucester Journal*, 20 August 1831.

30. Beaufort to Home Office, 15 June 1831, PRO HO 52/12.

31. *Monmouthshire Merlin*, 9 July 1831.

32. *Life of Warren James*, p. 7.

33. *Gloucester Journal*, 11 June 1831.

34. Beaufort to Home Office, 15 June 1831, PRO HO 52/12.

35. *Gloucester Journal*, 11 June 1831.

36. *The Times*, 15 August 1831. Bowdlerisation in original.

37. *Gloucester Journal*, 11 June 1831.

38. Magistrates to Home Office, 11 June 1831, PRO HO 52/12.

39. *Life of Warren James*, p. 7.

40. Ibid., *Monmouthshire Merlin*, 18 June 1831.

41. *Life of Warren James*, p. 8.

42. *Monmouthshire Merlin*, 18 June 1831.

43. Ibid.
44. Ibid.
45. Ibid., 11 June 1831; *Gloucester Journal*, 18 June 1831, 25 June 1831; and see the warrant sworn for James' arrest before the riot began, Depositions in the trial of Warren James, PRO Assizes 6/2.
46. *Monmouthshire Merlin*, 18 June 1831; *The Life of Warren James*, p. 12.
47. *Gloucester Journal*, 13 August 1831.
48. Ibid., 2 July 1831.
49. *Life of Warren James*, pp. 11—12.
50. *The Times*, 15 August 1831.
51. *Life of Warren James*, p. 15.
52. Ibid.
53. See Nicholls, *The Forest of Dean*, Ch. 7; and H. G. Nicholls, *The Personalities of the Forest of Dean* (1863), p. 180.
54. E. J. Hobsbawm, *Industry and Empire*, 3rd edn (Weidenfeld and Nicolson, London, 1969), p. 130.
55. E. P. Thompson, *The Making of the English Working Class*, rev. edn (Penguin, Harmondsworth, 1968), p. 81.
56. Duke of Beaufort to Home Office, 15 June 1831, PRO HO 52/12.
57. *Gloucester Journal*, 11 June 1831.
58. *Resolutions of a meeting of the Free Miners and Colliers of the Forest of Dean*, 5 March 1832.
59. *Monmouthshire Merlin*, 1 January 1831.
60. *Forester*, 2 June 1831.
61. Ibid., 26 May 1831.
62. Ibid., 2 June 1831.
63. Ibid., 26 June 1831.
64. Ibid.
65. Ibid.
66. Ibid.
67. Ibid.
68. Ibid., 2 June 1831.
69. The last returns from the election were in by 1 June. M. Brock, *The Great Reform Act* (Hutchinson, London, 1973), Ch. 6.
70. *Forester*, 9 June 1831.
71. Duke of Beaufort to Home Office, 15 June 1831, PRO HO 52/12.
72. *Gloucester Journal*, 11 June 1831.
73. Ibid.
74. Nicholls, *The Forest of Dean*, p. 110.
75. Duke of Beaufort to Home Office, 15 June 1831, PRO HO 52/12.
76. Register of Cases and Law Officers' Opinions (1828—43), Commissioners' Case on the Memorial of the Free Miners, 1829, p. 2.
77. *Boundaries Report* (1829), p. 2.
78. *Gloucester Journal*, 20 August 1831.
79. *The Life of Warren James*, p. 8.
80. Paar, *The Great Western Railway in Dean*, Ch. 10; and Gloucester Record Office Q/Rum 124—5.
81. *Award* (1841).
82. *Forester*, 4 August 1831.
83. *DFC*, 4, p. 24.
84. *Forester*, 4 August 1831.
85. *DFC*, 4, p. 9.
86. Ibid., p. 7.
87. Ibid., p. 19.
88. *Forester*, 4 August 1831.

89. *DFC*, 4, p. 20.
90. *Memorial of the Free Miners and Quarrymen, praying that their Rights and Privileges be not abolished, as recommended by the Dean Forest Commissioners* (PP, 1836, X/vii), p. 78.
91. Ibid., p. 79.
92. *Monmouthshire Merlin*, 19 November 1836.
93. Ibid., 17 June 1837.
94. *SCW* (1849), p. 135; *Monmouthshire Merlin*, 1 July 1837.
95. *Gloucester Journal*, 17 June 1837.
96. *Monmouthshire Merlin*, 19 May 1838.
97. Ibid.
98. The Hon. Augustus Henry Moreton and the Hon. G. C. Berkekey. They took 2,996 and 3,153 votes respectively, against 2,962 for Lord Edward Somerset. *Gloucester Journal*, 29 December 1832. In 1831, assured of failure, Somerset had withdrawn on the eve of the poll. *Monmouthshire Merlin*, 14 May 1831.
99. Ibid., 17 January 1835.
100. Ibid., 14 May 1831.
101. Ibid.
102. Ibid., 20 June 1832.
103. Ibid., 21 July 1832, 28 July 1832, 4 August 1832.
104. *Gloucester Journal*, 1 December 1832.
105. *Monmouthshire Merlin*, 17 October 1835.
106. Chief Constable to Home Office, 26 August 1842, PRO HO 45/248.
107. Newnham Magistrates to Home Office, 3 September 1842, PRO HO 45/248.
108. Superintendent of Police to Home Office, 25 August 1842, PRO HO 45/248.
109. Newnham Magistrates to Home Office, 3 September 1842, PRO HO 45/248.
110. Ibid.

Chapter 4

1. *Monmouthshire Merlin*, 8 December 1834.
2. 'The Church in the Royal Forest of Dean', *Churchman's Family Magazine* (August 1865), p. 141.
3. See A. Campbell, 'Honourable Men and Degraded Slaves' (Warwick PhD, 1977).
4. *Forester*, 7 July, 8 and 15 September 1871.
5. Dean Forest, Coal and Iron Mine Rentals, PRO LRRO 12/113, 114; Register of Free Miners, PRO LRRO 5/8.
6. R. Meade, 'The Iron Industries of Gloucestershire, Forest of Dean', *Mining Journal*, 18 March, 1 April, 1876.
7. R. Hunt, *Mineral Statistics of the United Kingdom* (Geological Survey, 1867, 1868, 1870).
8. Meade, 'The Iron Industries of Gloucestershire'.
9. *Report of the Dean Forest Mining Commissioners*, 1871 (hereafter *DFC* 1871), PRO F.26/19, p. 20.
10. Ibid., p. 55.
11. *Forester*, 20 September 1884.
12. *Dean Forest Mercury*, 1 December 1882.
13. Ibid.
14. It is no novelty now to argue that the miners' job required the exercise of skill. See C. Fisher and J. Hagan, 'Piecework and some of its Consequences in the Australian Printing and Coal Mining Industries, 1850—1930', *Labour History*, 25 (1973); F. Reid and A. Campbell, 'The Independent Collier in Scotland' in Harrison (ed.), *The Independent Collier*; and the introduction to Campbell, 'Honourable Men and

Degraded Slaves'. The account given here of the coal seams and the miner's work in the Forest of Dean is based on H. R. Insole and C. Z. Bunning, 'The Forest of Dean Coalfield', British Society of Mining Students, *Journal*, V, VI (1881); J. S. Joynes, 'Description of seams and some of the methods of working coal in the Forest of Dean', ibid., XI (1889); and the trade reports from the Forest which appeared in the *Colliery Guardian*, 1860—90.

15. T. Mountjoy, *Sixty-two years in the Life of a Forest of Dean Collier* (London, 1887), pp. 41—2.

16. *Report* of the Mines Inspector, South Western District, 1883 (PP XIX, 1884), p. 273.

17. *Forest of Dean Examiner*, 22 May 1874.

18. Ibid., 2 January 1874.

19. Insole and Bunning, 'The Forest of Dean Coalfield', p. 78.

20. *Forest of Dean Examiner*, 27 September 1873.

21. *Forester*, 6 October 1871.

22. *Forest of Dean Examiner*, 14 November 1873.

23. Ibid., 18 November 1873.

24. *Colliery Guardian*, 31 July 1885.

25. See for example, ibid., 3 August and 7 September 1867.

26. *Forest of Dean Examiner*, 25 October 1873.

27. Ibid.

Chapter 5

1. *Miner and Workman's Advocate*, 25 June 1864.

2. Ibid., 9 July 1864.

3. *Forester*, 30 December 1870.

4. Ibid., 4 November 1871.

5. Ibid., 7 July, 8 and 15 September 1871.

6. Ibid., 15 September 1871.

7. Ibid., 22 September 1871.

8. Ibid., 24 November 1871.

9. Ibid., 8 December 1871.

10. *Forest of Dean Examiner*, 2 August 1873. The lodges were at Cinderford, Ruspidge, the Tump, Cinderford Bridge, Little Dean, Ruardean Woodside, Ruardean, Point Inn, Drybrook, Lyndbrook, Blakeney, Broadwell Lane End, Coalway Lane End, Coleford, Whitecroft, Bream, Yorkeley, Berry Hill.

11. *Potteries Examiner*, 11 April 1874.

12. This account of the organisation of the union and the work of the miners' agent is based on the detailed reports of the monthly delegate meetings in Dean which appeared in the miners' 'official organ', the *Forest of Dean Examiner*, in 1873, 1874 and 1875.

13. *Forest of Dean Examiner*, 2 and 9 August 1873, 3 July 1874, 12 February 1875.

14. *Forester*, 6 October 1871.

15. Ibid.

16. Ibid., 8 September 1871.

17. *Forest of Dean Examiner*, 2 August, 19 December 1873, 20 January, 31 July 1874, 30 July 1875.

18. Ibid., 30 August 1873, 19 December 1873, 23 January 1874.

19. *Forester*, 6 October 1871.

20. *Forest of Dean Examiner*, 31 July 1874.

21. On the syndicate see Chris Fisher and John Smethurst, 'War on the Law of Supply and Demand: the Amalgamated Association of Miners and the Forest of Dean Colliers, 1869—1875' in Harrison (ed.), *The Independent Collier*.

22. *Potteries Examiner*, 8 November 1873.
23. *Forest of Dean Examiner*, 2 August 1873.
24. Ibid., 1 April 1875.
25. Ibid., 22 September 1871.
26. Ibid., 13 October 1871.
27. See for example, 'Fallacies of the Strike', ibid., 3 November 1871.
28. Ibid., 20 October 1871.
29. Ibid., 27 December 1871.
30. Ibid., 6 October 1871.
31. *Forest of Dean Examiner*, 2 August 1873.
32. Ibid., 28 November 1873.
33. *Forester*, 24 November 1871.
34. Ibid., 23 September 1870.
35. *Forest of Dean Examiner*, 7 November 1873.
36. Ibid., 21 November 1873.
37. Ibid., 5 December 1873.
38. Colonel Kingscote, elections, Gloucester Record Office, D471/X9.
39. *Forest of Dean Examiner*, 5 December 1873.
40. See R. Harrison, *Before the Socialists* (Routledge and Kegan Paul, London, 1965), p. 293.
41. *Forest of Dean Examiner*, 6 February 1874.
42. Ibid.
43. Ibid., 6 March 1874; *Forester*, 13 February 1874.
44. Mountjoy, *Life of a Forest of Dean Collier*, p. 1.
45. Ibid.
46. Ibid., p. 12.
47. Ibid., p. 17.
48. Ibid., p. 12.
49. Ibid., pp. 38—9.
50. *Forest of Dean Examiner*, 30 August 1873.
51. Ibid., 3 July 1874.
52. Ibid., 20 September 1873.
53. Ibid., 27 September 1873.
54. Ibid., 30 August 1873.
55. Ibid., 19 June 1874.
56. Ibid., 27 February 1874.
57. Ibid., 30 August 1873.
58. Ibid., 2 August 1873.
59. Ibid., 27 September 1873.
60. Ibid., 6 November 1874.
61. *Forester*, 20 September 1870, 22 September 1871.
62. *Forest of Dean Examiner*, 30 August 1873.
63. Ibid., 14 November 1873.
64. Ibid., 18 November 1873.
65. *Forester*, 16 May 1878.
66. *Forest of Dean Examiner*, 21 August 1874.
67. Ibid., 11 December 1874.
68. Ibid., 13 November 1874.
69. Ibid., 30 July 1875.
70. J. H. Porter, 'Wage Determination by Selling Price Sliding Scales, 1870—1914', *Manchester School of Economic and Social Studies*, XXIX (1971).
71. *Dean Forest Mercury*, 15 December 1882.
72. Ibid., 25 August 1882.
73. Ibid., 8 December 1882.
74. *Bainsley Chronicle*, 5 March 1881. On Rymer see Chris Fisher and Pat Spaven,

'Edward Rymer and the Moral Workman' in Harrison (ed.), *The Independent Collier.*
75. *Dean Forest Mercury*, 1 December 1882.
76. *Forester*, 28 October 1882.
77. *Dean Forest Mercury*, 15 December 1882, 14 November 1884.
78. Ibid., 8 and 15 December 1882.
79. Ibid., 15 June 1883.
80. *Miner's Advocate and Record*, 18 October 1873.
81. Ibid., 26 July 1873.
82. Ibid., 26 September 1874.
83. *Dean Forest Mercury*, 16 March 1883.
84. *Forester*, 21 October, 2 December 1882.
85. R. Hunt, *Mineral Statistics of the United Kingdom, 1874* (Geological Survey, 1875).
86. *Dean Forest Mercury*, 16 February 1883.
87. Ibid., 22 December 1882.
88. Ibid., 2 March 1883.
89. Ibid., 16 March 1883.
90. Ibid., 6 April 1883.
91. Ibid., 6 and 20 April, 11 and 18 May, 13 July 1883.
92. Ibid., 25 September 1885, 14 May 1886.
93. Ibid., 15 June 1883.
94. Ibid., 30 November 1883.
95. Ibid., 11 December 1885.
96. Ibid., 8 January, 28 May, 18 June 1886.
97. Ibid., 16 July 1886.
98. Ibid., 25 May 1883.
99. Ibid., 24 December 1886.

Chapter 6

1. *SC*, 1874, pp. 177—8.
2. Ibid., p. 173.
3. Ibid., p. 176.
4. *Forester*, 4 March, 8 April, 10 June 1870.
5. Ibid., 8 April, 20—7 May, 10 June 1870.
6. Ibid., 4 March 1870.
7. *SC*, 1874, q. 2,413.
8. *Forester*, 20 May 1870.
9. Ibid., 27 May 1870.
10. Ibid., 13 May 1870.
11. Mountjoy, *Life of a Forest of Dean Collier*, pp. 10—11.
12. *Forester*, 20 May 1870.
13. Ibid., 15 July 1870.
14. Ibid., 23 September 1870.
15. Ibid., 27 September 1872.
16. Ibid., 18 July 1873.
17. Ibid., 28 November 1873.
18. *Forest of Dean Examiner*, 6 February 1874.
19. *Forester*, 7 July 1871.
20. Ibid., 6 February 1874.
21. Ibid., 13 February 1874.
22. Ibid.
23. Memorandum left at the Treasury in March 1874 by Colonel Kingscote MP, PRO F.16/48; *Forester*, 17 April 1874.

24. *Forester*, 24 April 1874.
25. *Forest of Dean Examiner*, 22 May 1874.
26. Ibid.
27. *SC*, 1874, q. 2,248.
28. Ibid., q. 2,316.
29. Ibid., qq. 3,062—3, 3,094, 3,139, 3,615—16.
30. Ibid., qq. 3,199—201, 3,263—316, 3,618—26, 3,709—11, 3,739, 3,760—2, 3,789—873.
31. Ibid., pp. 9—10.
32. Ibid., p. iv.
33. Ibid., q. 2,338.
34. Ibid., qq. 2,384—8.
35. Ibid., qq. 2,635—43.
36. Ibid., pp. v—vi.
37. *Forest of Dean Examiner*, 4 September 1874.
38. Ibid., 5 March 1875.
39. *Forester*, 1 April 1875.
40. *Forest of Dean Examiner*, 19 March 1875.
41. *Forester*, 10 December 1874.
42. Ibid. Other letters appear at 17 and 24 December 1874 and 14 January and 18 February 1875.
43. Ibid., 18 February 1875.
44. *Forest of Dean Examiner*, 9 April, 23 April and 7 May 1875.
45. Ibid., 21 May 1875.
46. Ibid., 4 June 1875.
47. Ibid., 30 July 1875.
48. *Forester*, 11 March 1875.
49. Ibid., 22 April 1875.
50. Ibid., 13 May 1875.
51. G. Shaw Lefevre, *English Commons and Forests* (London, 1894), pp. 262—3.

Chapter 7

1. Registers of Free Miners, PRO LRRO 5/8.
2. *Return showing the number of Free Miners in the Forest of Dean* (PP, 1875, LX), p. 639.
3. Grants of Gales, PRO LRRO 5/8.
4. *SC*, 1874, q. 2,726.
5. *Award*, 1841, p. 168.
6. Ibid., p. 171.
7. *DFC*, 1971, p. 33.
8. Ibid., p. 39.
9. Ibid., p. 40.
10. Dean Forest (Mines) Act, 34 and 35 Vict. c. 85, s. 19.
11. *DFC*, 1871, p. 17.
12. *Award of Forest of Dean Mining Commissioners of 1871*, PRO F.26/21, pp. 1—3.
13. *DFC*, 1871, pp. 28—9.
14. T. Forster Brown, Memorandum upon the Commissioners' Minute of the 30th of October 1872, PRO F.3/884.
15. Deputy Gaveller to Commissioners of Woods, 16 November 1882, PRO F.3/311.
16. *Colliery Guardian*, 2 February, 3 March, 6 June 1867.
17. Ibid., 2 February 1867.

18. Ibid., 21 September 1867.
19. Ibid., 9 May 1868, 18 July 1868, 24 December 1869.
20. *SC*, 1871, p. 29.
21. T. Forster Brown, Memorandum upon the Commissioners' Minute of the 30th of October 1872, PRO, F.3/884.
22. Ibid.
23. *Forester*, 21 February, 5 September 1878.
24. Ibid., 26 August 1880.
25. A. Thomas and E. Crawshay to the Commissioners of Woods and Forests, 6 November 1882, PRO, F.3/311.
26. T. Forster Brown to the Commissioners of Woods, 16 November 1882, PRO, F.3/311.
27. Commissioners of Woods to Treasury, 19 April 1883, 22 October 1883; Treasury to Commissioners of Woods, 26 April 1883, 27 October 1883, PRO, F.20/79; Memoranda on the Deep Gales, PRO, F.3/311.
28. A. Thomas and E. Crawshay to Commissioners of Woods, 29 March 1883, PRO, F.3/311.
29. *Dean Forest Mercury*, 7 September 1883.
30. Ibid., 5 October, 26 October, 30 November 1883.
31. Ibid., 16 November 1883.
32. Ibid., 14 November 1883.
33. Ibid., 18 April 1884; and T. Forster Brown to Commissioners of Woods, 23 June 1884, PRO, F.3/313.
34. T. Forster Brown to Commissioners of Woods, 8 April 1884, PRO, F.3/312.
35. W. B. Brain to T. Forster Brown, 13 May 1884, PRO, F.3/313.
36. List of Owners of Deep Gales, PRO, F.3/311.
37. *Dean Forest Mercury*, 18 April 1884.
38. Commissioners of Woods to Treasury, 26 April 1884, PRO, F.20/79.
39. *Dean Forest Mercury*, 2 May 1884.
40. Ibid.
41. Ibid., 23 May 1884.
42. Ibid., 20 June 1884.
43. Ibid., 11 July 1884.
44. Petitions in Favour of and Opposed to the Dean Forest Bill, PRO, F.3/313.
45. *Miners' Advocate and Record*, 14 March 1873.
46. Ibid., 18 April 1874.
47. Ibid., 10 October 1874.
48. Ibid., 25 October 1873.
49. Ibid., 10 May 1873.
50. *Dean Forest Mercury*, 27 April 1883.
51. Ibid., 16 February 1883, 20 July 1883.
52. Ibid., 28 February 1884.
53. Ibid., 9 and 23 January 1885. Blake had begun as a clerk in the Post Office, later becoming a public accountant and real estate and insurance agent. In 1875 he had won the seat of Leominster, which the Conservatives had held for 50 years, as an advanced Liberal and nonconformist candidate.
54. Ibid., 16 January 1885.
55. Ibid.
56. Ibid., 24 April 1885.
57. Ibid., 21 September 1883.
58. Ibid.
59. Ibid., 28 September 1883.
60. Ibid., 2 January 1885.
61. Ibid., 2 May and 9 May 1884.
62. Ibid., 13 June 1884.

63. Ibid., 3 September to 1 October 1886.
64. Ibid., 3 September 1886.
65. Ibid., 24 September 1886.
66. Ibid., 10 September 1886.
67. Ibid., 2 January 1885.
68. S. J. Elsom, *The Dean Forest Freeminers' Rights* (Coleford, 1885).
69. *Dean Forest Mercury*, 22 May 1885.
70. Ibid., 23 May 1884.
71. Ibid., 11 June 1884, 25 June 1884.
72. Ibid., 26 December 1884.
73. Ibid.
74. See United Deep Gales, PRO, F.3/320—4.
75. *Report of the Select Committee on Dean Forest Bill and Minutes of Evidence* (PP, vi, 1904), pp. 7—8.

Chapter 8

1. Deputy Surveyor to Commissioners of Woods, 13 July 1854, PRO, F.3/735; The fence month lasted from 20 June to 20 July and the winter heyning from 22 November to 4 May each year.
2. *Dean Forest Mercury*, 25 November 1898.
3. Deputy Surveyor to Commissioners of Woods, 7 June 1898, PRO, F.3/264.
4. *SC*, 1874, qq. 2,454—67.
5. *Forester*, 5 April 1877.
6. Vicar of English Bicknor to Commissioners of Woods, 4 December 1865, PRO, F.3/735.
7. Deputy Surveyor to Commissioners of Woods, 27 March 1856, PRO, F.3/263.
8. Steward of the Verderers' Court to Solicitor to Commissioners of Woods, 19 April 1856, PRO, F.3/263.
9. Ibid., 9 April 1856.
10. Deputy Surveyor to Commissioners of Woods, 27 March 1856, PRO, F.3/263.
11. Ibid., 3 May 1856.
12. Ibid.
13. Ibid.
14. Solicitor to Commissioners of Woods, 1 May 1856, PRO, F.3/263.
15. Deputy Surveyor to Commissioners of Woods, 17 March 1859, PRO, F.3/263.
16. Ibid.
17. Ibid.
18. Ibid.
19. Ibid.
20. Solicitor to Commissioners of Woods, 18 January 1860, PRO, F.3/263.
21. Deputy Surveyor to Commissioners of Woods, 28 July 1864, PRO, F.3/735.
22. Solicitor to Commissioners of Woods, 6 September 1864, PRO, F.3/735.
23. Deputy Surveyor to Commissioners of Woods, 28 July 1864, PRO, F.3/735.
24. Statement of Keepers as to cases of pound rescue, 9 August 1864, PRO, F.3/735.
25. Ibid.
26. Solicitor to Commissioners of Woods, 2 November 1865, PRO, F.3/735.
27. Ibid; Dean Forest Drifts, 6 December 1898, PRO, F.3/735.
28. Ibid; Solicitor to Commissioners of Woods, 2 November 1865, PRO, F.3/735.

29. Deputy Surveyor to Commissioners of Woods, 8 December 1865, PRO, F.3/735.
30. Ibid.
31. Ibid.
32. Ibid.
33. Vicar of English Bicknor to Commissioners of Woods, 4 December 1865, PRO, F.3/735.
34. Ibid.
35. Vicar of Christchurch to Commissioners of Woods, 9 December 1865, PRO, F.3/735.
36. Ibid.
37. Alfred Goold to Commissioners of Woods, 12 December 1865, PRO, F.3/735.
38. *Forester*, 23 December 1870.
39. Deputy Surveyor to Commissioners of Woods, 8 December 1865, PRO, F.3/735.
40. Ibid.
41. Ibid; and note of John Gardiner dated 12 December 1865 on the letter of the Vicar of Christchurch to the Commissioners of Woods, 9 December 1865, PRO, F.3/735.
42. Solicitor to Commissioners of Woods, 2 November 1865, PRO, F.3/735.
43. *SC*, 1874, pp. iv—v.
44. Ibid., p. 9, q. 19.
45. Ibid., qq. 9—13.
46. Ibid., p. iv.
47. Ibid., q. 810.
48. Ibid., qq. 1,986—9, 901—2, 936, 1,035—43, 3,256—9.
49. Ibid., qq. 1,986—9.
50. Ibid., qq. 3,776—9.
51. Ibid., q. 3,898.
52. *Forester*, 3 September 1874.
53. Ibid.
54. Ibid., 22 May 1874.
55. Ibid., 29 May 1874.
56. Ibid., 4 March 1875.
57. Ibid. and 8 March 1875 to 6 May 1875.
58. Ibid., 4 March 1875.
59. Ibid., 5 May 1875.
60. *SC*, 1874, qq. 2,819—21.
61. Deputy Surveyor to Commissioners of Woods, 17 March 1859, PRO, F.3/263.
62. Solicitor to Commissioners of Woods, 18 January 1860, PRO, F.3/263.
63. *Dean Forest Mercury*, 14 September 1883.
64. Ibid., 2 January 1885.
65. Ibid., 23 May 1884.
66. Deputy Surveyor to Commissioners of Woods, 19 July 1884, PRO, F.3/313.
67. *Dean Forest Guardian*, 11 May 1894.
68. *Dean Forest Mercury*, 9 February 1894.
69. Deputy Surveyor to Commissioners of Woods, 19 May 1894, PRO, F.3/263.
70. Ibid.
71. A. D. Pringle to Commissioners of Woods, 30 April 1895, PRO, F.3/558.
72. Deputy Surveyor to Commissioners of Woods, 15 May 1895, PRO, F.3/558.
73. Ibid.
74. Chief Constable to Commissioners of Woods, 5 May 1895, PRO, F.3/558.
75. *Dean Forest Mercury*, 17 May 1895.

76. Ibid., 3 May 1895.
77. Deputy Surveyor to Commissioners of Woods, 15 May 1895, PRO, F.3/558.
78. Deputy Surveyor to Commissioners of Woods, 10 November 1895, PRO, F.3/558.
79. Deputy Surveyor to Commissioners of Woods, 4 October 1897, PRO, F.3/558.
80. Ibid.
81. Deputy Surveyor to Commissioners of Woods, 27 November, 4 December, 15 December 1897, PRO, F.3/558.
82. *Dean Forest Guardian*, 18 February 1898; *Dean Forest Mercury*, 18 February 1898.
83. Deputy Surveyor to Commissioners (n.d., [1898]) PRO, F.3/559.
84. Chief Constable of Gloucestershire to Commissioners of Woods, 26 February 1898, PRO, F.3/559.
85. *Dean Forest Guardian*, 8 April 1898.
86. Deputy Surveyor to Commissioners of Woods, 23 April 1898, PRO, F.3/559.
87. Commissioners of Woods to Solicitors, 25 April 1898, PRO, F.3/264.
88. Memorandum on Depasturing of Sheep in Dean Forest, 8 December 1893, PRO, F.3/263; Memorandum on Drifts of Sheep in Dean Forest (n.d., [1893]), PRO, F.3/735.
89. Memorandum on Depasturing of Sheep in Dean Forest, 8 December 1893, PRO, F.3/263.
90. Memorandum on Drifts of Sheep in Dean Forest (n.d., [1893]), PRO, F.3/735.
91. Memorandum on Depasturing of Sheep in Dean Forest, 8 December 1893, PRO, F.3/263.
92. *Dean Forest Mercury*, 12 January 1894.
93. Ibid., 26 January 1894.
94. Ibid., 3 February 1894.
95. Deputy Surveyor to Commissioners of Woods, 19 May 1894, PRO, F.3/263.
96. Ibid.
97. Deputy Surveyor to Commissioners of Woods, 15 May 1895, PRO, F.3/558.
98. Deputy Surveyor to Commissioners of Woods, 19 May 1894, PRO, F.3/263.
99. Ibid.
100. A. D. Pringle to Commissioners of Woods, 30 April 1895, PRO, F.3/558.
101. Memorial to Commissioners of Woods, 11 June 1895, PRO, F.3/558.
102. R. J. Kerr to Commissioners of Woods, 28 May 1895, PRO, F.3/558.
103. *Dean Forest Mercury*, 17 May 1895.
104. Ibid., 2 May 1895.
105. Ibid., 17 May 1895.
106. Commissioners of Woods to Treasury, 1 March 1898, PRO, F.3/559.
107. Ibid; and *Dean Forest Mercury*, 18 February 1898.
108. Ibid.
109. Ibid; *Dean Forest Guardian*, 18 February 1898; Deputy Surveyor to Commissioners of Woods, 1 March 1898, PRO, F.3/559.
110. Memorandum of E. S. Howard, Commissioner of Woods, 29 June 1898, PRO, F.3/264.

Sources

1. Public Record Office

Crown Estate Commissioners

Crest 2, Land Revenue and Record Office, Unfiled Correspondence and Papers.
Crest 8, Land Revenue and Record Office, Commissioners of Woods, Forests and Land Revenues, Early Treasury Letter Books.
Crest 9, Land Revenue and Record Office, Commissioners of Woods, Forests and Land Revenues, England and County, Letter Books and Treasury Report Books.
Crest 22, Land Revenue and Record Office, Commissioners of Woods, Forests and Land Revenues, Solicitor's Department, Letter Books.
Crest 23, Land Revenue and Record Office, Commissioners of Woods, Forests and Land Revenues, Solicitor's Department, Registers of Cases.
Crest 25, Land Revenue and Record Office, Commissioners of Woods, Forests and Land Revenues, Minute Books.

Forestry Commission

F.3, Director of Forestry for England, Correspondence and Papers, Dean Forest.
F.16, Records of the Deputy Surveyor's Office, Dean Forest.
F.17, Director of Forestry for England, Maps, Plans and Drawings.
F.20, Director of Forestry for England, Miscellaneous Books.
F.26, Miscellaneous Records, Dean Forest, Deputy Gaveller's Office.

Home Office

HO 40, Disturbances, Correspondence and Papers.
HO 41, Disturbances, Entry Books.
HO 43, Domestic Letter Books.
HO 44, Domestic, George IV and later.
HO 52, Counties Correspondence.

Land Revenue and Record Office

LRRO 12, Rentals.

2. Scottish Record Office

RH 4/40, Wemyss Mss.

3. Dissertations

Campbell, A. 'Honourable Men and Degraded Slaves' (Warwick PhD, 1977)
Hainton, G. 'The Development of Elementary Education in Gloucestershire, 1698 — 1846' (Bristol MA, 1953)
Porter, J. H. 'Industrial Conciliation and Arbitration, 1860 — 1914' (Leeds PhD, 1968)
Spaven, P. 'Accommodating the Miners' (Warwick PhD, 1978)
Williams, D. R. A. 'Elementary Education in the Forest of Dean, 1698 — 1870' (Bristol MA, 1963)

4. Parliamentary Papers

(a) Bills
For the Increase and Preservation of Timber in Dean and New Forests (1, 1808).

194

For ascertaining the Boundaries of the Forest of Dean, and for inquiring into the Rights and Privileges claimed by Free Miners of the Hundred of St Briavels, and for other purposes (11, 1830; 1, 1830 — 1; 1, 1831).

For vesting the Office of Constable and Keeper of the Forest of Dean in the Commissioners of Woods and Forests (111, 1836).

To empower the Commissioners of Her Majesty's Woods, etc., to confirm the Titles to, and to grant Leases of Encroachments on the Forest of Dean (111, 1837 — 8).

For regulating the working of Mines and Quarries in the Forest of Dean, and Hundred of St Briavels (111, 1837 — 8).

To divide the Forest of Dean into Ecclesiastical Districts (11, 1842).

To provide for the Relief of the Poor in the Forest of Dean (11, 1842).

To constitute the Extra-parochial Parts of the Forest of Dean and Hundred of St Briavels' into a District for the Relief of the Poor (11, 1844).

To make further provision for the management of Her Majesty's Forest of Dean (11, 1861).

To make further provision respecting the opening and working of mines and quarries in Her Majesty's Forest of Dean (1, 1871).

To ascertain and commute commonable rights in Her Majesty's Forest of Dean, and for other purposes relating thereto, and to mines and quarries in the Hundred of Saint Briavels, in the county of Gloucester (1, 1875).

Bill to facilitate the opening and working of certain of the lower series of coal seams in the Forest of Dean, and in the Hundred of St Briavels in the County of Gloucester (11, 1884).

(b) Royal Commissions and Select Committees

Reports I — XVII of the Commissioners appointed to inquire into the state and conditions of the Woods, Forests and Land Revenues of the Crown (1787 — 93).

Reports I — IV of the Dean Forest Commissioners to the Lords of the Treasury (XXXVI, 1835).

Report from the Select Committee on Woods, Forests and Land Revenues of the Crown (XIV, 1833; XV, 1834).

Reports I — III of the Dean Forest Mining Commissioners (XXIX, 1839; XXVIII, 1840; XII, 1841).

Reports of the Royal Commision on the Employment and condition of children in Mines and Manufactories (XV, XVI, XVII, 1842).

Report of the Royal Commission on the State of the Population in the Mining Districts (XVI, 1844; XXVII, 1845; XXIV, 1846; XVI, 1847; XXVI, 1847 — 8; XXII, 1849; XXIII, 1850; XXIII, 1851; XXI, 1852).

Report from the Select Committee on the Woods, Forests and Land Revenues of the Crown (XXIV, 1847 — 8; XX, 1849).

Report of the Royal Commission on Trade Unions (XXXII, 1867; XXXIX, 1867 — 8; XXI 1868 — 9).

Report of the Commissioners appointed to inquire into the several matters relating to coal in the United Kingdom (XVIII, 1871).

Report of the Royal Commission on the Truck System (XXXVI, 1871; XXXV, 1872).

Report from the Select Committee appointed to inquire into the present dearness and scarcity of coal (X, 1873).

Report from the Select Committee appointed to inquire into the laws and rights affecting Dean Forest (VII, 1874).

Report of the Royal Commission on the Sanitary laws (XXXV, 1871; XXXI, 1874).

Report from the Select Committee on Woods, Forests and Land Revenues of the Crown (XVI, 1889; XVIII, 1890).

(c) Annual Reports

Reports of the Surveyor General of Woods, Forests and Land Revenues (1787 — 1809).

Reports of the Commissioners of Woods, Forests and Land Revenues (1812 — 99).
Reports of the Inspectors of Mines (1854 — 99).
Mineral Statistics of the United Kingdom (1882 — 99).

(d) Miscellaneous

Report from the Commissioners of Woods to the Treasury recommending Measures for ascertaining the Boundaries thereof, and inquiring into the Rights of Free Miners, and Answer (XXIX, 1830).

Memorials sent to Government by Inhabitants of Dean Forest, in favour of or opposed to the Dean Forest Bill (XLVII, 1836).

Return relating to the Forest of Dean (XXXVI, 1872).

Return for 1872 — 3, with respect to each country (exclusive of the metropolis), of name and address of every owner of one acre, and upwards, with estimated acreage and annual gross estimated rental of the land, etc., of individual owners, and of the number of owners of less than one acre, with the estimated aggregate acreage, and the annual gross estimated rental of the land, etc, of such owners; together with the estimated extent of commons and waste lands (LXXII, 1874).

Return of the number of free miners in the Forest of Dean on the register on 1st January 1874, and on 1st April 1875, with an estimate of those who are supposed to have died or left the district (LX, 1875).

Return relating to the Forest of Dean for each year 1871 — 84 (LXII, 1884 — 5).

Returns relating to the Forest of Dean (L, 1893 — 4).

5. Newspapers and Periodicals

Barnsley Chronicle, 1881
Beehive, 1862 — 72
British Miner (Miner and Workman's Advocate), 1862 — 5
Cannock Chase Examiner, 1873 — 7
Chepstow Express, 1865 — 6
Chepstow Chronicle, 1867 — 86
Chepstow Mercury, 1867 — 74
Chepstow Mercury and Volunteers' Gazette, 1863 — 74
Cinderford Journal, 1868 — 9, 1874 — 86
Cobbetts's Weekly Political Register, 1831
Coleford Times, 1863 — 86
Colliery Guardian, 1861 — 86
Dean Forest Guardian, 1885 — 1900
Dean Forest Mercury, 1882 — 1900
Derbyshire and Leicestershire Examiner, 1873 — 7
Durham Chronicle, 1866
Forest of Dean Examiner, 1873 — 7
Forester, 1831
Forester, 1870 — 84
Foresters' Halfpenny News, 1877 — 86
Glasgow Sentinel, 1873 — 4
Gloucester Chronicle, 1831 — 8
Gloucester Herald, 1827 — 8
Gloucester Journal, 1800 — 38
Gloucester Mercury, 1828 — 9
International Herald, 1872 — 4
Labour League Examiner, 1874
Labour Press and Miners' and Workman's Examiner, 1873 — 8
Lydney Herald, 1863

Lydney Journal, 1865 — 7
Lydney Observer, 1875
Miners' Advocate and Record, 1873 — 4
Monmouth Free Press, Monmouthshire, Herefordshire, Forest of Dean and South Wales Advertiser, 1876 — 7
Monmouthshire Gazette and Coleford and Forest of Dean Circular, 1849 — 50
Monmouth, Glamorgan and Brecon Herald (South Wales Times and Star of Gwent), 1853 — 86
Monmouth Telegraph for Gloucester, Monmouth, Cinderford, 1863 — 9
Monmouthshire Chronicle, Hereford, Gloucester, Forest of Dean and South Wales Reporter, 1875 — 84
Monmouthshire Merlin, 1829 — 31
National Reformer, 1872 — 3
Northern Star, 1843
Potteries Examiner, 1871 — 81
Shropshire Examiner, 1873 — 7
South Staffordshire Examiner, 1874
Tamworth Miners' Examiners and Workingmen's Journal, 1873 — 6
The Times, London, 1831 — 98
Wednesbury, West Bromwich and Darlaston Examiner, 1874 — 8
West of England Examiner, 1874
Western Mail, 1873 — 5
Wigan Observer, 1869 — 74

6. Books and Articles

(All works published in London unless otherwise stated)
Addis, J. P. *The Crawshay Dynasty* (University of Wales Press, Cardiff, 1957)
Albion, R. G. *Forests and Sea Power* (Harvard, 1926)
Aldcroft, D. H. and P. Fearson (eds.) *British Economic Fluctuations 1790 — 1939* (1972)
Allen, V. L. 'The origins of industrial conciliation and arbitration', *International Review of Social History*, IX (1964)
Arnot, R. Page *The Miners* (George Allen and Unwin, London, 1949).
Ashton, T. S. *Economic Fluctuations in England, 1700 — 1800* (1959)
—— and J. Sykes *The Coal Industry of the Eighteenth Century* (University of Manchester Press, Manchester, 1929)
Bellows, J. 'Relics of Ancient British Forest Life', *Transactions of the Bristol and Gloucester Archeological Society*, VI (1881 — 2)
—— and M. Holland *A Week's Holiday in the Forest of Dean* (Gloucester, 1880)
Beveridge, W. H. 'The Trade Cycle in Britain before 1850', *Oxford Economic Papers*, 111 (1940)
Brock, M. *The Great Reform Act* (Hutchinson, London, 1973)
Brown, A. J. Youngson 'Trade Union Policy in the Scots Coalfield, 1855 — 1885', *Economic History Review*, 2nd ser. VI (1953 — 4)
Brown, I. D. 'Notes on the District of the Forest of Dean', Woolhope Club, *Transactions* (1898 — 9)
Brown K. D. (ed.) *Essays in Anti-Labour History* (Macmillan, London, 1974)
Buddle, J. 'On the Great Fault called the Horse in the Forest of Dean Coal-Field', Geological Society, *Transactions*, 2nd ser. VI (1842)
Burchill F. and R. Ross *A History of the Potters' Union* (Ceramic and Allied Trades Union, 1977)
Burgess, K. *The Origin of British Industrial Relations* (Croom Helm, London, 1975)

Challinor, R. *Alexander MacDonald and the Miners* (CPGB History Group Pamphlet 48, 1967 — 8)
——*Lancashire and Cheshire Miners* (Newcastle, 1972)
——and B. Ripley *The Miners' Association* (1968)
Clements, R. V. 'Trade Unions and Emigration, 1840—1880', *Population Studies*, IX (1955—6)
——'British Trade Unions and Popular Political Economy', *Econ. Hist. Rev.*, 2nd ser. IV (1961—2)
Coats, A. W. 'The Classical Economists and the Labourer' in A. W. Coats (ed.) *The Classical Economists and Economic Policy* (Methuen, London, 1971)
Cole, G. D. H. *A Short History of the British Working Class Movement, 1797—1937* (George Allen and Unwin, London, 1937)
——'Some Notes on British Trade Unionism in the third quarter of the nineteenth century', *Int. Rev. of Soc. Hist.*, 11 (1937)
Collins, H. 'The English Branches of the First International' in A. Briggs and J. Saville (eds.) *Essays in Labour History* (Macmillan, London, 1967)
Coltham, S. 'George Potter, the Junta and the Beehive', *Int. Rev. of Soc. Hist.*, V, VI (1965)
Conder, E. 'Some notes on the purlieus of the Forest of Dean', *Trans. BGAS*, XXIX (1906)
Cooke, A. O. *The Forest of Dean* (1913)
Cox, J. C. *Royal Forests of England* (1905)
Crawley Boevey, S. M. *Dean Forest Sketches* (1887)
Cross, A. L. *Eighteenth Century Documents relating to the Royal Forests* (Macmillan, New York, 1928)
Dobb, M. *Studies in the Development of Capitalism*, rev. edn (Routledge and Kegan Paul, London, 1949)
Drew, C. *The Forest of Dean in Times Past Contrasted with the Present* (Coleford, 1841)
Edwards, N. *The History of the South Wales Miners* (1926)
Einzig, P. *The Control of the Purse* (1959)
Evans, E. W. *The Miners of South Wales* (Cardiff, 1961).
Fryer, W. H. 'Notes on the iron ore mines of the Forest of Dean, and on the history of their working', *Trans. BGAS.*, XXIX (1906)
Fynes, R. *The Miners of Northumberland and Durham*, new edn (Wakefield, 1971)
Galloway, R. L. *A History of Coal Mining in Great Britain*, new edn (David and Charles, Newton Abbot, 1969)
——*Annals of Coal Mining and the Coal Trade* (2 vols., Newton Abbot, 1971)
Gayer, A. D., W. W. Rostow and A. J. Schwartz *The Growth and Fluctuation of the British Economy* (2 vols., Clarendon Press, Oxford, 1953)
Griffin, A. R. *The Miners of Nottinghamshire* (National Union of Mineworkers, 1955)
Hammond, J. L. 'The Industrial Revolution and Discontent', *Econ. Hist. Rev.*, 1st ser. 11 (1930)
Hammond, J. L. and B. *The Rise of Modern Industry*, 2nd edn (1926)
Harrison, R. *Before the Socialists* (Routledge and Kegan Paul, London, 1965)
——(ed.) *The Independent Collier* (Harvester Press, Hassocks, 1978)
—— G. B. Woolven and R. Duncan (eds.) *The Warwick Guide to British Labour Periodicals, 1790—1970* (Harvester Press, Hassocks, 1977)
Hart, C. E. *The Extent and Boundaries of the Forest of Dean* (The Author, Woodgate, Gloucester, 1947)
——*The Verderers and Speech Court of the Forest of Dean* (John Bellows, Gloucester, 1950)
——*The Commoners of Dean Forest* (British Publishing Co., Gloucester, 1951)
——*The Free Miners of the Forest of Dean* (British Publishing Co., Gloucester, 1953)
——*Royal Forest* (Oxford University Press, Oxford, 1966)

——*The Industrial History of Dean* (David and Charles, Newton Abbot, 1971)

Heath, C. *Historical and Descriptive Account of Chepstow and Neighbourhood*, 6th edn (Monmouth, 1913)

Hicks, J. R. 'The Early History of Industrial Conciliation in England,' *Economica*, X (1930)

Hobsbawm, E. J. *Labouring Men*, 3rd edn (Weidenfeld and Nicolson, 1968)

——*Primitive Rebels*, 4th edn (Manchester University Press, Manchester, 1974)

——and G. Rude *Captain Swing*, rev. edn (1973)

Holland, W. H. 'Notes on the Iron Trade in the Forest of Dean', *Transactions of the Stroud Natural History and Philosophical Society* (1881)

Insole H. R. and C. Z. Bunning 'The Forest of Dean Coalfield', British Society of Mining Students, *Journal*, V, VI (1881)

Jevons, H. S. *The British Coal Trade*, new edn (David and Charles, Newton Abbot, 1969)

Jevons, W. S. *The Coal Question*, rev. edn (1906)

John, A. H. *The Industrial Development of South Wales* (University of Wales Press, Cardiff, 1950)

Jones, D. *Before Rebecca* (Allen Lane, London, 1973)

Joynes, J. S. 'Description of seams and some of the methods of working coal in the Forest of Dean', British Society of Mining Students, *Journal*, XI (1889)

Kemp, B. *King and Commons, 1660—1832* (1959)

Kerr, R. J. 'The Customs of the Forest of Dean', *Trans. BGAS*, XLIII (1921)

Lefevre, G. Shaw *English Commons and Forests* (1894)

Loes, E. 'The Forest of Dean', *Architect*, 21 September 1878

Longley, F. E. *The Forest of Dean* (n.d.)

McCormack B. and J. E. Williams 'The miners and the eight hour day, 1863—1910', *Econ. Hist. Rev.*, 2nd ser, XII (1950—60)

McCready, H. W. 'British Labour and the Royal Commission on Trade Unions, 1867—9', *University of Toronto Quarterly*, XXIV (1955)

——'British Labour's Lobby, 1867—75', *Canadian Journal of Economics and Political Science*, 22 (1956)

Machin, F. *The Yorkshire Miners* (Barnsley, 1958)

Meade, R. 'The Iron Industries of Gloucestershire, Forest of Dean,' *Mining Journal*, 1 April 1876

Moore, R. *Pit-men, Preachers and Politics* (Cambridge University Press, Cambridge, 1974)

Morris J. H. and L. J. Williams *The South Wales Coal Industry, 1841—1875* (Cardiff, 1958)

——'The South Wales Sliding Scale', *Manchester School of Economic and Social Studies*, XXVIII (1960)

Morse, R. *Lays of the Forest and Other Poems* (Newport, 1836)

Mountjoy, T. *Sixty-two years in the Life of a Forest of Dean Collier* (1887)

Muir, E. *Local Government in Gloucestershire, 1775—1800* (Bristol, 1969)

Musson, A. *British Trade Unions, 1800—1875* (Macmillan, London, 1972)

Nef, J. U. *The Rise of the British Coal Industry*, rev. edn (2 vols. David and Charles, Newton Abbot, 1966)

Nicholls, H. G. *The Forest of Dean* (new edn 1966; 1st edn, 1858)

——*Personalities of the Forest of Dean* (1863)

——*Iron Making in the Olden Times* (new edn, 1966: 1st edn, 1866)

Nicholson, I. B. *National Landlordism in the Forest of Dean* (National League, 1881)

Nisbet, J. 'History of the Forest of Dean in Gloucestershire', *English Historical Review*, XXI (1906)

Osborn, F. M. *The Story of the Mushets* (Thomas Nelson, London, 1952)

Paar, H. W. *The Severn and Wye Railway*, 2nd edn (David and Charles, Newton Abbot, 1971)

——*The Great Western Railway in Dean*, 2nd edn (David and Charles, Newton Abbot, 1971)

Peacock, A. J. *Bread or Blood* (Gollancz, London, 1965)

Pelling, H. *A History of British Trade Unionism* (Penguin, Harmondsworth, 1963)

——*Popular Politics and Society in Late Victorian Britain* (Macmillan, London, 1968)

Pollard, S. 'Trade Unions and the Labour Market, 1870—1914', *Yorkshire Bulletin of Economic and Social Research*, 17 (1965)

Porter, J. H. 'Wage bargaining under conciliation agreements, 1860—1914', *Econ. Hist. Rev.*, 2nd ser. XXIII (1970)

——'Wage determination by selling price sliding scales, 1870—1914', *Man. Sch. Econ. and Soc. Studies*, XXXIX (1971)

——'Coal miners and conciliation', Society for the Study of Labour History, Bulletin 26 (1973)

Tilly, C., L. and R. *The Rebellious Century, 1830—1930* (Dent, London, 1975)

Townley, H. *English Woodlands and their Story* (1910)

Trotter, F. M. *Geology of the Forest of Dean Coal and Iron-ore Field* (Memoirs of the Geological Survey of Great Britain, England and Wales, 1942)

Webb, S. *The Story of the Durham Miners*, 1662—1921 (1921)

Webb, S. and B. *The History of Trade Unionism* (1920)

Welbourne, E. *The Miners' Unions of Northumberland and Durham* (Cambridge, 1923)

Wickenden, W. S. 'Whitsuntide and other customs in Dean Forest', *Gentlemen's Magazine*, XLII (1822)

Williams, J. E. *The Derbyshire Miners* (George Allen and Unwin, London, 1962)

Wright, T. The Roman iron district of the Forest of Dean and its neighbourhood', *Gentlemen's Magazine*, XXXVII (1852)

Anon.,

'The Church in the Royal Forest of Dean', *Churchman's Family Magazine*, August (1865)

'The Free Miners of the Forest of Dean', *Penny Magazine*, 19 August 1843

The Life of Warren James. The Reputed Champion of the Forest of Dean, Descriptive of the Forest Riots, including an Account of John Harris, Alias Poisefoot. By a Resident Forester (Monmouth, 1831)

'Methodism in the Forest of Dean', *Wesleyan-Methodist Magazine*, XLVIII (1825)

'The petition of the Methodist Society of Colliers in his Majesty's Forest of Dean, to the Methodist ministers in conference assembled', *Wesleyan-Methodist Magazine*, XLVIII (1824)

'Religious Instruction in the Forest of Dean', *Wesleyan-Methodist Magazine*, iii (1829)

Index